C000197515

Board Meetings in the Bath

The Knebworth House Story

Board Meetings in the Bath

The Knebworth House Story

Chryssie Lytton Cobbold

Methuen

First published in Great Britain 1986
by Methuen London Ltd
11 New Fetter Lane, London EC4P 4EE

Printed in Great Britain by
Richard Clay (The Chaucer Press Ltd), Bungay, Suffolk

British Library Cataloguing in Publication Data

Cobbold, Chryssie Lytton
Board meetings in the bath: the
Knebworth House story.
1. Knebworth House (Old Knebworth,
Hertfordshire)
I. Title
942.5′82 DA690.K6/

ISBN 0–413–41650–X

To David,
my husband and joint director,
who has contributed so much
to the writing of this book.

Contents

List of Illustrations

Preface

I sometimes wonder if I am the only company secretary who goes to board meetings with nothing on. At Knebworth it seems natural. My husband, David, the chairman and only other director of the company, works all day for BP in the City of London. When he gets home in the evenings, we spend an hour or so of precious time together in a magnificent Edwardian cast-iron bath rounded at both ends – complete with telephone and bottle of wine.

It is a moment of peace and a chance to discuss the events of the day and plans for the future. Luckily I do not have to keep board minutes, but I have on occasion signed formal documents while trying to keep them out of the water.

The problems have been many and varied – but there have been quite a few laughs as well. This book is a light-hearted account of how one family has struggled to keep a huge crumbling home alive for the benefit of future generations both of the family and of the public.

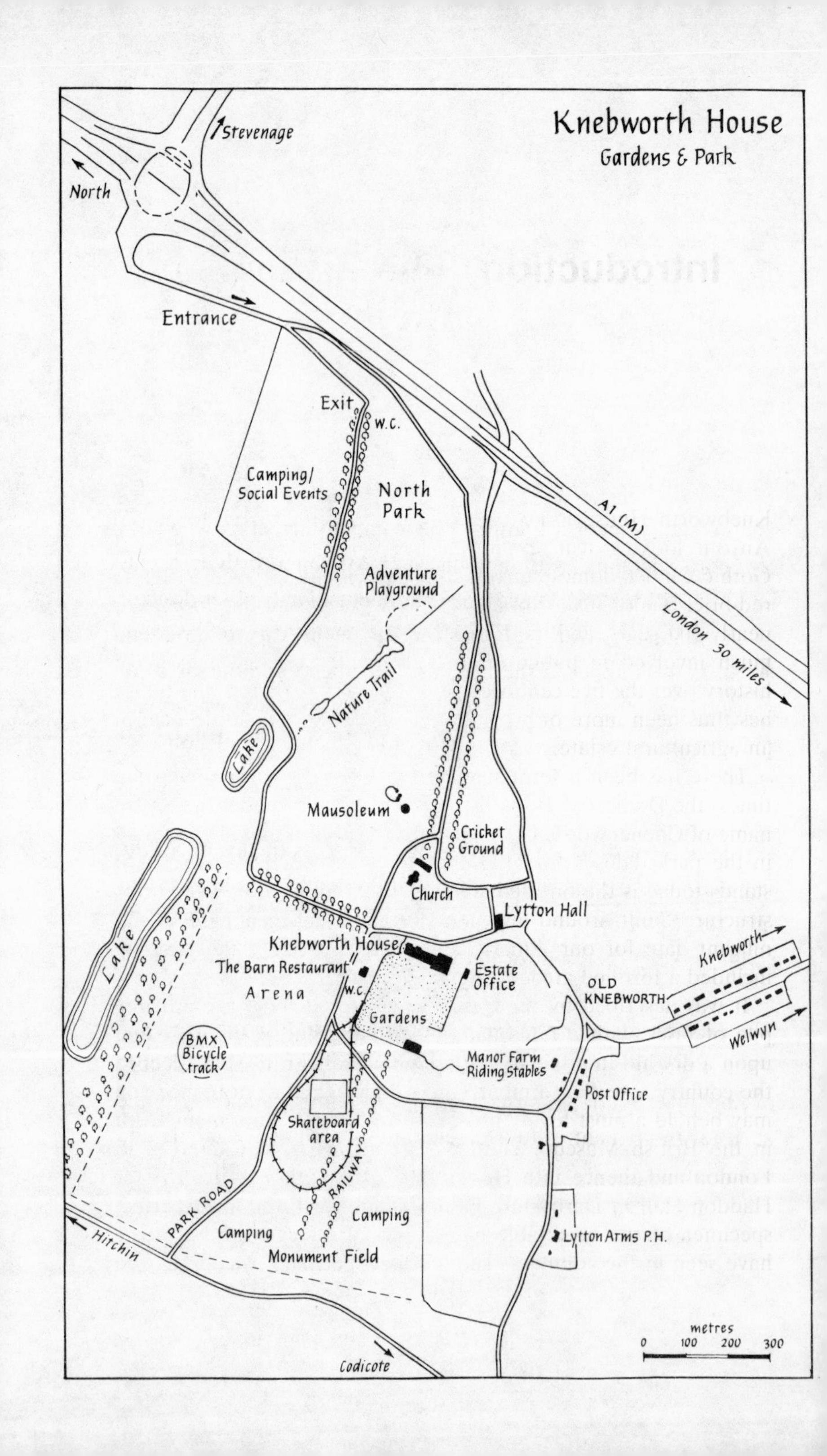
Knebworth House
Gardens & Park
Stevenage
North
Entrance
Exit
W.C.
Camping/
Social Events
North
Park
A1 (M)
London 30 miles
Adventure
Playground
Nature Trail
Lake
Mausoleum
Cricket
Ground
Lake
Church
Lytton Hall
Knebworth House
The Barn Restaurant
Estate
Office
Arena
W.C.
OLD
KNEBWORTH
Knebworth
Gardens
BMX
Bicycle
track
Manor Farm
Riding Stables
Welwyn
Post Office
Skateboard
area
RAILWAY
PARK ROAD
Hitchin
Camping
Camping
Lytton Arms P.H.
Monument Field
metres
0 100 200 300
Codicote

Introduction | The history of the house

Knebworth House is no palace, but an architectural nonsense. Anyone looking at it now would find it hard to believe that the Gothic copper domes, turrets and battlements conceal a simple red-brick Tudor manor house. It has been in the same family for nearly 500 years, and the Lyttons who have lived here have been much involved in public affairs, giving the house a flavour of history over the five centuries. Being close to London, the house has thus been more of a commuter residence than the centre of an agricultural estate.

There has been a settlement at Knebworth since pre-Norman times, the Domesday Book listing a royal manor under the Saxon name of Chenepworde or 'Village on the Hill'. The parish church in the park dates from 1120 and is still in use. The house as it stands today is the one remaining wing of a two-storey red-brick structure, built around an open courtyard between 1492 (a significant date for our American visitors) and 1530; the building included a fortified arched gateway of earlier date.

It was described by Sir Henry Chauncey in 1700 as, 'A large pile of brick with a fair quadrangle in the middle of it, seated upon a dry hill in a fair large park, stocked with the best deer in the country, excellent timber, and wooded, and from thence you may behold a most lovely prospect to the East.' In a manuscript in the British Museum entitled 'Excursions from Camerton to London and thence into Herts, 1805', the author writes: 'After Haddon Hall in Derbyshire I think Knebworth the most perfect specimen of the hospitable habitations of our ancestors which I have seen in the country.' The 'perfect specimen' was destroyed by Mrs Bulwer-Lytton in 1811, and the 'most lovely prospect to the East' is now Stevenage New Town. But Knebworth is still a hospitable habitation and as such we feel is worth preserving if possible for future generations of Lyttons.

The builder of Knebworth was Sir Robert Lytton, who purchased the manor from Sir Thomas Bouchier in 1490. The property had belonged to his father-in-law half a century earlier, so the family connection goes back to the early fifteenth century. Sir Robert Lytton was a close friend and confidant of Henry Tudor, and fought in the battle of Bosworth in 1485 at which Richard III was defeated, bringing the first of the Welsh Tudors to the throne of England. Sir Robert became Under Treasurer of the Exchequer and Privy Councillor to the new King Henry VII. We have recently purchased a letter from the King instructing Robert to buy shoes for his children.

Sir Rowland de Lytton, the great grandson of Robert, commanded the forces of Hertfordshire and Essex at Tilbury Port in 1588. His wife was related by blood to Queen Elizabeth I, who is traditionally supposed to have visited Knebworth that year, and the Queen Elizabeth state bedroom is named after her. As she spent her youth in the Palace at Hatfield, ten miles from Knebworth, she may well have come over to visit her relations – though I very much doubt whether she stayed overnight. Both the Queen Mother and Queen Elizabeth II have used the room to powder their noses on visits to Knebworth in recent years, however, so the room has some authenticity!

Sir William Lytton succeeded his father Sir Rowland in 1615. He was Knight of the Shire and represented Hertfordshire in the Long Parliament. In the early days of the Civil War he supported the cause of Parliament against the King, and Pym, Hampden and Faulkland visited him at Knebworth. He was later one of the forty members of Parliament who were imprisoned in 'Hell Hole', a cellar under the House of Commons, by Colonel Pride; this was known as 'Pride's Purge'.

His son, again Sir William, was the last Lytton to follow in the direct succession and on his death in 1705 he left the estate to his great-nephew, Mr Strode, on condition that he assumed the surname of Lytton. But Mr Lytton Strode died young and without children, so the property passed to his first cousin by marriage, William Robinson Norreys.

The Norreys were a Welsh family, tracing direct descent from Meredith ap Tudor, the grandfather of Henry VII. They brought the Tudor rose into the Lytton coat of arms and provided a romantic link with Sir Robert Lytton, the builder of Knebworth, who had fought and served with Henry Tudor. William changed his name to Robinson-Lytton. He was a Jacobite sympathiser and was only prevented from joining Bonnie Prince Charlie's rebellion by his wife, who, fearing for his safety, locked him in the stables at Knebworth. She was a Manchester businessman's daughter, and from the portrait of her with her family, which hangs in the State Drawing Room, she certainly looks capable of anything.

But in 1762 William's son, John Robinson-Lytton, died without an heir, and the property passed again through the female line to John's nephew, Richard Warburton, an antiquarian who had a magnificent library of books. This great library, as we shall see, was to prove an early inspiration to his famous grandson, but sadly had to be sold on Warburton's death to pay his debts.

Yet again there was no male heir, and the property passed to Richard Warburton's daughter Elizabeth, who was married to General Bulwer of Heydon Hall in Norfolk, where she lived with her three sons: William, who succeeded to the Bulwer estates; Henry, a politician and diplomat who is best known as the biographer of Palmerston and was created Lord Dalling; and Edward, the youngest and her favourite, to whom she was to give her Knebworth estates. Mrs Bulwer was a formidable lady. On the death of her husband in 1807 she moved with Edward to Knebworth, determined to rehabilitate the property. Her father, Richard Warburton-Lytton, had not lived at Knebworth, preferring to be surrounded by his books in a small house in Broadstairs, so Knebworth had been unoccupied for fifty years since the death of her great-uncle, John Robinson-Lytton, in 1762.

The unstable and complicated inheritance of Knebworth in the eighteenth century is doubtless the reason why there is very little of the Georgian period in the house; there are none of the sash windows and classical porticoes that were so frequently added to earlier English houses in that period. The fifty years of neglect can be the only justification for Mrs Bulwer's decision in 1811 to demolish three of the four sides of 'the most perfect specimen' of red-brick Tudor architecture and cover the remaining wing with fashionable stucco. But however much subsequent generations may criticise her for such an act of vandalism, she brought life and love back to Knebworth and laid the foundations for the next 150 years of its history.

A woman of strong character and individuality, she is the subject of many stories. She quarrelled with the rector, and not only refused to go inside the church but forbade every other inhabitant in the village to do so on pain of incurring her displeasure. She herself conducted daily prayers and regular Sunday services in her own drawing room. She planted trees around the church, so she should not see it from her windows, and built a mausoleum in the park so she would not have to be buried in the churchyard. But she also built almshouses and was a popular benefactor to the villagers.

If Mrs Bulwer had laid the foundations, it is to Edward Bulwer-Lytton, her son, that Knebworth owes its character and perhaps its golden age – but this was not to be until after his mother's death in 1843. Edward grew up at Knebworth; he was a talented boy and had written his first book by the time he was fifteen. He was inspired by his grandfather's extensive library ('I was Solomon in all his glory,' he later recalled, 'and surrounded by all his seraglio') and was desolated when the books had to be sold. As an undergraduate at Cambridge he had a brief affair with Lady Caroline Lamb, whose home was at Brocket, a short ride from Knebworth, and one of his early poems is dedicated to her. She was responsible for introducing him to Rosina Wheeler, a beautiful but penniless girl from County Limerick; after a stormy engagement they were married in 1827. Mrs Bulwer was furious. She strongly disapproved of Rosina, refused to receive her daughter-in-law and stopped her son's allowance. Rosina never came to Knebworth, and by all accounts she led a miserable life.

The couple lived near Pangbourne. Edward was obliged to make frequent visits to London to further his literary career, and Rosina was left alone a lot – shunned by her husband's family and short of money. Her two children were taken away from her at birth, as was fashionable in those days, and put out to wet nurses in the village, so she seldom saw them. She and Edward quarrelled incessantly.

In an effort to make amends, Edward took Rosina to Naples in 1833. He was very impressed by Pompeii and his best known novel, *The Last Days of Pompeii*, resulted from the trip. Unfortunately, the same could not be said for the harmony of his marriage, and in 1836 a deed of separation was signed. The success of *Pompeii* established Bulwer-Lytton in the forefront of contemporary novelists; his financial problems were solved and socially he was much in demand. He was a Whig and MP for Lincoln and St Ives, supporting the Great Reform Bill of 1832. Later on, however, the influence of his friend and literary colleague Disraeli caused him to switch his allegiance to the Tories, and he became Colonial Secretary during the 1860s while Disraeli was Foreign Secretary. It was the only time in British history that there have been two famous novelists in the same Cabinet.

When his mother died in 1843, Edward at last inherited Knebworth, and with the money he had made from his writing he set about turning the house into the romantic fairy castle of his dreams. His mother's severe stucco was embellished with minarets, copper domes and gargoyles of every size and description. Interior decorations were by John Crace, the pupil of Pugin – extravagant, heraldic, with heavy curtains and exotic wallpapers and a central theme of dedication to Henry VII and his Tudor ancestry.

Parted from his wife, Bulwer-Lytton set up house alone in his Gothic extravaganza and Knebworth became a centre of pilgrimage for artists, politicians, poets and men of letters. He was interested in the occult and for a time had a resident medium at Knebworth; he was also a Rosicrucian. Charles Dickens was a close friend, performing in amateur theatricals at Knebworth, and together he and Bulwer-Lytton founded the Guild of Literature and Art. The purpose of the Guild was to assist impoverished artists by providing pensions and rent-free accommodation, and the Institute of the Guild of Literature and Art was built at Stevenage, two miles from Knebworth, in 1865. Sadly, the chosen artists never wanted to live there, so the idea never took on and the building was eventually demolished by the Stevenage Development Corporation in 1951.

Lord Lytton of Knebworth, as Bulwer-Lytton became in 1866, was without doubt the most colourful individual to live at Knebworth. His influence on the house is still very strong, and it is his ghost which roams the passages. His life is a fascinating story in itself.

Lord Lytton's only daughter, Emily, died of typhoid at the age of sixteen. His son Robert had poetical aspirations, but his father decided that one author in the family was enough and encouraged him to become a diplomat. Robert did write, but under the *nom de plume* of Owen Meredith. He married Edith Villiers in 1864 and they had seven children.

It was while Robert was Minister of Legation in Lisbon that Disraeli, as a gesture to his old friend Bulwer-Lytton who had died a few years previously, offered him the Viceroyalty of India. Robert was unambitious, unconventional and suffered from ill health, so it was with some misgivings that he accepted one of the most prestigious and taxing positions in history. Their eldest son Rowland had died from the effects of whooping cough at the age of six, and the second son Teddy had also died in infancy, of congested lungs. It was with their three daughters, Betty, Constance and Emily (aged eight, six and a year), along with their English servants, that Lord and Lady Lytton travelled to India in 1876.

In 1877 Queen Victoria was proclaimed Empress of India, and Robert as Viceroy held a spectacular Durbar in Delhi for the occcasion. As a reward for his services in India, Robert was made the 1st Earl of Lytton and Knebworth became the home of his large collection of Indian artefacts: gifts from Maharajas, tiger skins from shooting expeditions, letters and dairies.

The Lyttons had two more children: Victor, who became the 2nd Earl of Lytton, and Neville, the youngest, who was a distinguished artist. During the short time that Robert and Edith lived at Knebworth after their return from India, and before Robert was sent to Paris as ambassador, they found the house far too small for a family to live in. Another floor was added to the house to serve as nurseries, and a mock Tudor wing on the south side to accommodate the extra servants. Robert died as ambassador in Paris in 1891, shortly after his sixtieth birthday, from a cerebral haemorrhage. Edith became a lady-in-waiting to

Queen Victoria in 1895 and was with her when she died. She continued at Court with Queen Alexandra until 1905, and thereafter lived in Knebworth village in a house designed by her son-in-law, Edwin Lutyens, until she died at the age of ninety-five.

Their eldest daughter Betty married George Balfour; Constance became a suffragette and never married. Frustrated in her efforts to be arrested because as 'Lady Constance Lytton' she was always sent home with a scolding, she cut off her hair, wore glasses and as Jane Warton succeeded in getting herself arrested and put in jail. Her health never recovered from her experiences in prison, where she was forcibly fed and suffered a heart attack. Confined more or less to her bed for the rest of her life, she wrote a book on women in prison and the suffragette movement which helped to improve prison conditions for women at that time. Emily, the third daughter, married the famous architect Edwin Lutyens.

Victor was born in India in 1876 and married Pamela Plowden in 1902. The young couple moved into Knebworth and with the help of their brother-in-law they tried to rid Knebworth of the then unfashionable Victorian decorations. Ceilings were ripped out and replaced with plainer designs, colourful Crace wallpapers and Spanish leather were stripped from the walls, which were then painted in softer Edwardian colours. Heavy brocade curtains came down to let the light in. The gardens were completely altered: the formal Victorian beds disappeared and large lawns with avenues of pleached limes took their place. Gertrude Jeykll, Edwin Lutyens's great garden collaborator, designed a herb garden for Knebworth in 1907, but for some reason they never got round to building it at the time.

To help defray the cost of maintaining Knebworth in the period up to the First World War, the house was often let and the family stayed in their London home. At one time it was let to the Grand Duke Michael Alexandrovitch, the Tsar of Russia's younger brother, who having made a socially unacceptable marriage to a divorcée decided to exile himself from Russia for a time. There are some wonderful photographs showing large Russian bear rugs covering the floors of the house and family groups of Russians wearing fur hats posed in the gardens.

In 1923 Victor, the 2nd Earl, was appointed Governor of Bengal and so returned with his family to the India of his birth, and to

Government House, Calcutta, where he had lived with his parents. For four months in 1925 Victor acted as Viceroy and the family moved to Delhi – 'Uncle Ned' Lutyens was busy building the city of New Delhi at the time.

After returning from India, Victor became British delegate to the League of Nations in Geneva, and in 1935 headed the League of Nations Commission to Manchuria to report on the Japanese invasion. When his eldest son Antony was killed in a flying accident in 1933 he published a book of his son's letters from school days called *Antony: a Record of Youth*. It was controversial at the time, some people feeling that it wasn't quite 'right' to publish such intimate material. Tragically, his second son Johnny also died young, killed during the war at El Alamein.

Pamela Plowden, Victor's wife, was a great beauty and was admired by many, including Winston Churchill, who wrote to his mother on one of his polo trips to India in 1896: 'I was introduced yesterday to Miss Pamela Plowden, who lives here. I must say, she is the most beautiful girl I've ever seen; we're going to try and do the city of Hyderabad today together, on an elephant.' Winston was twenty-one at the time and Pamela's father was British Resident in Hyderabad. They remained close friends all their lives, and a portrait of the Banqueting Hall painted by Winston on one of his visits to Knebworth hangs in the house. She died in 1971 at the great age of ninety-seven.

In addition to their two boys, Victor and Pamela had two daughters – Hermione and Davinia. When Victor died in 1947 he left the property at Knebworth to his elder daughter, Lady Hermione, so once again Knebworth passed through the female line. The title, Earl of Lytton, went to Victor's younger brother Neville, who was an artist living in Paris. He had married Wilfrid Scawen Blunt's daughter Judith, creator of the famous Arab stud at Crabbet Park in Sussex, on another of whose properties their grandson, the 5th Earl, now lives.

Lady Hermione had married Cameron Fromanteel Cobbold, known to all as Kim, and had three children. They never expected to inherit Knebworth, but after Johnny's death, when her father said he wanted Knebworth to be hers, they moved to a cottage in the village at Knebworth so that the children could grow up there. It was wartime and Knebworth House was the temporary home of the Frobel Institute, a teachers' training college.

Kim Cobbold had joined the Bank of England in 1933 and was an executive director throughout the war, managing the foreign department and exchange control. He was made Deputy Governor and then became Governor in 1949 at the very young age of forty-four. On his retirement from the Bank in 1961 he was created Lord Cobbold of Knebworth, and in 1963 he was appointed Lord Chamberlain to the Queen.

Kim and Hermione lived at Knebworth, but their lives were centred in London. Knebworth was used for weekends, children's holidays and entertaining. Life after the war was very different for people with large houses; Knebworth had suffered three lots of death duties in a very short time, and staff were expensive. So the mock Tudor wing was pulled down and the south side of the house was converted for 'fifties' living. The large kitchen was turned into a hall and dining room for the family and one of the pantries made into a modern kitchen. The copperware was sold off to help pay for the work, and in any case there was nobody to clean it. The family slept on the top floor and lived in one half of the ground floor. The rest of the house was covered in dust sheets in the winter and opened up in the summer for the public to visit at weekends.

This was the Knebworth I first visited in 1958.

Chapter 1 Planning the agenda

In 1958 I was eighteen and doing a 'London season'. I had been invited for the weekend to Knebworth House by Lord and Lady Cobbold's eldest son, David, whom I had met at a dance the week before. Attracted by my low-cut green dress and long hair, he had wandered over and asked 'Are you a mermaid?' 'Yes,' I replied, 'and I live in the sea off Hartland Point in north Devon.' Which was more or less true. I was brought up in a large, rambling twelfth-century Abbey, half a mile up a narrow valley from the wild Atlantic coast in Devon. My childhood had been spent with my three sisters and brother on the rocky beaches and steep red cliffs at the bottom of our drive, prawning and baiting lobsters out of shallow pools in the summer, looking for caves and old wrecks in the winter.

In spite of my grandmother's complaints about my mother having been taken at the age of eighteen all the way to London from their home on Exmoor to find a husband, only to end up six months later marrying my father, who lived in Devon only twenty-five miles away, my mother decided to launch her four daughters in London too. She rented a flat in London opposite Harrods for the duration. My two elder sisters were married off successfully at eighteen and nineteen years old, but I was proving more of a problem. Having left school at barely sixteen, and being too young for London, I was sent off to Rhodesia (as it was then) to stay with my grandparents.

They had emigrated in 1947, as my grandmother suffered from arthritis and the Exmoor damp made life miserable for her. So, both in their sixties, they bought themselves 40,000 acres of farmland sixty miles north-west of Salisbury (Harare) and, with a herd of Jersey cows and all their favourite belongings, moved to Africa.

I loved it out there. I spent my time going for long rides with my grandfather or sitting behind a bush bird-watching with my grandmother, armed with binoculars. My grandmother kept a well-stocked medicine cupboard, and the Africans who lived on the farm would come to her with their ailments and she would do what she could for them. One morning a woman arrived with a badly burnt toddler who had fallen in the fire. My grandmother did her best for the child, gave the mother some tea and a bag of sugar and told her to feed the baby with it for shock. The following morning six more mothers arrived at the door with their babies, all with burnt bottoms. They had sat them in the fire hoping to be given free tea and sugar! My grandmother was horrified. There were many lessons to be learnt about life out there, and I was sad when the time came to go back to England – but excited at the prospect of a London season.

My mother's and my choice in boyfriends for me were very different, but when Lady Cobbold wrote to my mother and invited me to stay for David's twenty-first birthday party, my mother was delighted. David was considered respectable, and she set about persuading me to go. David had seemed nice enough at the party the week before, but I had my current boyfriend and felt I had made enough new friends in three months in London to last a lifetime. However, rather than argue, in the end I went.

I suppose I was exceptionally spoilt at that time. A lot of dances were held in beautiful houses in the country, and I am shocked now at how unobservant and ignorant I was of the histories and beauty of these houses. I was not particularly impressed by Knebworth House, but it did have a certain aura about it (or could it have been David?) which by the end of the weekend had me captivated.

The party was mostly made up of undergraduates and I did not know anyone, so I found some cushions in the back of the fishing cottage by the lake and went to sleep. By about 5 a.m. most of the guests had departed, and David woke me up and suggested a row on the lake. The nightlights in jam jars around the lake were going out, a mist hung over the water and it was beginning to get light. It was all very romantic. I was glad I had agreed to come after all!

The following weekend I went to stay at Clandon in Surrey with my godmother, Lady Onslow, for my cousin Teresa's coming-out dance. I knew David had been invited to the ball and was excited at the prospect of seeing him again, but sadly I developed a sore throat and high temperature on the day of the party and Lady Onslow put me firmly to bed. There was no question of my being able to go to the party.

The family did not live in the big house, which was normally shut up, but in a smaller manor house in the park. Clandon had, however, been opened up specially for Teresa's dance. Everyone went off to the party and I was left alone in the smaller house feeling miserable. Suddenly there was a tap on the window and David's face appeared amongst the wistaria; he was wearing white tie and tails. With great excitement I let him in. Teresa had told him where I was and, having talked his way around the night-watchman who was guarding the house, he had seen the light on at my window and a convenient creeper outside! He refilled my hot-water bottle, got me a drink and sat on my bed chatting. I did not mind a bit any more about missing the dance.

All hell was let loose the next day, however. As always seemed to happen with my most innocent adventures, it turned into a major drama. I had told Teresa about David's visit the night before and she had told her brother Michael. Michael was about twenty-one, in the army and I think keen about me at the time. He stormed into my bedroom and stood in full military regalia at the end of my bed swearing at me. He then went off to tell his mother. I couldn't understand why he was so angry, although rumour had it that he had tried to climb up the wistaria during the night too, but hadn't been able to manage it.

My godmother came in and delivered a grand tirade, ending up by saying she was going to ring my mother and tell her I needed a psychiatrist. By this time my temperature had gone up to 104 degrees and, fed up with being shouted at and thinking it was time I went home, I got out of bed and tried to walk down the passage. I passed out and had to be carried back to bed by a rather contrite Michael. Lady Onslow rang not only my mother but David's father to complain about our behaviour – anyone would have thought we had spent the evening making mad passionate love or pinching the silver. I certainly felt in no condition to do more than talk and have some company, but at that age I found adults expected the worst of me. Maybe they judged me by their own standards?

My parents decided they had better meet David, so as soon as I was well enough to travel we went down to Hartland together. Luckily they liked him very much and we had an idyllic week, walking on the cliffs and sunbathing.

The season in London was drawing to a close. David was off around the world for the long vacation and I went to Ibiza with some friends. In the autumn of 1958 I went back to London and started my first job, working for Worth in Grosvenor Street. I was in the sewing-room making clothes for the autumn and spring collections. It was an easy job, but long hours – 8.30 a.m. to 6 p.m. with only half an hour for lunch. As I had usually been up all night at a party, I used to sleep in my lunch hour, slumped over my sewing-table or on the grass in Berkeley Square. I was paid £3 a week, which went up to £3 10 shillings a year later.

During the next two years I spent many weekends at Cambridge and at Knebworth with David. Accommodation at Cambridge was a problem, as my mother always insisted I took a girl friend with me when I went to visit David. I had a long-suffering friend, Zara Heber Percy, who used to come with me, and when David was in digs we would stay in his landlady's spare room. When he was in college I sometimes spent the night in college too, which meant hiding underneath the bed every time the house porter or bedder came in. Taking baths in Trinity College was also nerve-racking as there was a large gap at the top and bottom of the partitions, and I was always scared of being discovered.

The weekends I spent at Knebworth were rather awe-inspiring. It was not the house – I was used to living in a big house and if anything Hartland was rather larger than Knebworth (we also lived in the whole house, whereas many of the larger rooms at Knebworth were shut up). I just felt completely out of my depth, and seldom opened my mouth. Conversation at home barely went further than the weather and the dogs, but at Knebworth they discussed politics, careers and topical subjects, and laughed at jokes that I did not think funny at all. I was glad when David and I could escape to walk in the bluebell woods, or swim in the lake.

Except for nursery tea, meals were taken in a small dining-room on the ground floor in what had been part of the old kitchen, the present kitchen having been moved into one of the pantries. Sunday breakfast was always sausages, and one had to be there punctually otherwise they were all divided up between the two golden labradors before one got there. 'Nanty', the old family nanny, lived up on the top floor in the nurseries, and still tidied up after David and his younger brother Rowland, who was at Eton (Susan, their elder sister, was married and living in Singapore). Nanty was usually to be found in the nursery, knitting a scarf or jumper for 'her boys', and her meals came up to the top floor on a tray in a lift operated by a hand-pulled rope.

Nursery tea was a daily ritual when all the family gathered together, even though there were no longer any children left in the nursery, and after tea we played games such as racing demon. Here at last I was able to make some impression. Having played a lot with my mother and my grandmother, both excellent players, I was quick and usually won. Kim, who traditionally won at racing demon, was very surprised to be beaten by this silent girl and it was the beginning of a long friendship.

In the evenings we bathed and changed into long skirts for dinner. The main guest bedrooms were on the first floor, while the family slept on the top floor. At night David would creep downstairs and along the passages to my room, trying hard to avoid the worst of the creaking floorboards. In those days before the pill one could not sleep together 'properly', but a lot of exciting cuddling went on!

In July 1960, David came down from Cambridge and, not really sure what he wanted to do in life, decided to go into banking; his father was Governor of the Bank of England at the time, so could advise and help. As a trainee, David was to do three months in Hamburg and three in Paris, and then go to New York for a year. I made plans to follow him abroad, but my mother squashed them all. I was invited to spend the summer holidays with his family in the south of France, but again my mother said no. It was all very frustrating.

I was sulking at home in August when I got a telegram from

David: 'COMING BACK MEET ME BARNSTAPLE STATION TUESDAY EVENING LOVE DAVID.' I met him off the train and he proposed to me on the station platform. We drove back to Hartland to announce the welcome news to my parents – they must have been very relieved. I was determined to go with David to Paris in the New Year, so it meant getting married before we went. The date was set for 7 January. My mother complained that three months was not nearly long enough to prepare for a wedding, and the weather would be so much nicer in April, but we were adamant – anyway, my parents had been married in January and who cared if it rained?

We were married in St Nectan's Church on the cliff above the Abbey at Hartland; a gale was blowing off the Atlantic and it did pour with rain. But it was a wonderful wedding – with 400 guests all of whom my mother somehow managed to put up in house-parties – and I was reluctant to leave after the reception, I was enjoying myself so much. The Bank of England chauffeur drove us to the Imperial Hotel in Exeter, where, shedding confetti everywhere, we were shown to a freezing cold bedroom, with twin beds and a single-bar electric fire.

We tried to revive our flagging spirits over dinner with a bottle of champagne but everything seemed flat after the excitement of the last few weeks. The second night of our honeymoon was spent in a cramped *couchette* on a train to Paris and was not much better. I was in a state of nervous exhaustion and David was wondering what on earth he had let himself in for! His bachelor days had come to an abrupt end at the age of twenty-three, and he was now setting off to his first job, saddled with a naive young wife who had scarcely been away from home or family before.

Our small two-roomed flat in Paris was in the unfashionable district of Courbevoie and looked on to a railway station which was the equivalent of Clapham Junction. David started work at the Banque de Paris et des Pays Bas the day after we arrived in Paris, so it was not much of a honeymoon. I had never managed to get even as far as French 'O' level at school, and my cooking was not up to much either, so my time was taken up trying to buy food and then cooking it. David used to come home for lunch. In those days French banks closed for two hours, providing plenty of time for a siesta, and more often than not we would wake up at five o'clock – too late for David to go back to the office. Luckily no one in the bank seemed to notice that he was not there.

When we returned to Knebworth after our three months in Paris, Nanty unpacked our suitcases. She was horrified at the sight of David's clothes, and I was given a stiff lecture on how to scrub cuffs and collars, iron shirts and hankies, and roll his socks into balls.

After a quick visit to my parents, where I celebrated my twenty-first birthday, we travelled to New York on the *Queen Mary*. We stayed with friends in New Jersey to start with, and then moved into a scruffy residential hotel in Brooklyn Heights. It had the most spectacular view from Staten Island over the harbour and most of Manhatten, but the cockroaches were too much for me and I persuaded David to move to two unfurnished rooms round the corner in Joralemon Street. Our furniture consisted of packing cases, a stained mattress from the Salvation Army in Brooklyn, and the best family silver, which my parents had given me for a wedding present.

To supplement David's meagre pay as a Morgan Guaranty trainee, I took a job looking after a small boy. It did not last long, as I was soon pregnant and either lying in bed or hanging my head over a basin being sick. The doctor said I was not to put a foot to the ground for two months, so poor David had to rush back in his lunch hour across Brooklyn Bridge to empty bedpans and cook my lunch, which usually came straight back again. We had not had time to make many friends, so it was a lonely time for me, and David says now there were times when he felt like throwing himself off Brooklyn Bridge, he got so desperate. But he never showed any of this to me and was very supportive. The only thing I could eat without being sick was chocolate cake and David made do with TV dinners, so shopping was fairly simple. We sold our precious Austin Healey sports car to pay the medical bills.

Henry Fromanteel Lytton Cobbold, 9lb 8oz, was born in Long Island College Hospital on 12 May 1962. In the Knebworth tradition David had added the name of Lytton at the time of our marriage and apparently all Cobbolds have to have Fromanteel among their names, although it sounded rather a mouthful to me. I had a rough time having the baby. I was covered in bruises from the straps they had put round my chest, arms and ankles to hold me down, and David, who was not allowed into the delivery room and had to sit outside, said the doctor came out covered in blood from the scratches I'd given him. Eventually they gave me a general anaesthetic.

When I came to, it was night-time and I found myself in a room with another girl. I woke her up and asked if she knew whether I had had a baby or not. She said she thought I had but did not know what sex it was. I lay in bed feeling my flattened tummy and wondering whether I dared to shout for a nurse. I didn't dare and it was some hours before a nurse bustled in and told me I had a bouncing baby boy. She then asked me to get out of bed as she wanted to make it for me. I got out and promptly fainted, so was put smartly back again, and the baby was brought in crying.

The nurses were very disapproving as I wanted to feed the baby myself, and Americans did not approve of breast-feeding at that time. They dumped him in my arms and told me to get on with it. No one showed me what to do and they fed him on bottles in the nursery when they took him back, but I persevered for a few months. David used to come in the evenings, though he was only allowed to see his son through glass in the nursery. At least he was easily recognisable – he was almost the only white baby and twice the size of any of the others! We called him 'the bishop' with his little flock.

After three days I was sent back to our flat, nervously clutching my baby. My mother very kindly flew out to help me for a week or so, volunteering to do the shopping, cooking and housework, but refusing to have anything to do with the baby. In spite of having five of her own, she confessed to being completely ignorant as far as babies were concerned. We had all been brought up by monthly nurses, nannies and nursemaids.

Henry cried incessantly. Dressed in a long vyella nightie from England, a matinée jacket and bootees, and wrapped firmly in a woollen shawl as I had seen babies at home, he went redder and redder in the face and eventually started choking – at which point I rang the paediatrician. The doctor looked at him with pity, stripped all his clothes off and asked if we were trying to cook the wretched child? The temperature was in the nineties. He needed no clothes on at all! As a parting shot he said, 'It's a good thing for him he's going back to England to live. Uncircumcised and with a name like Henry he would never survive in the States!'

Luckily Henry was tough, and with the help of Doctor Spock's *Baby Book* he survived. As soon as I felt fit enough, I pushed the pram down to the rectory in Brooklyn and rang the bell. The rector opened the door and I showed him the baby and asked him if he could perform the 'Churching of Women' service for me. A look of amazement crossed his face. 'In all my years as a priest I've never been asked to do "the Thanksgiving of Women after Childbirth",' he said, 'but I'd be delighted to do it for you.' I was equally surprised. I thought everyone had the service performed after having a baby – my mother and both my elder sisters had. I met the rector at church a few days later, and Henry lay in his pram in the aisle and, for once, did not scream at all while we went through the service. I liked the words, they were so wonderfully old-fashioned.

Two months later we went back to England and Nanty took Henry off to the nursery at the top of Knebworth House. His American cotton jumpsuits were regarded with horror, and out came David's old vyella nighties, matinée jackets and bootees. I tried not to mind too much, it was wonderful to get some sleep at last.

It was now 1962 and my parents-in-law were thinking about the future of Knebworth House. Lord Cobbold had been appointed Lord Chamberlain to the Queen, and they used the house quite often for entertaining ambassadors and foreign guests. Talk about the future of the house at that time revolved around the possibility of giving it to Hertfordshire as a university, or to an American college; at one stage it nearly became the site for the University of the Air. Anyway, we none of us thought at that time that it would be possible for it to remain a family home for another generation. Kim was definitely against any such idea. He did not want us to be burdened with the expense and worry of a large crumbling house, which he himself had struggled so hard to keep going.

David and I spent the winter of 1962-3 in a small cottage in the village. It had no heating, and as that winter was one of the coldest on record, we would wake up to find the water that had dripped into the bath frozen. Our feelings towards each other became rather strained, not helped by the cold, and so we decided to move to London. We found a large flat in Drayton Gardens, SW10, and were both far happier; I had lots of friends, and the flat to redecorate, and David joined the Bank of London and South America. Unfortunately, however, we were only in London for three months before we were posted to Zurich.

We took an au pair with us to Zurich, and with a three-bedroomed flat things were definitely looking up. Skiing in the winter and water-skiing on the lake in summer – it was a good period in our lives, although our first few weeks were marred by my having a miscarriage, made more complicated by the fact that we knew neither a doctor nor where to find a hospital in Zurich. Not easy in the middle of the night!

Our next attempt was more successful. After I had spent another long period in bed, Peter Guy Fromanteel was born in Mannerdorf Hospital on Lake Zurich on 25 November 1964. This was a much less traumatic event than my experience in America; the hospital expected David to help with the delivery and breast-feeding was considered the normal thing to do.

In February 1965 we were sent to Barcelona for two years. I was getting quite deft at travelling with babies and our lives became very baby-orientated. My memories of our time in Spain are a blur of seaside picnics and hot sunny days in our garden, with gin at ten shillings a bottle! David's job as assistant to the manager of the bank was very boring; the first morning that he turned up, the manager said, 'I have never had an assistant before and I don't need one now.' From then on he hardly addressed a word to him.

As David had no particular job to do in the bank, he took to looking after the stranded tourists who had lost or run out of their money on holiday and were waiting for more to come through from England. He would bring them back to stay in the house, and some stayed quite a few days (usually the attractive female ones). David then got hepatitis and after three months in bed was invalided home.

We moved back to our London flat, where I suffered yet another miscarriage. Planning not to have any more babies for a while, we settled down to enjoy our London life, only to find six months later that I was expecting again. At the same time a large house in Knebworth village had become empty, so we decided to move to Knebworth; and, typically, we managed to move into the house and have the baby all in the same week. The baby was another boy, born on 31 July 1968, named Richard and known by his brothers as Basil Brush!

We loved our life at Knebworth. Park Gate House had a big garden and we built a swimming pool. Commuting for David was easy and Nanty, now in a cottage of her own, would always have the children when needed. They were happy, carefree days. Looking back on those years, I realise that life has never been so easy since and I really appreciated the time I had to enjoy my children and my home. It was marred for me by only one thing. When David and I first married we had both agreed that we would never send the children to boarding school, though maybe as teenagers the boys would go to Eton. But in 1970, when Henry was eight, David changed his mind and, despite my tears and misery (and Henry's), off he was sent to Wellesley House in Broadstairs, Peter following two years later.

They could never understand why they had to go away to school. Henry was an individualist, bright and original; Peter was the comic and show-off, and made us all laugh. Boarding school changed them both – they became quieter, more introverted and lost a lot of their individuality. They would now hang around the house in the holidays waiting to be organised, instead of inventing their own amusements. But they were certainly better behaved and tidier, and we knew they were getting a good education.

Living in Knebworth village, we quickly became involved with the big house and its problems. My parents-in-law were finding the house more and more of a burden, and they longed to build themselves a comfortable bungalow for their retirement. Plans to give Knebworth away to a good cause had fallen through: people had been interested but were frightened off by the state of the building, riddled as it was with dry rot and every sort of beetle.

David and I were young and energetic; the sixties had seen a huge expansion in car ownership and tourism, and the idea of 'the stately home' had been pioneered at Woburn, Longleat and Beaulieu. Suddenly it occurred to us that we could perhaps keep Knebworth as a home. Knebworth House had always been open in a small way even before the war, either by request to the owners or, as in the fifties and sixties, on Saturday and Sunday afternoons. We thought that by opening up the park and adding some new attractions we could make the house pay for itself. The question was, what attractions should we have?

The house had lots of interesting history to offer and 250 acres of parkland for picnicking and putting on events. It was only thirty miles north of London, 6 million people lived within a thirty-mile radius, and it was on the doorstep of the fast-growing New Town of Stevenage. The great leisure boom was beginning, and it seemed that Knebworth had as good a chance as any of being successful.

Our first task was to convince David's parents that our plans for the house were practicable. We arranged a dinner with them and carefully rehearsed what we were going to say. David loved the house, and we both felt it would be sad to be the ones to give it up after 500 years. It would be hard work, but we felt full of energy and keen to take on the challenge. The dinner went better than expected. David's mother was obviously delighted that there was a possibility of keeping the house in the family, but his father was rather more reserved, worrying that it would be a millstone round our necks and that David's City career would suffer. He knew all too well the weariness of coming back from a hard day in London to face a desk full of estate matters. But there was no other solution for the house except to sell it.

After dinner we went back to our house full of excitement, although rather nervous. In convincing the parents that we could make the house and park pay for themselves, the full realisation of what we had let ourselves in for began to dawn.

Chapter 2 | Taking the plunge

Having now convinced the family and ourselves that it was worth having a go at running Knebworth House and park as a viable concern, we thought of little else. In 1969 David obtained a year's sabbatical leave from his job in the bank, and I advertised for a nanny for the children.

The advertisement read, 'Do you like boys? Can you ride, swim, play football, and drive a car?' I had sixty-seven replies, and chose a Yorkshire girl called Patricia Razey. She had been a dentist's receptionist up until then, could not cook and had not looked after children before, but she looked strong and enthusiastic and I had a hunch that she would learn. I was right. She's still with us after seventeen years and is a proficient cook, nanny, decorator, gift-shop manager, engine driver and much else besides. On her first day she was dropped off by three men in a sports car; she was wearing a bright yellow suit and floppy hat, and had a huge plastic rabbit under her arm for the children. She was an immediate success.

In 1970 David's parents had begun designing their log house in the woods half a mile from the house. They would be sufficiently close to feel part of Knebworth still, but far enough away from the crowds of visitors that we expected. It would be a year or two before it was built, so we continued to live at Park Gate House.

We decided to devote our first year to seeing how the existing arrangements for opening the house went, visiting other stately homes to gather ideas and generally making detailed plans for 1971. We increased the entry price to the house from three shillings and sixpence (17½p) for adults and two shillings (10p) for children, to five shillings (25p) and two shillings and sixpence (12½p). To justify the increase we set up a small exhibition in the picture gallery as well.

The exhibition was to mark the centenary of the death of Charles Dickens and to act as a tribute to the friendship of Dickens and Edward Bulwer-Lytton. They had met in the late 1830s at the home of Harrison Ainsworth, publisher of the *Monthly Chronicle*, and become fast friends. In November 1850, Dickens brought his amateur theatrical group to perform in the Banqueting Hall at Knebworth. It included many of the big names of the day: Douglas Jerrold, Mark Lemon, John Forster, John Leech, Georgina Hogarth, Augustus Egg and of course Catherine Dickens, his wife. They acted a play by Ben Jonson called *Every Man in His Humour*. The play was so successful that Dickens and Bulwer continued to put on further performances around the country, to raise money for their ill-fated Guild of Literature and Art and the Guild Houses at Stevenage that later fell victim to the Stevenage Development Corporation.

There is a lot of correspondence between Dickens and Bulwer-Lytton in the Muniment Room at Knebworth, and David spent days doing research for the exhibition. We had to buy display stands and lighting, and arrange for lettering and photography to be done. It was all quite expensive and I worried that we would not get our money back on it. I always worry about the money we spend. David says everything we do is a good investment for the future, but I am not always convinced.

The house was open at weekends from April to September, and from two to five during the week. So on hot sunny afternoons David and I forced ourselves away from our garden and swimming pool at home and went over to Knebworth House. David joined Mrs Martin, the curator, in talking to visitors, checking on the exhibition and planning how to lay out the house for the larger number of visitors we hoped to attract the following year. I spent my time selling tickets and guide books at the entrance or working with the tea ladies in the Lytton Hall (built originally to house the 1st Earl's Viceregal Indian collection), cutting sandwiches and making pots of tea. We decided we would have to build a larger restaurant in the park for the following summer, but I reserved judgement on whether or not I was prepared to run it myself!

The house obviously needed a lot doing to it, and many of Bulwer-Lytton's gargoyles and battlements were crumbling, so we put signs up all round the house saying 'Beware of falling masonry'. The roof was in an appalling state and there was dry rot, fungus and an alarming variety of wildlife in the house. We planned to do the repairs during the winter months and (optimistically) when the money started coming in. The fourteen acres of garden were a problem too. The garden staff had dropped from fourteen gardeners fifty years ago to just one in 1970, the wilderness had encroached and only the lawns and rose beds remained. They were not going to be an attraction yet, and would be expensive to get back into shape and maintain. We contemplated scrapping them altogether and just letting the park come up to the house, but that did not seem right somehow. We never expected to be famous for our garden like Sissinghurst in Kent or Levens Hall in Cumbria, but the area did need to look smart and tidy, so we gave the hard-working gardener two boys to help him and hoped the problem would solve itself.

The house and garden on their own were not large or special enough to bring in the numbers needed to pay for their upkeep, so we were going to have to look to the 275 acres of parkland for extra attractions. We talked over the idea of a garden centre with a local company who ran one in Stevenage. The biggest problem seemed to be that we needed to charge people to come into the park during the summer months and it was difficult to separate the two, as we had only one entrance into the park. Customers wanting just the garden centre would end up being charged the admission fee as well, so unfortunately it never really worked out.

We looked at safari parks at Woburn and Longleat, but decided that our 275 acres of parkland could not compete with these much larger parks; in any case, I did not particularly like the idea of large foreign beasts roaming our park. Other houses had motor museums, beautiful gardens and so on; we had to think of something new. We were very impressed by the adventure playground at Doddington in Gloucestershire and it seemed to go with the country park image that we wanted to project; we also needed something for the children to do while their parents went round the house.

By the end of the summer our heads were buzzing with ideas.

Everything seemed possible: 8000 people had visited the house and the exhibition had been proclaimed a success, earning quite a few good reviews. The *Economist*, writing about the various Dickens exhibitions that summer, said: 'The most evocative of all has been the small one which David Cobbold prepared at Knebworth House near Stevenage (where Dickens wrote part of *David Copperfield*) to celebrate the long friendship of Dickens and Bulwer-Lytton.' We were thrilled.

During the week, David talked to the local authorities and planners; before we did anything we needed to find out the local authorities' attitude to the venture. Luckily, they were delighted that we wanted to take the house on, and there was a recognised need for more recreational facilities for the quickly expanding local population – Stevenage, Welwyn and Letchworth all had 'new towns'. It is important to be on good terms with local residents, and one of the first problems was access to the house and park; we were not going to be popular if we brought a lot of extra traffic through Knebworth village. The A1 motorway runs right through the estate and there was an exit roundabout to which a new spur road could be added straight into the park, eliminating all traffic from the small picturesque village of old Knebworth. It would make Knebworth the only stately home to have its own entrance directly off a motorway (and it still is).

We decided to open the house and park six days a week, Tuesday to Sunday, from 11 a.m. to 5 p.m. from April to October. It would be uneconomical to have to heat the whole house during the winter months, when few visitors would come anyway, and this period could be used for repairs and upkeep.

Neither David nor I wanted to be tied to the estate office, and David would in any case be going back to London soon as his sabbatical was up and we needed his salary to live on. So we started looking for a manager. There was already an estate agent and secretary who dealt with problems relating to the estate such as rents and repairs. Besides the house there are 1000 acres of farmland let to three tenant farmers, 750 acres of woodland and 275 acres of parkland.

We hired Michael Tebbut, who had been the manager at Bowes-Lyon House Youth Centre in Stevenage. There were not many, if any, managers who had experience in house-opening fifteen years ago, as most people muddled along on their own or used their agents, and Michael seemed capable and a good organiser. We also needed an accountant and another secretary as the office was growing. We wrote a list of all the things we needed to organise and do before our big opening the following spring:

Build the new drive off the motorway
Move the tithe barns to make a restaurant
Build a kitchen and loo block
Construct an adventure playground in the park
Find a stable manager and start a riding stables
Find a farrier and get the old forge working
Prepare the house for large numbers of people
Find someone to write a new guide book
Discuss plans for a Fairy Garden in the gardens
Look into the possibility of rebuilding the old maze
Discuss plans for building a two-foot narrow-gauge railway line
Start a gift shop
Make signs, buy litter baskets, tickets etc.
Find summer staff to help run it all . . . and so on!

We did actually manage to do all those things, some more successfully than others.

David went back to the City during the autumn, but found it impossible to concentrate when so much was happening at home. The bank could not be expected to grant indefinite sabbatical leave, so he decided to give up his banking career for a while. I was glad of his presence at home even if it did mean we were short of money. We ran into our first big problem with the new road, which had to be cut through thirty acres of land rented to one of our tenant farmers. We had discussed the project with him and got his agreement, but nothing had been put in writing.

The road-building contractors moved in early on New Year's Day, 1971, with all their heavy equipment. The next thing we knew there was an angry farmer banging on our door, claiming we had not completed a contract with him. It was an expensive start. He ordered the contractors off his land and we had to pay him a lot of money in order to carry on with the road. It was built to take 2000 cars an hour, with six pay gates in operation at the North Lodge entrance, and was 10 feet wide and 2 miles long. It took three months to complete and cost £50,000, the Countryside Commission giving their first major grant to a private development and contributing £25,000 towards the cost.

We decided that the park was to be used for car-parking, picnicking, horse-riding, an adventure playground and a deer park. There had been deer in the park up to 1914, when Lloyd George put a tax on deer parks to help pay for the First World War. A lot of deer parks were closed down as a result, and although the tax was short-lived, fences soon fell into disrepair and few people bothered to replace them. At Knebworth it meant seven miles of new deer fencing would have to go up around the park, but as we needed to secure the park anyway, to make sure everyone came in at the correct entrance and paid, it seemed to solve two problems at once. We had to make sure that all existing footpaths were left open, as well as the entrance to the church, and we built rickety narrow ladders over the seven-foot deer fence where the public footpaths crossed the park, so only a fairly determined walker would attempt to get in!

We also thought that riding and livery stables would go well with the country park image, and we both enjoyed riding at the time (though we have not had time to do any since). Both my father and my grandfather had owned packs of hounds in Devon and I had hunted all over Exmoor as a child, so I felt fairly knowledgeable about horses. David was keen as well, although his early experiences had been less enjoyable – his elder sister had made him clean the tack all the time, with dire threats of being locked in the stables if he did not do it.

There were some disused farm buildings in the village, perfect for stables, so during the winter of 1970 we hired a stables manager and converted the buildings. There were records in the house going back to the 1700s about the farrier at Knebworth forge. If we were going to run the stables as a school with livery and hacking facilities, it made sense to reinstate the forge, the idea being that the farrier would be right on the spot for shoeing the stable horses.

This was all right in theory, but within six months our newly hired stables manager and farrier were not on speaking terms.

Another farrier had to be brought in from miles away at great expense to shoe our horses, while our resident farrier found that making wrought-iron flower pots and chastity belts for selling to the tourists was far more lucrative and less hard work than shoeing. So it was not a great success. Neither were the stables, for some reason. The horses always seemed to have sore feet, coughs or ringworm, and of course big appetites – but at that stage we had yet to find out.

We took on a maintenance team, which we were certainly going to need. It was headed by Derek Spencer; we showed him around the house and park and explained our plans and ideas, but he looked sceptical. 'Might keep me busy for a year,' he said, 'then what?' Fifteen years later, he has not been allowed to forget that remark! The list of 'things for Derek to do' has never got any shorter.

His first job was to build the adventure playground. Most of the playground was made out of wood and rope and was more like an assault course, the *pièce de résistance* being a thirty-foot high, four-lane astroglide slide. It cost £6000 and paid for itself in the first year. We also put in a hut for the St John's Ambulance people, but this proved to be very expensive. We found that if you have a first-aid post, everyone immediately wants sticking plasters, bandages and aspirin. Far better to have nothing on show, and if someone looks in bad shape you can always dig out the necessary from under the cash desk.

We needed a restaurant and lavatory block near the house, but did not want to spoil the park with a new building. So we planned to move two 400-year-old tithe barns from the estate, and build a kitchen and loo block between them. One of the barns would have to be dismantled and put up again in its new position, but the other we decided to move in one piece. This was to be done by a firm called Pynfords between Easter and Whitsun, when the ground would be drier. In the meantime I was to make do with a marquee in the park. As we were now going to be open from 11 a.m. visitors would want more than a cup of tea and sandwiches, so I bought two gas rings and some large frying pans so that they could have hamburgers and hot-dogs. I had not taken into account, however, how much shopping and carrying this was going to involve.

Organising the summer staff was quite a problem as well. There was no shortage of people wanting to work, but they all had summer holidays booked, or a family wedding or some day they could not manage, so I had to shuffle them around all the time and hope they turned up at the right time. There was an empty cottage in the village, and I had the bright idea of putting four foreign students in it for the summer in order to have 'on site' help. However, this wasn't a great success. First, I had to furnish the cottage, including making curtains, and then it was felt that if we fed the students at home we wouldn't have to pay them so much, so I ended up having to cater for an extra four hungry teenagers. There was also the language problem, getting them up in the mornings – never easy – and making sure they were happy and not getting into trouble.

Meanwhile, David was tactfully trying to reorganise the house for larger numbers. Mrs Martin had been the curator in the house for my parents-in-law for many years and none of us knew how she would take to all our changes. She was, not surprisingly, suspicious of our ideas and told David he would never get more than 350 people round the house in one day, David proved her wrong on the first bank holiday Monday when 1500 people poured through the house, the secret being a new one-way route round the house with wardens in each room instead of guided parties. She rose to the challenge nobly, approved of the new glossy guide book Sybilla Jane Flower had written for us, set up a gift shop in the hall, reorganised her staff and did a wonderful job until her retirement six years later. But there were obviously some tricky moments. David's parents were still living in the house and I found it easier to let him handle the house side of things and to keep myself busy in the office or park.

David's one-way system was, and still is, a great success. Visitors enter the house through the garden door on the west side of the house into the entrance hall, which was given its present form in the early 1900s by Sir Edwin Lutyens. In the hall stand fifteen high-backed hall chairs with grisaille decoration, about half of which are the original ones from the seventeenth century, the remainder being copies which Edward Bulwer-Lytton had made in the 1830s. They're stately-looking chairs but amazingly uncomfortable to sit on. The Banqueting Hall is the first room the visitor enters, and it is rated as one of the most beautiful rooms in England; the beautiful oak screen and Minstrels' Gallery is the oldest part of the room, dating from 1610–20, and the rest of the panelling is fifty or sixty years later. The rosewood Banqueting Hall table dates from the late eighteenth century, and reproductions of it are now sold all over the world; the twelve chairs are eighteenth-century and made of applewood. The table is laid up with Nymphenburg china which had been Edward Bulwer-Lytton's wedding present to Rosina, and the Italian crested glass was made up for Robert Lytton during his time as Viceroy – neither are candidates for the dishwasher! There are also two Jacobean sofas in the room which were taken from James I's state bedroom at Wanstead. Portraits show Sir Robert Lytton, who was the great favourite of Henry VII, and his great grandson Sir Rowland Lytton, painted in 1585; the painting of Sir Rowland's wife, Anne St John, is by Marcus Gheeraerts, one of the most fashionable painters of his day. A painting of the Banqueting Hall by Sir Winston Churchill hangs at one end of the room, and there is a motto around the cornice of the hall written by Sir Edward Bulwer-Lytton:

> Read the rede of this old roof tree
> Here be trust safe, opinion free,
> Knightly right-hand, Christian knee,
> Worth in all, wit in some,
> Laughter open, slander dumb.
> Hearth where rooted friendships grow
> Safe as altar even to foe.
> Home where chivalry and grace
> Cradle a high-hearted race.
> If thy sap in these may be
> Fear no winter, old roof tree.

From the Banqueting Hall, the visitor passes into the White Drawing Room, which was the dining parlour of the original house. The room was extensively remodelled by Bulwer-Lytton and was known as the Oak Drawing Room until the beginning of this century, when it was transformed into its present state by Lutyens. The furniture has been collected over the years: the sofa is Hepplewhite, the tortoiseshell and ivory cabinets are Italian of the early part of the eighteenth century and a cabinet veneered with tortoiseshell and framed with ebony and ormolu is seventeenth-century Flemish. There is also an inlaid writing-desk with lots of secret drawers; our daughter is the only member of the family who knows where they all are. The octagonal 'dolphin' table was painted in 1923 by the late Lady Plymouth as a gift for Pamela, Countess of Lytton. The paintings are particularly interesting, and the finest is undoubtedly the portrait by Sir Peter Lely of Ruth, daughter of Sir Francis Barrington and a first cousin of Oliver Cromwell. She married Sir William Robinson, and died in 1645 shortly after this portrait was painted. William Robinson in his elegant and richly-beribboned costume is one of the small group of portraits executed by Samuel van Hoogstraeten during his visit to England in the 1660s.

The Library was made by Sir Edward Bulwer-Lytton. The decoration of the room has been radically altered since his day, but the shelves still retain the greater part of his collection. Bulwer himself wrote over seventy volumes of novels, plays, poems and essays, all of which are represented in the Library in various editions. There is a sketch by G. F. Watts of Robert, 1st Earl of Lytton, over the fireplace; the finished portrait is in the National Portrait Gallery. The marble roundel set into the Lutyens fireplace shows him in his later years and was made by Sir Alfred Gilbert as a model for his memorial in St Paul's Cathedral. Over the fireplace is a motto, a quotation from Virgil, which was chosen by Bulwer as applicable to his Library – *Hic Vivunt Vivere Digni* ('Here live those only that are worthy to live'). There is also a splendid seventeenth-century Dutch musical clock, with mechanical figures and windmills. Every three hours – at three, six, nine and twelve o'clock – it plays 'Greensleeves' and a shepherd walks across the face of the clock, followed by a flock of sheep and his wife brandishing a stick. There is also a woodman chopping wood, a man fishing, and in the background the windmills turn. It didn't work when we moved in and, although we've had it restored, it's always breaking down.

The visitor then moves on to the staircase, again the creation of Bulwer-Lytton. The double flight of oak stairs surmounted by lions bearing armorial shields and a magnificent pair of Nubian slaves is typical of his extravagant ideas of decoration. The collection of arms at the foot of the stairs is of varying periods, the majority dating from the seventeenth century, and includes one suit of armour presented to Bulwer-Lytton by his friend, the novelist Harrison Ainsworth. Family portraits cover the walls. The life-size, full-length portrait of Victor, 2nd Earl of Lytton, in his Garter robes was painted by his brother Neville, and the latter's self-portrait and a portrait of his niece, Lady Cobbold, also hang on the staircase. Adding a lighter touch is a portrait of our children in jeans and T-shirts.

The two small rooms off the landing are devoted to illustrating the life, literary career and friendships of Edward Bulwer-Lytton. The portrait over the fireplace was painted by E. M. Ward in 1854 and depicts the novelist sitting in the room where he always worked, smoking one of his long cherry-wood pipes. Bulwer-Lytton had a passion for smoking. 'A pipe', he says in *Night and Morning*, 'is a great soother – a pleasant comforter. Blue devils fly before its honest breath. It ripens the brain: it opens the heart and the man who smokes, thinks like a sage and acts like a Samaritan.' This was probably because the pipe normally contained opium. Bulwer's favourite pipe is preserved in this room, as is the crystal ball into which he would gaze for hours.

The State Drawing Room is the next room. This is one of the finest surviving examples of Victorian interior decoration and a perfect example of the revival of interest in the High Gothic which was to turn upside down the world of English architecture and decoration. The designer John Crace and Bulwer-Lytton worked closely together, and the decorative scheme expresses the ideas of both men – quite outrageous even for the tastes of the next generation. The only reason that the decoration has remained in this form is that the room is in the farthest corner of the house and nobody ever went in! There is a large portrait by Daniel Maclise representing Caxton's printing press in one corner of the room; it was painted in 1850 and left to the Lytton family by John Forster, the friend and biographer of Dickens.

Going back into the main part of the house, through the Minstrels' Gallery, you come to the first bedroom, the Falkland Room, named after the Viscountess Falkland, daughter of the last Sir Rowland Lytton. It is hung with hand-painted Chinese wallpaper of the eighteenth century, and there is a small Chinese pagoda in the room which was the inspiration for a scene in Charles Dickens's novel *David Copperfield* – 'the Chinese house for Jip with little bells on the top', which Dora and David Copperfield bought for her dog.

The Hampden Bedroom recalls the Lyttons' association with the Parliamentarian cause. We refurbished it in the style of an Edwardian nursery and it contains a dolls' house made for Mrs Bulwer in the eighteenth century and a cradle dating from about 1775, two Edwardian children's four-poster beds and two Edwardian cots. It also has a large collection of children's clothes, nursery books and toys; we had a hard job keeping our children out of the room, and occasionally they would creep in to ride on the rocking horse and sit on the musical chair. Mrs Bulwer's Bedroom contains many of the small objects and pictures (such as portraits of her favourite dog, and her dressing-table set) which hung in this room during her lifetime, thirty years of which were spent at Knebworth as a widow. The Queen Elizabeth Room is the most impressive bedroom and the great oak carved bed dominates the room; the paintings are from the Elizabethan period.

This concludes the tour of the house and visitors then go down the back stairs and back into the front hall past the gift shop. They have a chance to look down into the Picture Gallery, but we don't allow people into it except for special occasions, as the family use it.

We opened for business on Good Friday, 1971. The road was built, the stables and adventure playground were operational, the house was looking good and the gardens just passable. Before Easter we had a grand opening of our new two-mile drive, through the park from the motorway and up the 300-year-old chestnut avenue to the house. David had fallen in love with and bought a landau a few months earlier, and the stables manager had found a horse to pull it. My mother-in-law cut the red ribbon and the children piled into the landau for the ride up the new road. We hoped our dalmatian would remember its ancestry and be a carriage dog, but it got under the horse's feet almost immediately and got trodden on, then refused ever to go near a horse again.

Visitors poured into the park – we had quite a lot of local

publicity and many people were curious. Any apprehensions we may have had about people turning up disappeared, although of course we were uncertain and anxious about how the organisation would work out. The barns were yet to be moved, but my marquee was open for lunches and teas; lavatory facilities were for the moment in some port-a-loo cabins; a large hut served as a gift shop, and plans for a steam railway were going ahead.

By the end of Easter weekend I could hardly move, my back ached so much. I had carried so many crates of fizzy drinks and cooked pounds of hamburgers . . . and I was pregnant once again. As I had gone through yet another miscarriage the year before I had to try to be careful; but it was impossible – there was so much to do and I was hopeless at sitting and giving orders. When I went into the hospital in Welwyn Garden City with my miscarriage, the doctor had said, 'All right, then, what did you do to try and get rid of the baby?' I protested that I had not done anything and I wanted the baby. He then told me I had more than my quota of 2.6 children and should not want any more anyway. But we had set our hearts on having a girl, so I retired to bed and chewed my nails, wondering how everyone was getting along without me.

The barn-moving had begun over Easter. Pynfords put bailey-bridging around the one that was to be moved intact, jacked it up, placed sixteen huge wheels under it and pulled it with a steam traction engine two-thirds of a mile across the park. It was the largest building ever to be moved in England, and the publicity brought a lot of people to watch. It was supposed to take five days to move, but ended up taking five weeks; there were many frustrating delays and I thought it would never get there. Easter Sunday was an embarrassing day. The press had been invited for the first day's moving, but the preparations were not complete and, when pulled, the barn would not move. The rain was sheeting down and we had to try and keep the journalists happy with endless whisky and hot soup.

Charlie, the driver of the traction engine pulling the barn, regularly got bored and disappeared to 'his office' – his name for the Lytton Arms. When all was ready he had to be extracted from the pub and guided back to his engine. On the first pull the engine went backwards instead of the barn going forwards. But it got there in the end, and not a single tile fell off the roof!

The two barns make very attractive restaurants, and although our original idea was that they should be used for daily visitors they quickly became popular for weddings, banquets and dances. I sat up in the evenings making huge curtains for them in order to be ready for their opening. Simmonds, some local caterers who were already running the restaurants at Hatfield House and Waddesdon, had asked if they could run the Barns Restaurant for us, and I willingly handed over the catering to them, the smell of frying hamburgers and onions being more than my now delicate stomach could handle.

Nevertheless, I got out of bed for Whitsun weekend and gave myself a sitting-down job, taking the money and lifting the tops off the fizzy drink bottles. There was a 3d. deposit on the empty bottles, and after a while I began to get the feeling that more bottles were coming back than I had sold. I then discovered that children were pinching the discarded empties from under the side of the marquee and bringing them round over and over again for 3d. a time!

The adventure playground was proving a tremendous draw. We'd hired a beautifully painted gipsy caravan from Lady Bangor (who has a large collection of fairground equipment at Wookey Hole) for the summer, and two of the foreign students sat in it and looked after the playground. The lavatories at the playground were not finished, but a large round yellow septic tank sat waiting to be put in the ground with a piece of rope staked around it and a sign saying 'please keep off'. But, as we soon discovered, no one reads notices – or if they do they don't think they apply to themselves. Two children climbed through the spout into the tank and another sat on top. The ones inside managed to roll the tank right over, squashing the child on top underneath. The child was badly injured and lost an eye, and his parents sued us. It was a bad start and a strong lesson to us; we have never had a serious accident since then and the playground is generally thought to be safer than the slides and swings in concrete municipal playgrounds.

David's grandmother Pamela, Lady Lytton died in June 1971. She was ninety-seven and living in the nearby manor house. She had become completely blind and more or less bedridden by the end, and I don't know how much she took in about what we were doing at Knebworth House, but she was pleased that we were continuing to keep the house in the family. I hate funerals and was relieved that I had an excuse not to go to hers, as I was still stuck in bed trying to keep the baby. Henry was at prep school but Peter was at the village school and Richard was at home all the time, so I had plenty of company; but I did not see much of David. He was often late coming back in the evenings and I started feeling deserted and hostile towards the attractive Swedish and Austrian girls we had virtually living with us. Everyone seemed to be having a good time except me, and I got thoroughly fed up.

Our house and garden were getting very neglected as I was not able to do anything to them. I did not have a gardener at that time because I had been doing it all myself, but now I could not even pick the flowers for the house. David did spend one afternoon up a ladder trying to tie up the wistaria, but the ladder slipped and he fell off on to the paving stones below. Badly bruised and winded, he staggered into the sitting room and lay on the floor groaning. I could not hear as I was upstairs in bed reading, but the Swedish au pair was hoovering the floor and continued to hoover all around him. He was eventually rescued by Pattie, and the au pair, when asked why she had not done anything to help him, said, 'Oh, I thought he was playing one of your silly English games.' Luckily, by July I was able to get up and start doing things again, and one of the first things I did was to get rid of the foreign students!

The biggest day we had that first year was an air display in August. It was run by the Barnstormers and included the Blue Eagles helicopters and a Spitfire, brilliantly piloted by ex-Red Arrow leader Ray Hanna. David was in his element over the air displays; he had learnt to fly on a Tiger Moth after school and had done national service in the RAF flying jets in Canada. He flew one of the Tiger Moths for the press preview the week before the show. I was less enthusiastic, however, as it meant having twenty airmen plus assorted wives and girlfriends to stay in the house or camping in the park for the weekend. Breakfast was a nightmare, trying to cook eggs and bacon for them all in my kitchen. But it was a very popular event and brought in about 5000 people.

By the end of August everything seemed to be working fairly

well, so David and I and the three boys and Pattie took a fortnight's holiday. We went down to the south of France and then up to the mountains to walk. I found walking rather a problem with my expanding waistline, but it was good to leave the pressures behind and be together as a family for a while.

Totalling up at the end of the first year, the cost of setting the whole venture up had been: the Barns Restaurant, £118,000; drainage, £12,000; roads and car parks, £70,000; fencing, £15,000; architects' fees, £19,000; equipment, £86,000; vehicles, £2000; miscellaneous improvements, £42,000. A horrifying bill of £366,000 which carried a bank interest of £40,000 a year. How we ever expected to pay that back and make money to repair the house as well, I do not know.

But 92,000 people had visited the park, 26,000 had been round the house and we were hailed by the press as 'the fastest-growing stately home in the business'. Nothing was going to stop us now!

Chapter 3 In at the deep end

Although we were now eighth in the stately home league – after Woburn, Longleat, Castle Howard, Beaulieu, Harewood House, Warwick Castle and Tatton Park – and the numbers of visitors had exceeded everyone's expectations, we were going to need even more next summer and would have to put the price up. Everything had cost so much money.

Because of our grant from the Countryside Commission, we had to get their permission to raise our prices, but as the park had still been under construction the previous summer we had only charged 20p a car. With a few more attractions and improvements to the adventure playground and railway, we planned to put the price back to 25p for adults and 10p for children, and the astroglide and railway were extra. We hoped there would not be too many complaints.

Meanwhile we had the winter to get through. The riding in the park was popular during the summer and the gymkhanas we had held had been well attended, but the winter months were not going so well. The daylight hours were short and the weather often bad. The horses could not go out at all if there had been a heavy frost and the ground was hard. We longed to build an indoor riding school, but the expense was prohibitive and even David did not think we could afford it. However, we did decide to extend the bridle path into the 700 acres of woodland beyond the park; in May the bluebells in the woods at Knebworth are the best in the country and the trees would provide a more sheltered ride in bad weather. We could not let the horses go all over the woods as the gamekeeper would have a fit, so in the autumn of

1971 we hacked a path through the brambles and bracken, painting yellow blobs on the trees to mark the track. It was very hard work and took quite a few weekends to complete. David was back in the City again and as I was now very large I did not like doing it on my own.

The keeper watched the proceedings with disapproval, then added his contribution after we had finished; this consisted of strands of wire strung at neck height between trees at places where he thought the riders might be tempted to go off the path. He was only protecting his pheasants, but it annoyed us a lot at the time and nearly killed David once.

The woods are full of game and there is a pheasant shoot at Knebworth. In 1971 this was run by David's father as a syndicate; he seldom shot himself but hired guns out to the local gentry. David shot when I first met him, and so did I. My father, being a very good and keen sportsman, must have been disappointed in having four daughters before his only son, and used to encourage us to go shooting and fishing with him. I took to the shooting though I never mastered the fishing – my line always ended up in a tangle. David said he gave up his shooting because I was better than him, but I was not. We were neither of us particularly enthusiastic, and at Knebworth we certainly did not want to spend our Saturdays chasing after pheasants; we preferred to ride or walk in the woods. But we joined in the shooting picnic lunches held in the fishing cottage by the lake.

Kim did give me his 20-bore gun, though, which I kept in my bedroom so I could shoot the rabbits out of the window when they were eating my plants. The gardens were full of rabbits, both at Park Gate House and at Knebworth. I tried to teach my boys how to skin and gut them, but I never had much success. Even when I plucked the pheasants, the entire family, including Pattie, held their noses and rushed from the kitchen.

I had little patience at that time with people who were squeamish. As children we made our pocket money from mole skins; my brother, younger sister and I had our own traps and we caught the moles, skinned them, rubbed salt on the pelts and pinned them out on boards. When my father went to London he would take a brown paper parcel of mole skins with him, and dressed in his city suit, bowler hat and umbrella, he would go into the London Fur Company in Brompton Road and exchange the mole skins for a pound or two. We got a shilling a skin. Thirty years later, when a friend said he longed to have a moleskin waistcoat, I had a go at trapping and skinning a couple of moles to see if I could still remember how to do it. I did, but I could not have made a waistcoat – I have definitely become less bloodthirsty with age.

The lake in the woods is stocked with trout each March, and there is a boat house with a couple of punts in it which is a lovely place to go for a quiet afternoon in the summer. David still sometimes holds birthday parties there. In winter there are always a few days when we can skate on the lake or go curling. David's grandfather was a keen skater and there is an assortment of old skates in the attic and heavy curling weights in the back of the fishing cottage.

We had expected the winter months to be fairly peaceful after our busy first summer. The house was closed, and although a lot of people still came into the park, closed or not, because they had always walked in it before and did not mean to stop now, it was not worth trying to take money off them during the winter – they could always say they were looking for the footpaths anyway. By the end of 1971 the Barns Restaurant was proving to be a tremendous success for local banqueting and dinner dances. We had been asked by several travel agencies if we could put on special evenings for large groups of Americans over here on 'incentive tours'. I discovered that 'incentive tours' were the prize for the person who sold the most of a particular product, such as Ford motor cars or International Harvester tractors, in their area during the year. Up to 400 salesmen and their wives would be flown over to England for a week or two and given a condensed sightseeing tour ending up with a big last-night party. We decided to try our hands at Elizabethan banquets for them.

David and I would greet them, dressed in Elizabethan costume, at the front door and take them round the house, then we would go over to the Barns for a banquet. Wenches in low-cut dresses would serve mead and sit on the gentlemen's laps. Minstrels would sing bawdy songs, while we sat at the High Table with Henry VIII (in the person of Terry Denton de Gray), signed guide books for the visitors and tried to avoid drinking too much mead. The evenings usually ended up with everyone doing a conga around the room, and some had to be carried into the coaches when it was time to leave. Mead is obviously far more potent than people realise. We made quite a few friends throughout 1972 and had lots of offers to go and stay with people in America, which we were to take up the following year.

Christmas 1971 was to be our last in Park Gate House before moving the family into Knebworth. The baby was expected in January but, like a lot of our plans, this did not work out quite as expected. Getting up early one dark morning in December to make David's breakfast before he went off to catch his train to London, I tripped and fell headlong down the stairs. I lay on the floor winded and terrified I might have damaged the baby, but I recovered my breath and decided I was more frightened than hurt.

Later in the day, I drove up to London to finish off some Christmas shopping and then went on to an Italian restaurant with David and his parents. During dinner the pains started. I was supposed to have the baby in Hertfordshire but could not risk driving home, so we rang my former London doctor. She told us to go straight to the Holland Park nursing home, and she would meet us there.

A short time later the baby was born. 'It's a girl – it's a girl,' David kept saying, his voice full of excitement. The baby was put into my arms, but my wonder soon turned to panic – she was blue and felt stiff and wrong to me. The doctor took her away quickly and spent the next half hour trying to clear her congested lungs by sucking with a straw. Eventually she wrapped her in tinfoil and rushed her to the Charing Cross Hospital, where she lay in an oxygen tent and incubator for two weeks. She had pneumonia and was very ill; it was a tearful time.

Christmas arrived, the boys all had chickenpox and there was no chance of the baby coming home. We went up to London to visit her in hospital, where the nurses had hung a Christmas stocking on the end of her incubator. Donning gowns and masks, we were allowed into the room to look at her in her glass box, but we couldn't touch her. Both David's mother and mine tried to persuade me to get a monthly nurse for the baby when she came out of hospital, but I knew Pattie and I would both be fighting to care for her – we didn't need anyone else. The baby was named Rosina after her notorious Irish ancestor, Rosina Bulwer-Lytton, and Kim after her grandfather. The boys regarded their sister with suspicion; they had hoped it would be another boy.

Life soon settled down again, and I was back at work. David wanted a flag for the top of Knebworth House; the Union Jack had been hoisted from the tower on appropriate occasions but for a permanent flag we were going to need to replace the old wooden flagpole. So a huge crane arrived in the courtyard and a long aluminium pole was somehow erected on top of the eighty-foot tower. I decided to try my hand at flag-making; the Cobbold coat of arms was a gold lion and two balls on a black background with two blue crowns on the top, and it was fun to make. I felt quite proud of my flag when it was finished and fluttering in the breeze, hoisted on the new flagpole. But I had not counted on the beating it would get from the wind – I found myself having to make two new flags each year.

We had got rid of the cattle in the park as they frightened some people and cowpats don't go with picnicking. Consequently, trying to keep the grass down was becoming a problem. The deer fence was complete but we needed the deer; they were expensive to buy and we couldn't afford them – everything was costing so much more than we had expected. Dr Dansie, a local doctor in Welwyn, was a deer expert, so we asked his advice and he said he would see what he could do. Soon after, he came back to us looking very pleased. A rich local businessman had come to him suffering from a heart attack, and the doctor had persuaded him that what he needed was a peaceful hobby, such as deer-watching, to keep his blood pressure down. The deer could be bought from Woburn Park, and Knebworth was the ideal place to put them. Mr Rourke could drive the few miles from his home in Welwyn in his Rolls Royce in the evenings and at weekends and watch his deer in our park. It seemed the perfect solution at the time, although we were to live to regret it. Fifteen fallow deer and fourteen Manchurian sika arrived first; the red deer were to follow. Red and fallow deer had always been found in England, but the sika had been brought from China a hundred years ago by the Bedfords for Woburn Park; we were the only other park to have them. We called our new gift shop the Sika Stores.

Another wildlife attraction was a bird garden which Michael and Ann Tunnicliffe set up in the park, to open the following summer. Ann was a daughter of Richard Chipperfield and had worked with her macaws in his circus. I have never liked animals or birds in cages, but the attraction of this bird garden was going to be the free-flying birds – although of course some cages had to be built and a pond made for the flamingoes. The flamingoes were supposed to have had their wings clipped before coming, but as soon as they were let out they flew straight off and disappeared over the park. We managed to get them back by the evening, but one had made a bad landing and broken a leg. I had to ring up our vet in the middle of the night to ask him to come and splint a flamingo's leg; he took some convincing that we were serious!

The free-flying pelicans and macaws were the most spectacular. The macaws would fly in formation around the garden, quite often lining up on both wing tips of a huge white pelican – an amazing sight. They would sit in a tree near where I was gardening and squawk at me. Ann Tunnicliffe knew them all by name; she would whistle for them and they would fly down from the trees and perch on her head and shoulders. However, the macaws were wreckers of trees and any tree that took their fancy would be stripped at an alarming rate; my parents-in-law were worried they would discover their new wooden house being built in the woods. It was nearly finished now and they had started moving in.

We were learning that free publicity is the best. I was brought up to believe that it was 'not nice' to be written about in the newspapers and I found it hard to be suddenly in the public eye, to have to change my attitude and chat up the press instead of avoiding them. If one could think up a good gimmick at least once a week, the local papers were very willing to do an article and take some pictures.

Even during the winter we managed to find some excitements for the press. In February we held a lawn meet for the local hunt, the Enfield Chase; it was the first time hounds had met at Knebworth for at least fifty years. David and I did not ride but we handed out the cherry brandy and worried about our new deer in the park. The Master assured us that his fox hounds would never go after deer, but I remembered some awkward moments on Exmoor in my youth when my grandfather's hounds had been tempted to go after the red deer, and I did not relax until the hounds were out of the park and into the woods.

A completely different event took place the week after when part of the RAC Rally was held in the park. The expected time for the trip around the two-mile circuit was set by the organisers at 2 minutes 17 seconds; this was beaten by 5 seconds and one of the cars veered off the track and ploughed through the spectators. Luckily no one was hurt, but it made the day more exciting and provided headlines for the local newspapers.

In the spring of 1972, a local motor club asked if they could hold regular autocross or grass-track motor-racing meetings in one corner of the park. There was plenty of room and it would mean four or five meetings spread throughout the year, so we said yes. The noise was rather excessive, however, and as the meetings were held on Sundays we had to make sure they stopped while the church service was in progress or no one could hear a word the rector said.

We were keen to include the church in the park opening, and one of the first things we did that spring was to hold the annual thanksgiving and blessing service of the Lullingstone Farm silk-worms. We had been talking to Zoe, Lady Hart-Dyke who ran the silk farm at Ayot St Lawrence. She was looking for somewhere to plant an orchard of mulberry trees for her silkworms, and we toyed with the idea of becoming part of her silk farm. It was her suggestion that the service should be held in the church in the park. It sounded a strange idea to me but Mr Rumsey, the rector, was willing, so Lady Zoe arrived with about eight ladies bearing large cardboard boxes full of silkworms, and we all trooped into church. The ceremony solemnly took place. I found it difficult to keep a straight face and I was glad I had not taken the children with me.

We found Sundays were so busy in the park that our visits to church with the children were becoming less and less frequent. But in spite of the crowds pouring in, I felt that Easter Sunday must be an exception and I really should take the family to church. So I chased them up. There were complaints all round and groans about not being able to find any tidy clothes etc, but I was firm and bundled them all into the car, through the park and into the family pew. Peter had tears streaming down his face but I refused to listen to anyone's complaints. Halfway through the second hymn, Peter was still sobbing and no amount of dirty looks from me would shut him up, so I grabbed his arm and marched him out of the church. Once outside I started swearing at him, until he sobbed that he had not had time to find his underpants and his willie had got caught in his trouser zipper and he was in agony. I tried hard to unzip him but to no avail, I stopped the manager on his way through the park and he couldn't do it either, so I had to take him to Stevenage hospital where a sympathetic doctor gave a quick jerk to the zipper and Peter was free, though scarred for life. I felt so guilty that I promised never to bully any of them into going to church again!

We had 8500 visitors over the Easter weekend in 1972, more people than we had had in the whole season in 1970. Most of the forthcoming summer weekends were booked for some event, but the biggest one was a 'Stately Steam-Up' which carried on over two weekends in July. Bill McAlpine, who owned our steam train, and Professor Weeks, a steam enthusiast from Newcastle, helped us to stage the event. About thirty traction engines came along with an Edwardian steam fair, with roundabouts, steam yachts and organs. In addition to our normal advertising in the local papers, Charlie, who had been responsible for moving the barn the year before, came with his traction engine and suggested we might all go pub-crawling in it as extra publicity for the steam event. It sounded a great idea and we spent a few evenings puffing and grinding our way around the countryside, visiting local inns. It was slow work and there was plenty of time to sober up between pubs!

The event was a huge success, the sun shone and the crowds flocked in – 16,000 on one Sunday. There were competitions for the engines, such as ploughing and obstacle races; there was a steam-pudding eating contest and, even more popular, a Miss Steam competition, which Julia Whitbread our local butcher's wife won. She posed for the press in a scanty bikini on a traction engine. The steam yacht was my favourite fair ride – a really sick-making experience that swung you backwards and forwards and lifted you from your seat and made your hair stand on end. A very eccentric vicar brought his own steam railway engine (he had a track in his garden in Leicestershire) and drove it round and round our two-mile track, hooting his whistle continuously until about midnight, when we had to coax him off his train with promises of pints of beer in the house.

Unfortunately, the event was a financial disaster. We learnt that you do not offer ten days of free beer to steam-engine drivers; all the profits had been drunk. In fact I think we even ended up owing the breweries money.

In July 1972, David's parents moved out of Knebworth House and into their new Lake House. We wanted to do a lot to Knebworth but did not have time during the summer months, so for the time being we camped on the top floor. The nursery was used as a kitchen, dining room and sitting room, though we seldom had time to sit down. Entertaining was out of the question; feeding seven of us was about as much as a Baby Belling stove and the nursery table could take, and washing had to be done in a sink in a small maid's cupboard. We were going to let Park Gate House furnished, so we needed to buy new dishwashers and so on, but that would have to wait until the end of the season when I had time.

The boys loved the freedom of the big house to run around in, and were fascinated by the visitors. I had to stop them throwing their toys out of the night nursery window on to the unsuspecting visitors' heads below, and the guides in the house were always shooing them back upstairs, although the visitors seemed to enjoy the fact that the house was lived in. Night-time was a problem, as the children decided it was spooky, so doors had to be left open and lights on. Certain passages and pictures were to be avoided after dark and there was a great reluctance to let me leave after the bedtime story. But the park was a continual source of amusement and they became very popular with their contemporaries; local school birthday parties were often held at the adventure playground.

The air display had been such a success the year before that we booked the Barnstormers again for the first Sunday in August. I went on strike over feeding them all in the nursery – there really wasn't room – so they camped in the park and we had a party for them on the Saturday night in the Barns Restaurant. But Sunday turned out to be a nightmare.

In the morning we were feeling fairly hungover, when Pattie

rushed into our bedroom at seven-thirty with Rosina in her arms. 'Quick, there's something dreadfully wrong with her,' she gasped. 'I went to pick her up and she had stopped breathing and had gone stiff and blue.' I grabbed the baby and David rushed to telephone the doctor. The doctor said take her straight to hospital, so we made a dash to the local hospital; she was by now lying white and limp in my arms and hardly breathing at all. She had had a bad cold all the week and apparently had been unable to clear her lungs properly. It was lucky that Pattie had picked her up at that moment – a few minutes more and she would have been dead. Rosina spent a few days in hospital, but fortunately did not have to be put in an oxygen tent. I never even noticed that it had poured with rain all day and the air display had been a disaster; low cloud had prevented a lot of the acts taking place and hardly anyone had come to watch.

The following weekend in August, there was a different emergency. The engine driver never turned up to drive our steam train, the manager was having a day off and David was busy in the office. Who was going to drive the train? Visitors were beginning to grumble. David looked at me; I shook my head. Where was Pattie? She was just about to take Richard and Rosina for a walk with the pram. 'I'll take the children for their walk,' I said firmly, 'you'd make a much better engine driver than me.' David gave her a quick lesson on how to start and stop and left her to it. The tourists were delighted; quite a queue had built up and the coaches were soon full to capacity. Pattie set off down the track and all went well until it came to stopping, when, suddenly realising that the train was not going to stop, Pattie shouted to her startled passengers to jump off quickly. The engine ploughed off the rails into the gravel in front of the Barns Restaurant. Luckily no one was hurt, but we needed a crane to get the engine back onto the rails and Pattie's train-driving career came to an abrupt halt.

The 1972 season drew to an end. We had boosted the numbers to 183,000, 35,000 of whom had been through the house, and instead of us looking for events, people had started writing to us asking if they could put something on in the park the following summer. Caravan clubs were busy booking a part of the park for weekend rallies. We had no facilities for the campers, only a water tap, but it didn't seem to matter – they brought everything with them. There were no problems and they nearly always paid to go into the house during the weekend. The coach trade and school parties still had to be worked on; we planned a new leaflet and advertising campaign for the following year.

It had been a very successful summer and the future looked optimistic. It seemed strange, closing the house and suddenly having no visitors around the place, but it did give us breathing space to sort our own lives out a bit. The move over to Knebworth House during the summer had been undramatic; we had taken quite a few weeks over it and I had collected a carload whenever I had a moment. Unpacking was a problem, however, as every cupboard and chest in Knebworth House was already full and in four years we had collected a lot of belongings. We stacked them in boxes and cases in empty rooms and left them until the end of the season. As my parents-in-law had always expected to give the house away they had not bothered to do much decoration, and the top nursery floor especially was in need of new paint, wall-paper, carpets and curtains.

As soon as we shut the house to the public in September and Henry and Peter had gone off to boarding school, and Richard had started at the day nursery in the village, Pattie and I began looking at paint colours and wallpaper books. Our task for the winter was to decorate the house. Major repair works had started on the roof and Derek, our maintenance manager, was busy organising that and trying to cope with the dry rot and beetle in the house as well. He would not have time to do any decoration and we could not afford decorators, so Pattie and I rolled up our sleeves, bought a couple of light aluminium ladders, borrowed some planks of wood from the timber yard and set to. We stripped off the old papers, which usually meant half the wall coming off with them, plastered the walls where necessary and filled up the cracks with polyfilla. We started on the top floor, which consisted of eleven rooms and a long passage. The rooms were large and some of the ceilings were over twelve foot high.

One bedroom had a huge ornate arched plaster ceiling, which Pattie and I painted orange and white. David waited until we had finished and then said he thought green and white would look better. He was away for a week on business, so we painted it over in green, as a surprise for him. He took one look and said it was hideous. Pattie and I cursed him but had to agree it was not right, so for the third time we painted it white all over – boring but safe. David and I never agree on colours and we usually end up with something which neither of us likes and is a disaster.

Henry, having been born in America, decided on stars and stripes for his room, so we painted a blue ceiling, stuck luminous stars all over it and hung red and white striped material on the walls. Peter could not make up his mind so we painted the panels in his room in ten different colours. Pattie had her own room next to Rosina, who was in the old night nursery, and Richard slept in the day nursery. We had made a television and play room for the children downstairs next to the kitchen, which was more practical for modern living than the nursery upstairs, but we had to rig up a baby alarm system from the top floor down to the kitchen on the ground floor in order to be able to hear Rosina in the evenings. There are forty-five stairs up to the top floor, so we didn't want to make any unnecessary journeys. We had a small private study and dining room downstairs, but seldom used them. Life revolved around the kitchen, where we put in an oil-fired Aga instead of the coal one that my parents-in-law had used. The kitchen has a dining area at one end, and the door opens out into a sheltered private courtyard where we have our meals out of doors whenever possible.

We could get away with modern wallpapers and materials in our bit of the house, but the brocades and Victorian papers suitable for the state rooms were going to be much more difficult to find and certainly more expensive. I was not going to be able to change my mind about the colour once I had done it either! But redecorating the public rooms was going to have to wait until we had a bit more money and the roof had been made watertight. We had put a heavy-duty blue runner carpet through the public rooms and up the staircase to protect the oak floorboards and keep the noise down. I already hated the colour. We had chosen it because it was called 'heavy duty'; it looked as if it would never wear out – and it hasn't. It still looks new fifteen years later and I am still trying to think of a way to get rid of it!

A lot of the furniture had woodworm, as I found out to my cost. A rather snooty man came to look round the house to see if it was suitable for his group of art collectors' yearly outing. He looked disparagingly around the house. 'What a pity the house was ruined with all this Victorian façade,' he said. 'It really is quite hideous.' Hating him but keen to get his business, I offered him a chair in the Library while I went to make a cup of tea. The chair, unknown to me, was riddled with beetle and collapsed in a cloud of sawdust when he sat on it. Full of apologies, I dusted the ruffled gentleman down and offered him another chair, which he hastily declined, and he left, never to be heard from again. After that incident we went through every piece of furniture looking for beetle holes and tapping for telltale signs of dust. It has become a regular winter job and makes the whole house stink of Rentokil.

The estimate for repairing the roof was over £100,000, so we planned to do it in sections and get as many grants as possible to help. That first winter they were mending the section over our bedroom. I was lying in bed with flu and I could hear the builders stomping around on the roof above me. There was a sound of sawing and suddenly a saw came straight through the ornate ceiling above my bed and continued to cut a large slice through it. I shouted and screamed but they could not hear me, so in desperation I got out of bed and went through the attic out on to the roof in my dressing-gown to tell them to stop. There is still a hole in the ceiling fifteen years later!

We were apprehensive about our first winter in the house. We were not going to be able to afford to have the heating on for more than a few hours a day and many of the window panes were either missing or cracked; the curved leaded windows made replacing the panes difficult, if not impossible. We divided the heating sytems up: one for the public part of the house, including six large reception rooms and the main staircase; and one for our part in which we included the state bedrooms, as we planned to use them for guest rooms as well. There was also a six-roomed flat at the top of the house for a caretaker. We kept the public side of the house on a thermostat to prevent it going below freezing; ours we had on for a few hours in the morning and again in the evenings, but we soon found that as long as one kept moving one kept warm. Luckily that is not hard to do in a house with sixty rooms and three floors.

Chapter 4 Drama

Sir Edward Bulwer-Lytton, 1st Lord Lytton, died in January 1873, so we decided that 1973 should be a special Centenary Year. Full of enthusiasm and energy, David and I planned 'An Evening with Dickens and Bulwer' and a special exhibition in the huge Victorian State Drawing Room. Sibylla Jane Flower, who had written our guide book and was planning a biography of Edward Bulwer-Lytton, came down to do the research for the exhibition, which was to be ready for an opening at Whitsun.

The evening's entertainment was to be a glass of hot punch from a Dickens recipe on arrival, ladled out by serving wenches in mob-caps; a tour of the house and exhibition; then, with everyone seated in the Banqueting Hall, the curtain would go up on a twenty-minute audio-visual show portraying the life of Bulwer-Lytton, followed by Charles Dickens arriving at the front door with his actor friends. David, dressed as his great-great-grandfather, Sir Edward, would greet them and they would then put on a play in the Banqueting Hall. After the play a Pickwickian banquet would be served in the Long Gallery, accompanied by musicians and singers in period costume. It was an ambitious plan and the work involved was enormous.

Most of the plays performed at that time were far too long and involved for modern audiences, particularly those written by Edward Bulwer-Lytton. In 1850 Dickens had produced and performed several in the Banqueting Hall at Knebworth, one of which was *Every Man in His Humour* by Ben Jonson, followed by *Animal Magnetism*, a lampoon on medicine and the occult The latter was light and short enough to suit most audiences, so that was the one we decided to do.

Derek had to build a stage and seating for the Banqueting Hall and tables for the dinner. The heavy red-plush stage curtains were my job, as were the costumes and plans for the food and girls to serve it. David was to research and write the audio-visual. We became so excited with the idea that we thought it was worth a trip to America to promote the evenings.

We had a new manager called David Condy, who had been an accountant at Petworth Estates in Sussex previously and was coping with the office side of the business. If we went to the States from January to March, it would leave two months to get everything ready for the opening planned for May. I felt sad and rather guilty at leaving the children for such a long time, but the older two were at boarding school and Pattie was like a second mother to them all by now. We planned our American tour with the help of the British Tourist Authority, who gave us a list of travel agencies in each city we were going to visit and helped us to get on to local TV chat shows and radio. David was to give a couple of lectures as well.

We flew in a Jumbo to New York on 17 January. Our first evening was a dinner with Gray Boone, owner and editor of *Antiques Monthly Magazine*. She criticised us for trying to sell Victoriana to Americans, when they had plenty of their own, but she was to give us a lot of good publicity and became a family friend. The dinner was delicious and we managed to stay awake in spite of it being the equivalent of 4 a.m. for us. The next day we spent talking to BOAC, who had just had another stately home owner trying to promote his house; he had been really tiresome so they were rather suspicious of us, but we became friends and they gave us some useful travel trade contacts.

It was exciting to be back in New York after ten years. One evening we went for a walk around Brooklyn Heights to visit our old home, and found groups of threatening-looking youths on the street corners, a few bedraggled beggar ladies and two men necking in a car outside our old house. The atmosphere had completely changed. Ten years before I used to travel back from New York City to Brooklyn Heights alone at night on the subway without a thought of danger, and David and I used to wander along the terrace overlooking Manhattan harbour after dark. Now it was locked in the evenings and there was a warning sign to keep clear of the area at night. Everyone had a story to tell about muggings.

We were thankful when we got back to our apartment. A good friend of ours, Humphrey Wakefield, had arranged for us to stay in his secretary's apartment – she kept very strange hours and her kitchen was full of ants, but it was wonderful to have a free bed. Humphrey also organised endless lunches and dinners with people who could help us with our promotion. He had lots of interesting friends, among them Andrea Cowden, a marvellous lady of seventy, who claimed to be one of Augustus John's mistresses and had a house full of his paintings. She regaled us with stories of Hollywood: Elizabeth Taylor and Howard Hughes were her specialities. She told me she had been mugged four times that year already and was very nervous about going out alone. Another personality was Ben Sonnenberg, who lived in Gramercy Park in a house full of fantastic paintings and furniture and was immensely rich.

The Americans are so hospitable, and we soon had lots of parties given in our honour. The Dickens Fellowship of New York held a lunch to commemorate the birthday of Charles Dickens while we were there, and David was asked to make a speech. He was very nervous and it was rather long and not very fluent – I don't think anyone minded, but he was very unhappy about it afterwards. We recorded a ten-minute interview for the 'Casper Citron Radio Show' on our last morning in New York. I had never done anything like it before and it was my turn to be nervous. I was shaking like a leaf and did it badly, which put me in a bad mood for the afternoon. I refused to visit any more travel agencies with David and went off shopping in Bloomingdale's by myself.

After four days in New York it was time to move on. It was a wonderful sunny morning, and as we drove over Brooklyn Bridge to the airport I felt very nostalgic for our early life there. Philadelphia was our next stop, and the president of the Art Museum showed us round as it was officially closed for a private party. They had a special exhibition on – 200 years of Philadelphia fashion, with an impressive display of costumes. The rest of the day was spent calling on more travel agencies from the address lists given us by the BTA.

We spent the night with a couple we had met at one of our Elizabethan banquets, who had the most extraordinary house full of stuffed game birds and fish and a human skeleton in a coffin in one corner of the living room. They also had four impossible children all under five years old, who stayed up until after midnight and then went to bed with a television blaring at the end of their beds. Joyce, who was twenty-four and completely worn out, said the only way she could get the oldest child to eat was to hold her on her back in the bath and force the food down her throat. There was a major panic in the mornings as their three-year-old had eaten some of the Disprin out of my sponge bag – luckily not too many.

We drove on down through Baltimore to Washington, visiting travel agencies and talking to local newspapers. We stayed in a lovely farmhouse in Willmington, where they put rum in the breakfast orange juice! Not being used to a big breakfast I began by refusing the waffles, eggs, bacon and hush-puppies I was offered, only to discover that one quite often never got given any lunch and by 4 p.m. I would be starving. Everywhere we went people were immensely hospitable and helpful, and the tourist agencies seemed interested in Knebworth House and the Dickens and Bulwer evenings.

We flew up to Pittsburgh and I got into a heated discussion with the person sitting next to me about the colour problem. He said that bussing school children would never work in the north; it might in the south as the southerners did not mind living with the blacks as long as they knew their place and did not get too big, but the northerners did not mind how big they got as long as they did not have to live with them! Being liberal-minded, and not realising the extent of the problem, I was shocked by his attitude.

From Pittsburgh it was Boston. A Boston agency promised to bring 3000 people over to visit us that summer, so that made the whole trip seem worthwhile. They never came, but it got us very excited at the time. We then went on to Toronto. David had a lot of friends from his air force and university days, so we got full newspaper coverage and David did two radio shows. I was made to go to a ladies' lunch in London, Ontario. I had never been to one before and thought it dreadful – I could not cope with ten females all trying to ask me questions about living at Knebworth House at the same time. I find men's company so much easier, they are not so overpowering and they don't gush.

We spent a week in Canada and then had to get to Detroit for a 6 a.m. TV show, so after a late dinner with some friends in London we drove straight on through the night. It was one of the most frightening drives I have ever had. It was snowing and the road was very slippery; there were convoys of huge lorries throwing up waves of slush, and David insisted on overtaking all the time as we were running late. In the end we arrived shaking but in plenty of time. We had to wait to go on to the show, and we got talking to a black girl who used to be a homicide reporter for the local paper. After two years, she told me, when she found herself wondering whether the pair of red boots of a murdered girl stuck up a chimney were her size or not, she knew it was time to find another job!

David is very good at television chat shows and radio. I hate them and am very nervous, but you spend a lot of time waiting around and I enjoy talking to the personalities waiting with us to do their bit. In New Mexico, a little later on, I made friends with an Indian who made jewellery from chalcedony, and he insisted on giving me a lovely turquoise ring when we parted. Another of the chat show guests produced a red rose for me from nowhere just before I went on.

Our next stop was Chicago, where we found a store called 'Lyttons' so had to go and buy something in order to get a 'Lytton' bag. We did a television show and then drove out to Lake Geneva, which was frozen over. Every sort of activity was taking place on the lake: ice sailing, ski boats, snow mobiles, even an aeroplane landed while we were there.

I had discovered Charles Dickens's *Notes on America* while I was in the States, and was fascinated by them. They are all about his visit to St Louis and Lebanon, Illinois, which were the next places we visited. We were put up in someone's house and David had to give a lecture on Bulwer and Dickens; this went off well, except that the two old ladies next to me were deaf and could not hear a word. David was longing for a drink by the time we got back to the house, but unfortunately for him our hosts were teetotallers. Grace, said before breakfast, caught us by surprise as well. In Lebanon, at least, nothing much seemed to have changed since Dickens's day.

We were only halfway through our tour and I was getting fed up with visiting travel agencies. I longed to have time to do some sightseeing. In Denver, David suggested that perhaps if we worked separately we could get through them faster and have more time to relax. So, armed with a list of addresses, I set off on my own. In the first agency I walked into, I went up to the man behind the desk and said with a bright smile, 'Good morning. This is my home in England [showing him the picture on the front of the guide book]. Would you be interested in bringing some of your clients over to visit us?' The man laughed loudly. 'You expect me to believe that?' he said. 'You're far too young to own a house like that.' 'No, I'm not,' I said crossly, 'and what's more I've got four children at home.' 'Sorry, lady, I'm not interested,' he said, going back to his writing. My confidence completely shattered, and fighting back the tears, I went to find David and resigned myself to tramping along behind him once more. To make amends, he took me up to Vale in the Colorado mountains for the weekend to ski.

San Francisco was so warm and colourful after the cold and grey of the north that all I wanted to do was relax. Still in rather a huff over travel agencies, I let David go off and do two radio shows, two newspapers and about fourteen travel agencies, while I shopped and basked in the sunshine. We then flew on to Los Angeles.

One morning in Pasadena there was a small earthquake at seven-thirty. It was like an underground train going along under the house, and David and I sat up in bed with a start – we had never experienced one before. But to our surprise his uncle and aunt, with whom we were staying, refused at breakfast to admit it had ever happened, although it had done $1 million worth of damage to buildings and was headline news in all the newspapers next day. Obviously the people who live there pefer to ignore the fact that they are sitting on a highly active seismic zone.

We had been travelling non-stop for six weeks now, and I found California so fascinating that I longed to stop and take it all in.

We did sightsee, but always in a mad rush at the end of a day's work, usually five minutes before the place concerned closed down for the night. Although we had been married for twelve years we had never been closeted together all day and all night before, and we now found ourselves always either in a hotel room or car or walking the streets. Luckily we got on well, but I felt the pace was a bit exacting and the travel agencies rather too numerous. However, David was determined to stick to the programme, so we battled on.

I had a fright during our stay in Las Vegas. By midnight I was tired of slot machines and floor shows and I went back to the motel, leaving David to carry on with the nightlife. I woke at 8 a.m. and he was still not back. I wondered what I would do if he never turned up, as he had the passports and all the money. I was so relieved when he did get back that I did not feel like being cross about what he had been doing all night!

We drove from Los Angeles right across America on our way back to New York, going through Dallas, Houston, New Orleans, Orlando and Miami. We had various adventures on the way, including a couple of brushes with the police. At one point we were followed by a car flashing its lights at us for quite a while; eventually we realised it was a police car and pulled over. They came over with their guns at the ready and made us get out and put our hands on top of the car. We had been speeding, why hadn't we stopped when they came up behind us? When we explained that in England police cars overtake and flag you down, they said that in America no policeman would pass you in a car as they might get shot at! They were very polite after they realised we were English and let us go. Another time, we went down a one-way street the wrong way in thick fog at 6 a.m., having frantically driven through New Mexico and the Painted Desert all night to try and get to Dallas for an early-morning television show. The police stopped us, and when we explained they said 'Follow us' and took us all the way to the studios, sirens blaring. Sadly we discovered we were a day too early, so they showed us to a hotel instead. We had missed the Painted Desert for nothing.

When we got to New Orleans we found that it was carnival time. Luckily we had a hotel room booked as the city was packed out. The BTA had booked us rooms in almost every city we visited, but they were always in the most expensive hotels and, as we were doing it as cheaply as possible, we usually cancelled and found a cheap motel instead. The streets were packed in New Orleans and soon got very sordid. By midnight one had to wade through thousands of plastic cups, corn husks and general filth; the crowds grew less attractive the drunker they became and many had passed out and were lying in the gutters amongst the rubbish. But the music in the clubs was fantastic. We sat squashed on the floor together listening to jazz all night.

We visited both Disneyland in Los Angeles and Disney World in Florida. The Disney expertise in tourist management is inspiring and we learnt many lessons and tricks of the trade, hoping to be able to apply some of them at Knebworth. We vowed to take the children there if we could ever afford it. America is a paradise for children, and quite a few adults too – I arrived home many pounds heavier from all the waffles and milkshakes I had devoured.

Altogether, we had visited 36 cities, 21 states and about 250 travel agencies; we had done 10 radio and 12 television chat shows and 3 lectures. It had been a marvellous tour and we hoped our efforts would pay off. A lot of agencies we visited in both the States and Canada expressed great interest in the project but said we had come too late; all their plans for the present year were already fixed.

There had not been any great dramas while we were away, but neither had there been a lot of action, and we were going to have to work very hard in order to be ready for the opening of the exhibition and the theatrical evenings. I discovered that Mrs Roberts, our gardener's wife, was a very good seamstress, so she helped me on the sewing side. She made the knickerbockers, bodices, skirts, sashes and mob-caps for the twenty serving-wenches, while I completed the stage curtains. I was going to need a couple of Victorian dresses to wear, so I made the dresses and found some old lace and ribbon in the attic to trim them with. We still had Bulwer's old smoking jacket, so David was fixed up. He had let his hair and moustache grow for the summer in order to look more Victorian. It made him look rather sinister!

The boys had white trousers and dark blue velvet jackets with silver buttons and black shiny pumps to wear. Henry and Peter looked disparagingly at theirs but Richard was very excited about his; he sat in the Minstrels' Gallery watching all the rehearsals for the play and knew every word by heart by the time we opened. He never missed a performance throughout the summer. I was surprised at how much he took in at five years old, but sadly he now says he can remember very little of that time.

Doreen Hamid, who ran Richard's nursery school, knew everyone in the village and she soon had a wonderful collection of local wenches willing to work on Tuesday and Wednesday evenings every week during the summer. They were to serve at the banquets, look after the guests and provide a chorus for the singing after dinner. The menu we chose was vichyssoise soup, a choice of game pie or turkey (in the States we had discovered that game pie was thought to be too strong for the average American's taste), garden vegetables, lemon sorbet and cheese and biscuits, accompanied by carafes of red and white house wine. We could fit 150 people into the house, but had no idea how popular it would be as we did not have many bookings in advance. The price for the whole evening's entertainment was £5. I had to buy china, glass and cutlery, and turn our dining room into a servery.

As I was going to have to be the hostess for the evenings, I could not be in the kitchen as well, so I found a cook, known as Fizzy, who lived in the next village and came in every day for weeks before to make the game pies and put them in the freezer. The gamekeeper was sent off to find pheasants, hares and rabbits, and the deer-keeper produced venison. The whole house stank for weeks of cooking game. My new kitchen was used to capacity, and it was difficult to find room on the Aga to cook the family lunch or a place to eat in.

Meanwhile, David and Sybilla were working on the exhibition. They borrowed pictures and manuscripts from various sources: Her Majesty the Queen, the National Portrait Gallery, the Victoria and Albert Museum, and many private collections. The exhibition was to be opened by Lord Blake, Provost of Queen's College, Oxford. He had written a life of Disraeli, with whom Bulwer-Lytton had had a long friendship, and gave an excellent speech on Bulwer's life. Bulwer-Lytton wrote more than fifty books, including some of the best-known novels of the Victorian age, and in his career as a writer and politician he played a part in changing tastes in fashion. A remark in *Pelham*, one of his most successful novels, led to the fashion of black evening dress for men, which has lasted to the present day. He presided over the birth of Queensland in Australia and British Columbia in Canada, and campaigned for prison reform and the abolition of theatre censorship; he argued in the Commons that public taste backed by a vigilant press was the only civilised form of censorship. Bulwer was also a keen opponent of slavery.

About 150 people were invited to the official opening and more turned up. Lord Longford was among the guests, most of whom were from the literary world or the press. We gave them all lunch as well as drinks and ran out of food before the end, which was very embarrassing. I always over-cater, but Fizzy was inclined to under-provide. The press were all highly complimentary about the exhibition and felt it had been very professionally put together and presented. The first day we were open to the public David and Sybilla were adding some last-minute touches and were on their hands and knees in the State Drawing Room with hammers and nails, when the first visitors arrived. One lady nudged her companion and said, 'Cor, this family ain't got much – all them things is lent!'

The first two of the Bulwer and Dickens Evenings were fully booked. I was very nervous about the organisation of it all – there were so many things to be remembered at the last moment. The punch had been made and tested several times; it was a special Dickensian recipe with rum, brandy and lemon juice and a lot of sugar. The girls were all fixed up with their costumes and thought they knew what to do; and four old-age pensioners were going to come in during the evening to do the washing-up – we had no dishwashing machine, so everything would have to be done by hand. Fizzy was in charge behind the scenes: cooking, dishing up and organising the girls. David Condy, our manager, made a wonderful Mr Pickwick; we stuffed a pillow down his waistcoat and trousers and he looked just the part.

David was going to sit in a corner of the stage being his great-great-grandfather and smoking a long cherry-wood pipe. He would then host the dinner. The actors and actresses were found by Joanna Hobbs, who ran a theatrical agency and had found all the actors and minstrels for our Elizabethan evenings, and they were directed by Peter Tanner. The actors were all singers as well and during dinner would sing such songs as 'Come into the Garden, Maud' and 'The Gendarmes', finishing with 'Just a Song at Twilight'. The plan was that the actors should play Dickens and the original actors, as well as the parts they played in the actual theatricals. The music David chose to go with the audio-visual show was from the opera *Rienzi* by Wagner. It was the first opera Wagner ever wrote, and he adapted it from a book written by Bulwer-Lytton, so it seemed appropriate. The last train back to London left just before midnight, so we hoped to be cleared up by 1 a.m.

My job was to do the shopping for food, lay up the tables, make sure everyone had what they needed, collect actors from the station, greet guests at the door and take their tickets. During the performance, I had to shuffle everyone's place-names round in order to seat parties together. The tables took ten people each, so when we were a full house it meant strangers sitting next to each other, and one had to be a bit tactful about who went where and who was invited to the High Table with David and me. After the play had finished and everyone came into the Picture Gallery for dinner, I showed people to their places, and then hosted a table. At the end of the evening I had to stand by the door and say good-bye and thank them all for coming. I then helped clear up, after which, having seen the last helper home, I collapsed into bed. The two evenings a week were Tuesday and Wednesday; the preparation took up most of Monday and Tuesday, and Thursday and Friday were spent clearing up, so there was not much time for anything else.

The first night was 7 May and a lot of press and important guests had been invited. Then – disaster – Fizzy rang up. She was terribly sorry but she was in bed with chickenpox and was covered in spots, she couldn't possibly come. It was one of the busiest nights of my life as I dashed from the kitchen to the guests and back to the kitchen again. I actually prefer being behind the scenes, so in a way I quite enjoyed it – it made a wonderful excuse not to have to be polite to a lot of people I did not know. Friends came through to the kitchen to chat and it was proclaimed an enormous success.

Luckily Fizzy was back after a couple of weeks or I would never have survived the summer. As it was I got very over-tired and neurotic and began taking sleeping pills, which I had never touched before. By midnight I was longing for everyone to leave, so we could clear up and go to bed. But David, who always wakes up at night and had been sitting on the stage all evening smoking his pipe and then been keyed up talking to a complimentary audience during dinner, would insist on inviting all the actors and the guests he liked best to stay on for a party afterwards.

So after every evening lots more drink and glasses came out. The record-player was put on and tables pushed back. Everyone was thrilled at being given free drink and the party would run on into the small hours. The waitresses either got grumpy because they could not clear properly and wanted to go home, or they joined the party, egged on by David, and were not a bit interested in helping any more. The fact that it was always the pretty girls who were asked to stay on only added to my displeasure. When the occasional guest was still there for breakfast I became thoroughly bad-tempered.

There were always unexpected crises to be coped with. Some people would turn out to be vegetarian and want a salad (why could they not have let us know in advance?) and once a party of 100 Spanish-speaking tourists came straight from the airport off a flight from the Caribbean. They were going on to their hotel in London after the performance; hardly any of them spoke English and they were all suffering from exhaustion and jet-lag. They did not understand a word of the audio-visual or the play, hated the food and wished they were back in their hotel rooms asleep.

One evening the cast put some marijuana in David's pipe instead of tobacco – David was not a smoker and had certainly never smoked marijuana before. He always had difficulty in keeping the five-foot-long pipe alight and usually spent quite a while puffing away behind the scenes to get it burning before going onto the darkened stage and sitting in his corner. That evening he missed the chair altogether and fell off the stage into the laps of the front row, causing some surprise in the audience and fits of laughter in the green room!

There were some evenings when only about ten people had

bought tickets, and in order to fill up the seats we had to ring round frantically asking all our friends to bring guests for free. We did not have enough people to make it a financial success, although almost everyone who came thoroughly enjoyed the evening and was surprised at how professional and what fun it was. David still believes it is the best thing we have ever done at Knebworth. It was suggested that we should do another season the following summer: we would have plenty of time to talk to tour operators in the autumn when they were planning their itineraries for the following year. I said it was divorce if we did another season, and anyway by the following year David had decided to resume his City career.

Chapter 5 Bambi, jousting and rock festivals

Bambi arrived in our kitchen on a hot June afternoon in 1973. He was about twenty-four inches high and very wobbly on his legs. Some visitors had found him lying in a bed of bracken in the park, and, thinking he had been abandoned by his mother, they had picked him up and brought him up to the house. Hinds leave their fawns hidden for the first two or three weeks of their lives while they go off and graze, and the deer-keeper tried to find out from the people the exact spot where they had found him, so he could put the fawn back, but they could not remember which clump of fern they had taken him from. By now, anyway, it was unlikely that the mother would take her baby back, smelling strongly of humans. His only chance of survival was for us to look after and bottle-feed him.

The Dickens and Bulwer Evenings were in full swing and I had little time to nurse a baby red deer. But the family all promised to help. We made a home for him in the old woodshed which we had turned into a kennel for the dogs, and found some of Rosina's old feeding bottles. Dr Dansie said he would thrive best on gold-cap powdered calves' milk, and would need feeding every four hours, twenty-four hours a day to start with. He was actually rather sceptical about the fawn's chances of survival.

We had two dalmatians at that time, Tasha and a puppy called Lotta. Bambi soon decided he was a dog too and followed them everywhere. He could be persuaded only with great reluctance to go into the outdoor kennel last thing at night, otherwise he was bouncing around the garden with the puppy or getting under our feet in the kitchen. On rainy days he would sit on the sofa in the play room, watching television with the children. He was soon consuming three litre wine bottles of milk four times a day, and chewed through the rubber teats at an alarming rate.

Dr Dansie arrived one day to put rubber bands round his testicles. It seemed cruel, but apparently it was to stop his antlers from growing and was the most painless way to do it. A tame red deer with antlers would obviously pose some problems. It was difficult to believe at the time, but when fully grown they weigh 3-400 pounds and are over six foot tall with their antlers. As it was, he grew apace and became very strong.

The Tunnicliffes had two lion cubs for the summer. They had been born in one of the Chipperfield Safari Parks and their mother had been unable to feed them, so Michael and Ann were bringing them up in the bird garden. We had some wonderful summer afternoons on the lawn in front of the house with Bambi, two lion cubs, two dalmatians and all the children. The cubs, in spite of their young age, instinctively stalked Bambi and would try and trip him up by hitting out at his back legs with their paws. Bambi was completely fearless and butted them with his head. Pattie pushing the pram through the park with two dogs and Bambi running alongside became a familiar sight; he was a new attraction and the tourists loved him.

Our numbers were down by about 10,000 in 1973. The Dickens and Bulwer Evenings had taken up so much of our time that we had perhaps not concentrated on the park enough, or it could have been the weather. We had held another air display and again it had poured with rain all day. We thought that maybe we needed some new attractions, so when in July 1973 Max Diamond arrived in our office one day and suggested a jousting tournament for Knebworth, we listened with interest. He ran the Jousting Association of Great Britain, whose members went around the country putting on jousting tournaments, and also took part in films which involved medieval battles and knights. Most of them were stunt riders. He was looking for new premises for his horses and wondered if we had any stables to rent. We were becoming disillusioned with our riding stables – they were losing money and there were endless staff problems and sick horses. We were tempted by the idea of closing them down and earning some money by leasing out the stables instead.

Max suggested we went and saw one of their shows, which were on at the Tower of London during the summer. The Tower made a magnificent setting for a joust and it was all so colourful and seemed very dangerous. There were some nasty falls and the crowds loved it. We asked Max if anyone got badly hurt during the performances, and he said that out of the fourteen knights he had started with that summer, only two remained unscathed by the end of the season. One had lost an eye and there were countless broken bones and sprains. Max, known as the Black Gauntlet, was a striking personality with a shock of white hair and, dressed in black, he rode a white charger called Simon. He had broken every bone in his body at least once during his career as a knight.

It sounded like a good crowd-puller, so we settled enthusiastically on the idea of the Jousting Association coming to Knebworth and began selling up our stables operation. We closed the park and house at the end of September and packed away the exhibition, returning all the things we had on loan. The staging came down and the Banqueting Hall reverted to its original use. This Christmas was to be our first at Knebworth. With the builders on the roof, the house had been so chaotic the year before that we had gone to my parents in Devon.

The yearly Christmas estate party was held the week before Christmas. A huge Christmas tree covered in decorations stood in one corner of the Banqueting Hall, and all the people who worked for the estate came with their families for a big tea party. One of the family, dressed as Father Christmas, would come in and give everyone a present, and then we sang carols led by the rector. If someone could be prevailed upon to play the piano in the Minstrels' Gallery the singing was rather more tuneful. As a result of Lytton Enterprises (our new company), staff numbers with families had grown to over a hundred people, so it was quite a squash. I had to buy all the presents and wrap them up, which, with the family ones as well, was a major operation. I had difficulty remembering how old all the children were each year, so as to buy appropriate gifts. The adults all received a bottle of sherry.

We had all David's family to stay for Christmas that year: his parents, his sister Sue with her husband Christopher and their four children, and his brother Rowland with his wife Gus and their two babies and nanny. The whole house was lived in again, which was wonderful. The house responds to a party with tremendous warmth and atmosphere, and to have it full of children, Christmas decorations and presents was magic. It always makes me think that the hard work is worthwhile. We had our meals in the Banqueting Hall, seventy-five yards from the kitchen, so we worked up a good appetite for the next meal running back and forth. It was difficult to keep the food warm, but I had Pattie and a Swedish au pair to help, and the Hall looked so beautiful it was worth it.

Bambi caused chaos; he was not house-trained but insisted on joining in with the festivities. He ate everything in sight – the jigsaw puzzles, the decorations off the tree, the buttons off the children's jumpers – and if we shut him in the garden he either ate the roses or stood up against the window, banging on the panes with his hooves to be let in.

On Boxing Day we had a family pheasant shoot. We all went out with the dogs and Bambi came too, quite unperturbed by the guns banging away, walking in line with us while we beat through the woods. He had lots of energy and enjoyed going on rides; we often used to ride about three miles through the woods to a pub and stop and have a drink. Much to the amusement of the locals, Bambi would wait outside with the dogs and horses while we had our drink. But he became so large and unmanageable that eventually, with heavy hearts, we told him he was a deer and put him in the park. He was miserable and stood right up against the big front gates, where he could just see the kitchen window, and moped. Any chance of someone leaving a gate open, and he was through in a flash and knocking on the back door.

Meanwhile, the lion cubs, now nine months old, had grown big enough to go back to the game park. They were loaded into the back of a van for transporting up north, but the driver did not close the back door of the van properly and as they were going along the A1 the doors flew open and the cubs jumped out. The driver never noticed and continued north. A very surprised lorry-driver coming along behind narrowly avoided running over the cubs and drove to the nearest telephone box to call the police. They thought it was a hoax at first, but then more calls started coming in . . . 'two lions were spotted sitting on a motorway bridge watching the traffic go by . . .' The police took action.

Radio stations gave out warnings for parents to keep their children indoors and shut up their dogs, chickens, etc.

The cubs were eventually cornered in the middle of the night near a turkey farm, presumably getting hungry by this stage. The police were armed with guns, and volunteer searchers had large sticks, but luckily Michael Tunnicliffe was with them when the cubs were found. At the sound of his voice they jumped straight into his arms and were safely loaded back into the van.

By the early spring of 1974 the Jousting Association of Great Britain had moved into our stables and we planned a big joust for the Easter weekend. As Max had promised, the press loved it. He was a very good public relations man, with endless contacts in radio, television and the press, and jousting was newsworthy stuff. It was dangerous and spectacular. The horses were Andalucian and wonderfully wild; they had been trained originally for the Spanish bull-ring and pranced and danced on their hind legs, frothed at the mouth and turned on a penny.

David immediately decided to become a knight. Max taught him how to ride the tilt and strike the quintain while ducking smartly to avoid the spiked iron ball on a chain. On his first attempt the new knight, 'David of Knebworth', was swiftly run away with and last seen heading over the hill in the direction of Stevenage in full armour. The horse came back alone, cleared a twelve-foot deer grid and disappeared up the main road in the direction of its stables. David was found picking himself out of a large muddy puddle, the bridle having come apart in his hands. But he persevered and by Easter was considered good enough to join the tournament. According to the newspapers, it was the first time a member of the landed gentry had jousted in England for 500 years.

I turned down Max's offer to teach me to become a knight as well. I did not fancy galloping down the tilt with someone coming at me with a twelve-foot lance, trying to unseat me. I preferred to ride side-saddle dressed as a medieval maiden and join in the procession. There was a girl knight called Denise Sparkes, but perhaps she did not have four children to worry about – anyway, she was certainly braver than me.

Easter was a huge success and people poured in. We had been given some television coverage for the jousting which always helps enormously, and it was a good start to the season. Jousting was something all the family could enjoy; it was colourful and exciting.

In May we hosted the Renault Car Rally. It was a big affair and they organised two Concours d'Elégance, one for all cars built before 1939 and one for Renaults built in 1946 or later, as well as some driving tests for them. Besides the cars, they had a helicopter display, comedy cycling, sheep dog demonstrations and a large display of Renault cars past and present from the continent. The Radio One disc jockey Noel Edmonds arrived in Elton John's £16,000 Ferrari and gave the commentary on the parade, which consisted of 200 cars dating back to 1900. Rosina and I gave away the silver cups at the end of the day. We also had a few smaller car rallies planned for the summer; they seemed popular events, especially with the men, and were no trouble to put on.

Up to now we had concentrated on making the park a place for families to come and enjoy themselves. We had certainly never dreamt of going into the rock festival business, so when a music promoter called Freddie Bannister approached us wanting to put on a concert in the park we said no. In our minds, in the early seventies, pop concerts were something to be avoided. Various promoters had approached us wanting to put on outdoor concerts in the park, but valuing our local reputation and also being a trifle scared at the idea of having thousands of rock fans all over the place, we had always refused.

Freddie was very persuasive, claiming that we would never have heard of him or his concerts because although he had put on lots of concerts before there had never been trouble at any of them, so they had never hit the headlines. He said everything had a price and asked us to name ours. We suggested a five-figure sum, never dreaming he would accept, but he did and we found ourselves before long famous the world over as a rock venue.

That first concert of summer 1974 was planned for 20 July, which left two months to plan everything and get in a panic. Of course there were headlines in the local press as soon as the word got out: numbers of 25,000 people coming to Knebworth were mentioned; then there was a rumour that Led Zeppelin were to head the bill and it shot up to 100,000 people expected. The parish council held meetings about it, but Chief Superintendent Tom

Oliver, head of the Stevenage police division, thought it would be a good exercise for his men and they would not charge us any money for it, despite all leave being cancelled and everyone being on duty. There were endless meetings with the promoter, the Red Cross, St John's Ambulance, the police and the council, but at that stage no question of having to get a special licence.

Although it was only going to be a one-day event, starting at 12 a.m. and ending at 12 p.m., some of the fans were expected to arrive the day before and camp overnight, and some were expected to stay on into Sunday as well. It was as if one was preparing for a town the size of Stevenage to move into the park for forty-eight hours. Lavatories, water taps, lighting, food, market stalls, Red Cross and emergency posts, ambulances, fire engines and information centres all had to be organised – as well as fencing the huge arena and building the stage. We put the camp site outside the deer fence, and the arena was just in front of the north side of the house in the park.

For a month before the concert our beautiful park seemed to be full of heavy machinery digging latrine pits, constructing the stage and putting up hideous corrugated fences for the arena. Workmen camped in corners of the park in tents and caravans, their washing, dogs and children very much in evidence. The meetings became more intense. Led Zeppelin had dropped out and Freddie was furious and threatening to sue them. The line-up was now: the Alman Brothers Band, the Van Morrison Show (featuring the New Caledonia Soul Express), the Doobie Brothers, the Mahavishnu Orchestra (featuring John McLaughlin and Jean Luc Ponty), Tim Buckley and the Alex Harvey Band. The tickets were £2.75 in advance and £3.00 on the day. The names didn't mean much to us, we hadn't heard of any of them before; our musical tastes were still in the sixties, with the Beatles, the Kinks and Janis Ian.

Simmonds, the caterers for the Barns Restaurant, had taken our idea of Elizabethan Evenings to Hatfield House, and of course the Old Palace at Hatfield, where Queen Elizabeth I held her first council meeting, is the perfect place to hold Elizabethan Evenings. Our bookings immediately dropped off as everyone went there instead, so we parted company with Simmonds and J. Lyons Catering took over our catering in the park and Barns. This was their first summer and they did not think much of the plans for a pop festival and were not interested in doing the catering for it. Their line was more Buckingham Palace garden parties, Wimbledon and Gatwick Airport. The promoter was delighted and sold off the catering rights somewhere else. Lyons, I think, quickly learnt to regret that decision.

Mr Rourke began to panic about his deer, but we assured him they would not come to any harm (although we had no idea how it might affect them); the fans would be coming to listen to the music and would not be interested in the deer. Parents began ringing me up. Their offspring wanted to come to the concert – would it be safe for them? Again I had no idea; I could only say that ours would be there.

One morning about a month before the planned rock festival, a young Australian couple arrived at our door. They had come over to England for a holiday and had heard about the concert – was there any chance of them putting their camper somewhere on the estate and finding work until after the concert? Beginning to get quite excited about the concert and these being our first rock fans, I said 'yes' and showed them where to put their Volkswagen camper behind the offices, hoping David wouldn't mind. We were building a swimming pool in the courtyard in our private bit of the garden and David Brown, the Australian, got a job with the builders. I had cause to be grateful to him a few days later.

We had a rat problem in the house and one could hear them running round between the floorboards and the ceilings. 'Mice in gumboots', we explained to enquiring visitors, but something had to be done. The rat catcher came and put down poison, promising me that it did not hurt dogs. Tasha, the elder of our dalmations, was eight weeks pregnant at the time and was always hungry, eating everything she could find. She somehow found the poison, ate it, and proceeded to have a fit. It was quite dreadful – she kept trying to climb up everything in sight, and eventually got herself all the way to the top of the water tower and died; there was no time to get her to the vet. The puppies went on moving inside her for quite a while and I considered a quick Caesarian, but the thought of trying to keep eight or so premature puppies alive on baby bottles stopped me.

David was abroad on business for his bank, it was after five o'clock and the gardener had gone home. Only Richard and Rosina were in the house. I went and found David, our Australian rock fan; he was very sympathetic and came to help. As tears poured down my face we loaded Tasha on to a wheelbarrow and he dug a grave for her in the dog cemetery at the bottom of the garden, where we buried her alongside generations of Knebworth family dogs.

There are about fifteen graves in the dog cemetery, dating back to the last century. The inscriptions on the headstones give one an idea of the family dogs over the years: 'HERE LIES THE GREAT HEART OF A LITTLE DOG, 'BUDGET', DIED 1886'; 'HERE LIES OUR DEAR GOBLIN, 1909'; 'MAJOR: A VERY GREAT DANE, 1915'; 'RUBY, GIVEN BY THE MONASTERY OF RUBING, DIED 1929'; 'WILBERFORCE THE STRANGEST, 1932'; 'GEMMA THE PRETTIEST, 1934'; 'POOR LITTLE TOPSY, 1938', and so on. It was overgrown with grass and difficult to find, so I resolved to clean it and put in some flower beds around it with plants such as dog-violets and dog-roses, and to look out for some appropriate statues.

A few days before the concert, people started arriving. The camp site was not ready and did not open until Friday afternoon, but by that time there was quite a crowd. A steady stream of colourful people with knapsacks on their backs aproached the park from all directions. I was scared they would end up in some angry local resident's garden, so I drove around collecting them up in my car and dropping them at the campsite. Eventually, 25,000 people hitch-hiking to Knebworth were too much for my Renault, so I left them to walk.

The camp site on the Friday night was a wonderful sight: a mass of coloured tents, small fires (we had provided loads of wood to try and prevent any damage to our trees), people playing guitars and holding impromptu parties. There were two huge marquees for people who had not brought tents. My parents-in-law came in their evening clothes after dinner to have a look, and my mother-in-law put her head inside the marquees full of sleeping bodies and wished them all 'a very good night'. Everyone was very friendly.

Saturday was wonderfully hot and sunny. The gates of the arena opened at 5 a.m. and by 7 a.m. the arena was fairly full. David Brown, who had been to numerous concerts before, knew it was important to make a camp in the arena early on in order to get a good place; so he went down with sleeping bags, rugs and refreshments and a long pole with a flag on the top, so one could find the way through the crowds back to the site.

Henry and Peter were still at school and the younger children were a bit put off by the noise and so many people crowded together, but they came down at intervals during the day with books and packs of cards. Richard, aged six, was playing snap with one rock fan sitting on the grass next to us, when he got into a heated argument. The man asked Richard where he lived and when he said 'There', pointing to the house behind, the man said, 'Oh yeah, and I live in Buckingham Palace.' 'But I do,' said Richard. 'Tell me another,' said the man. I don't think he ever believed him.

David, our manager David Condy and Derek Spencer drove around the park with walkie-talkie radios all day, helping organise the traffic, the parking and the fans. Having been very apprehensive about the whole event, they found they were far too busy to be worried about it.

For someone who had never been to a giant rock festival before it was a fantastic experience . . . the sun blazing down on 60,000 denim-clad fans from all over the world sitting on the grass all day, contented and listening to the music, sharing their drink and dope around, babies running naked around the site and dogs frolicking in the grass. The sound system could produce 700 decibels and, according to the music press, was the loudest ever heard in England: 25,000 watts of sound – equal to the noise of seven low-flying aircraft or 125 full-sized discotheques, seven times the accepted 'pain threshold' – but I think that was just a bit of journalistic licence.

Fifty ten-seater circular tin loos with awnings over them and canvas partitions had been erected, and there was a continual queue for them. In spite of the 'gully cleanser' or 'sludge-gulper' machine, which emptied them at regular intervals, some overflowed and the paper was soon gone. I was glad I was within easy reach of the house.

British Rail had laid on special trains to Stevenage during the day and back to London on Saturday night, and St John's Ambulance were to take any casualties to the local hospital. Alcohol was not allowed to be sold in the park, so people arrived pushing Tesco supermarket trolleys full of beer, cider and wine; the atmosphere was pungent with the smell of bodies, beer, fish and chips and exotic smoke. The police kept a low profile and did not come inside the arena, at least not in uniform.

I thought the concert was wonderful. What had I been missing all these years? I was a natural hippy. I lay on the grass watching the clouds go by, soaking up the atmosphere and listening to the music from 7 a.m. until midnight, loving every minute of it. David came down into the arena to listen to the Alman Brothers at the end of the day; he was very happy too, the day had gone much better than he had ever expected. Everyone had behaved well, and the police and local authorities were pleased too.

It was after midnight by the time everyone had left the arena and headed for home or the camp site. The litter was unbelievable and we were open for our daily visitors at 11 a.m. David began frantically putting rubbish into black plastic sacks and I helped for a bit until, realising the futility of it, we stopped and went to bed.

There were rave reviews about the concert in the papers. The only complaint seemed to be that the rate-payers were going to have to foot the bill for the police and clearing up the litter in Stevenage and Knebworth, probably in the region of £10,000. The litter in the park took about two weeks to clear up, organised by a marvellous character called Captain Ollie. Lots of local children came and were paid by the plastic-bag full; they found bundles of fivers, watches, sleeping bags etc., so it was a popular job. The corrugated fencing and stage came down, the latrines were filled in and the place began to settle down to normal.

One group of hippies decided that Knebworth Park was a nice place to live and took no notice of our requests for them to leave. The weather was fine and they wandered around their encampment with little, or sometimes nothing, on. We eventually helped them pack up their belongings, drove them to Stevenage station and dropped them off to catch a train. They were back in the park again by the time we got back! So we put them back into the van and actually bought them tickets and saw them on to the train to London, which seemed to work.

David's grandfather Lord Lytton put the following notice up in the park before the war:

TO VISITORS

All ye who enter Knebworth Park
One moment pause these words to mark.
This property belongs to me
As visitors here welcome be.
As you proceed please feel a duty
Not to disfigure Nature's beauty
With remnants of a picnic meal,
Silver paper or orange peel.
If you are smokers, be so kind
As not to leave a trail behind
Of cigarette cards, matches, rags,
Empty packets or paper bags.
If you have such litter, leave it
In baskets furnished to receive it.
Give no cause to think you hateful
And I the owner will be grateful,
And ever gladly make you free
Of places that are loved by me.

One of our concert visitors added a few more lines:

Don't leave your roaches in the grass,
It's best to stash them in your boxes.
Remember, all you doped buffoons,
The Lord won't take to coker's spoons
And if you feel the urge to mate,
To procreate, to copulate,
Just think, not all will have your luck.
There'll be bad vibes if he sees you . . .
(get down and get with it).

Chapter 6 New challenges

Letting the house out to film companies can be a lucrative business on paper, though I am rather doubtful whether it is really worth it. In 1974 the rate was £250 a day for indoor shooting and £100 for outdoor, and it seemed a good idea, but over the years I have come to realise all the problems that go with it. You have to clear furniture out of rooms and store it, which entails wear and tear on the furniture and often the paint on the doorways it goes through. Film crews arrive at some ungodly hour in the morning and leave hours later than they told you in the middle of the night, and once they are let into the house you have to watch them every moment of the day and night. They are so used to working in studios that they think nothing of standing on a Chippendale chair with their boots on to change a light bulb, or getting out a paintbrush and touching up the eighteenth-century decoration around the doorways, changing doorknobs or taking out windows and putting in different glass. I watch in agony as the cameraman backs his camera to within inches of the ancestors on the wall.

They are always asking for things they have forgotten to get from the prop shop. Over the years I have lent them all kinds of objects – my silver hair brushes, white gloves, walking sticks, safety pins, even the dog – and you have to make certain they give them back afterwards or they end up very quickly in the back of the props lorry. The dog is about the only thing you can be sure of getting back and even she suffers indirectly. She hangs around the canteen truck and gets fed with everyone's soggy rolls and old sandwiches and has a figure to show for it!

In the autumn of 1974 we hired out the house to Anvil Films,who were making films of operas for television. Part of *Anastasia* and most of the film version of Evelyn Waugh's *Decline and Fall*, directed by Sir Ivan Foxwell, had already been filmed at Knebworth when David's parents lived in the house, but this was the first major film company that we had had. *La Traviata* and *Pagliacci* were the two operas they filmed, and the house reverberated for weeks with the sound of Valerie Masterson's and Kenneth Woolham's voices. I had to keep everyone quiet: no easy task with a small daughter who enjoyed screaming, two dogs that barked every time anyone came near the house and a telephone which rang incessantly – not to mention the workmen still on the roof. But as far as disruption went, it was not bad compared with future examples we were to encounter.

The 1974 season had been good and the rock festival had helped financially. There had been one or two disasters, however, the worst of which was the fourth air display in August when, instead of the expected 15,000, only 2000 had turned up. Yet again it had virtually been rained off and had cost a considerable amount of money to put on. The Rothmans Aerobatic Team had to be cancelled because of low cloud, but the Barnstormers just managed to do the 'girl on the wing' stunt. They strapped a sporting lady on to the wing of a Tiger Moth and flew her round and round just below the cloud. It looked terrifying. She had been going to be dressed in just a bikini, but because it was so cold and pouring with rain she ended up in jerseys and an anorak.

An unexpected excitement was the October 1974 general election. David, who had never expressed an opinion on politics to me before, arrived home from the City one evening in September and announced that he had joined the Liberal party for the coming election. He had been accepted immediately as prospective candidate for Bishop Auckland. What were the Liberal policies? Where was Bishop Auckland? All these things had to be discovered. We took Richard out of his day school and, with Rosina and Pattie, loaded ourselves into our minibus, taking our manager David Condy as David's agent. The fact that David Condy had been a staunch Conservative until that moment never worried David.

I was wondering whether to confess to my parents, both long-standing Conservatives, my defection to the Liberal party, or whether to try and get through the election without them finding out. It was a risk I decided not to take and confessed. Knowing us, they did not seem to be very surprised.

Luckily, when we arrived in Bishop Auckland someone from the Liberal party lent us an unfurnished house, which had been up for sale for two years and had not been lived in during that time. It was thick with dust and the upstairs loo leaked into the kitchen sink downstairs, but it was an improvement on six of us camping in the minibus. Liberal funds in Bishop Auckland (which we had by now discovered was in County Durham and one of the largest constituencies in the country, stretching from Darlington to the top of Teesdale), were non-existent and David was not planning to waste money on hotel bills. We slept in sleeping bags on camp beds.

In three weeks I learnt an awful lot more about County Durham than I had discovered about Hertfordshire in twelve years. I also learnt that I hate smoky pubs, politics and fish and chips. Every morning, after some rushed work on Richard's school books, we set off canvassing – knocking on people's doors and putting leaflets through their letter-boxes. I couldn't decide which was worse – having your fingers bitten off by an infuriated dog the other side of the letter-box when you pushed the literature through, or having some lonely old soul ask you in for a cup of tea and a look at her damp patches. A lot of people worked night shifts in that area and occasionally the doorbell would wake an unfortunate person who had just collapsed into bed after a hard night's work. Not surprisingly there would be a mouthful of abuse, and once I even had a full chamber pot emptied from an upstairs window.

Lunchtime was spent in a different pub each day. The landlords are very lenient as far as children are concerned and usually allowed them to sit somewhere in a corner, so there was no good excuse to take them back to the house for lunch. The smoke made my eyes sting, and the endless shandies and pork pies filled out my waistline. I also found it quite hard to understand the strong northern accent above the noise of the crowded rooms.

In the evenings Pattie and I took it in turns to babysit, while writing envelopes for mailing shots to be posted the following day. But it was usually me who was expected to be by David's side while he sat on some platform with the other two candidates in a different town or village hall each night, talking and answering questions on Liberal policies. Afterwards, it was off to the pubs or working men's clubs. David would disappear into the 'Men Only' bars to play cards and drink, and I would find myself sitting awkwardly in the Ladies' Lounge drinking more shandies and feeling out of place, wishing I was in bed.

One morning I shall never forget we lost Rosina. We took the children with us when we went canvassing, Rosina in a pushchair and Richard dragging his feet behind. This particular morning, Rosina was fed up and kept wriggling out of the pushchair, so Pattie put her back into the car with a bottle of milk and some biscuits and went off to finish her row of houses. When we all met back at the car – panic! The car door was open and Rosina had disappeared. We drove all round the streets searching for her and asking everyone we met if they had seen a small blonde two-year-old, but with no success. So we went back to the house to ring the police.

To our enormous relief, there was Rosina playing happily in the sitting room. Somehow, and I still cannot imagine how, she had walked back to the house where we had been staying, about half a mile away, crossing three busy streets. She had arrived at the door crying, still clutching her bottle, and the Liberal helper whom we had left in the house to answer the telephone had heard her and let her in. I nearly bundled the two children straight into the car and took them back to Knebworth, but there was only one more week to go before the election so we stayed.

There were some amusing moments. Tommy Taylor, Shildon party secretary, became a great friend; he is a flamboyant character who knows everyone and was full of amusing stories about the Shildon Waggon Works where he was a union convener. Tommy and Cathy Dixon treated us as part of the family and cooked enormous teas for us, and as we had a loudspeaker on top of the car there were endless possibilities for playing practical jokes. On one occasion David caused a stampede among a herd of heifers by bellowing like a bull across the countryside.

Everywhere we went the people could not have been more friendly and hospitable. Most people are liberal at heart, so it was not difficult to talk to them about Liberal policies and I got the impression (wrongly) that they were all going to vote for David. But I cannot say I enjoyed it.

Election day dawned and luckily David did not win, but he did not disgrace himself either. Bishop Auckland was a four-hour drive from Knebworth and it would have been a long way to go to visit his constituency; with a job in London and Knebworth House he really did not need any more to do. I put the three weeks down to 'experience' and went thankfully home to Hertfordshire.

I was happy to be back in the humdrum life of Knebworth again. We found that as well as rats in the ceiling, we now had rabbits under the floorboards in the Picture Gallery. Pattie found their entrance through a broken ventilation grille under the house and painted a doorway around it with a sign saying 'Peter Rabbit's house, open to visitors, 10p a visit'. Richard posed for press photographs in front of the new Stately Burrow.

Being the 'lady of the manor', so to speak, I found I was expected to participate in a lot of local events. I am afraid I am rather a disappointment in this respect, feeling that the lady of the manor quite rightly no longer has the enormous privileges of the past, so why should she devote precious time to a lot of boring functions? There always seem to be lots of married ladies complaining that they have nothing to do with their spare time, but my spare time is very precious to me. However, I picked out a couple of causes that I felt I could be interested in: the Church of England Children's Society boys' home in Knebworth, and the local girl guides. While the children were at the local Knebworth Nursery School, I also helped raise funds by starting the Knebworth Variety Club; my vocation is certainly not to be on stage, so I did the catering. I turned down all the fête-opening and other local groups, though, and I know I am often criticised for that. People did not like the way I slopped around in my wellies and paint-stained jeans either, but they are all used to me now!

David is always complaining that I slop around in jeans or overalls in the house, but I find I cannot work in a skirt or stockings. One Sunday a rather smart girlfriend of mine came to lunch. She was dressed in a navy blue tailored suit with a red shirt and a scarf around her neck, and after she had left David turned to me and said, 'Why can't you ever look like that?' At that moment Rosina, aged about seven, walked in and said, 'Who was that person dressed as an air hostess who was here for lunch?' She was very puzzled when I fell about laughing, and David has never been allowed to forget it. As children we were never allowed into the dining room in trousers, so I am fairly adept at changing from one set of clothes to another, but as my bedroom is three floors up I am not inclined to do it very often.

We had a chance to repay some of the hospitality we had received in Durham soon after we got back. A coachload of our supporters came down for the day and we gave them all lunch and showed them around the house and park. It was a long day for them but they seemed to enjoy the outing. On another occasion we were staging a massive jousting tournament in the courtyard in front of the house, with a medieval banquet in the Barns afterwards, for 300 Canadian bakers and their wives. So we invited Councillor Arthur Nye, Tommy Taylor and two journalists from Durham, Mike Amos (now editor) of the *Northern Echo* and Peter Bibby of the *Darlington Evening Dispatch*, both of whom had been very supportive of David's Liberal campaign.

The Gallant David of Knebworth was on top form and was a great hit with the ladies, sweeping them off their feet with a lordly kiss. A queue formed to test his ardour. Chivalry triumphed until a lady baker of at least fifteen stone joined the line. I saw his face go white as she drew nearer, and felt his back was doomed. But to tumultuous applause the deed was done and Honour – could that have been the damsel's name? – was satisfied.

Our Durham guests, dressed for the occasion much to their amusement in black tights, singlets and velvet caps out of the dressing-up trunk in our attic, had a ball. The Canadians found their Durham accents quite incomprehensible and were amused by Tommy's reaction when one of the horses disgraced itself in front of the guests. 'Great stuff, that,' he said. 'It'll do me leeks a power of good.' Mead and brown ale helped everything along, addresses were swapped and invitations across the seas were issued at the end of the evening. They have been back many times since, but will never forget that first evening.

We needed to think of a new attraction for 1975 and, as the weather is so dreadful most of the time, we thought a building full of 'one-armed bandits' might be a good idea. We put the idea to the council. Horrors! A storm of protest followed. 'Stately

Home wants to become a Casino' said the papers. We were turned down, but the local papers kept the story going for quite a few weeks – all good publicity.

Instead, we opted for a 90-foot-long, 23-foot-high inflatable plastic whale; children could climb inside its tummy and bounce around on a huge air cushion. We had the press preview on 14 February, so decided to call the whale Valentine. The Easter opening was very successful in spite of cold weather and mud, but Valentine kept splitting his sides, and stitching him back up was a particularly difficult and unpleasant task.

The next excitement was May Day, which was celebrated with special aplomb this year. 'Wocko', our new deer-keeper, was a keen Morris dancer. Besides being one of the best raconteurs of risqué jokes I know, he has a lot of musical talent and can often be seen checking on the deer fence in the park, riding a bicycle in grubby shorts and playing a violin. His Morris dancers put on a fertility dance for us. A maypole was erected and the performers wore the traditional breeches and crossed braces called 'baldricks' over basic shirts, with bells attached to their legs and straw boaters decorated with spring flowers. They charmed away evil spirits by waving white hankies around. Bambi came and joined in, although sadly a fertility dance was not of particular relevance to him . . . but he enjoyed eating the flowers.

In June the Welwyn Floral Decorative Society asked us if they could put on a flower show in the house one weekend. It sounded a lovely idea, and they filled the house with wonderful creations of different sorts of flowers. The house smelt delicious and the public loved it, but for the first time in my life I got hay fever; my eyes poured and I sneezed continually. We have never done it since, but the parish now does a yearly flower show in St Mary's Church in the park instead.

Another weekend in June, over 360 Alvis cars turned up for the National Alvis Club annual meeting, and later in the month we tried another, smaller Stately Steam-Up, but in spite of pre-publicity stunts, it was not very well attended – only 5300 compared with 20,000 two years before. The pre-publicity stunt had involved a 'human cannon ball' act, when Mary Connors, a pretty 22-year-old, was shot out of the mouth of a huge cannon into a safety net. Mary came down a week before the show, so the press could take some photographs. She arrived wearing overalls with her hair hidden under a cap. As a gimmick, and unknown to David who was in his London office, we told the press that David did not believe a girl would do anything as daring as that. He thought she was really a man in drag and was prepared to bet £25 that she was a man. So Mary climbed down the mouth of the cannon dressed only in bra and pants. As she shot out and flew towards the safety net – oops! her bra fell off. She was definitely a girl. The press photographers were delighted, and I handed the £25 over to Mary. David was told of his part in the operation before he read it in the *Daily Mail* the next day!

Talks about another rock festival for the summer of 1975 started in April. Pink Floyd were the big name; they did not mean anything to us at the time but we bought a record and liked the music. The same group of people came down to help Freddie Bannister with the organisation of the concert as the year before. Hal Christensen, an American from California; David Campbell (known as Thump), Freddie's right-hand man; and Barry Turner, a deep-sea diver and boat-builder from Bristol, were the three we got to know best. They came to the house for baths, meals and drinks, swam in the pool and often stayed overnight. They were all in their late twenties and had been part of the 'hippy scene' of the sixties; they were good fun and made the festival time very memorable. David somehow managed to join in the party at night and go off to his office in London each morning in the right frame of mind, if a bit sleepy.

The festival was planned for 5 July. Obscure relations and previously unheard-of friends rang up before the concert wanting tickets and a bed for the night, so there was no shortage of people around. The concert was a sell-out. For the first time we had to get a special licence from the council, as our normal music and dancing licence only covered 15,000 people and there were obviously going to be more than that. The police wanted to do all the parking and traffic control, to which we of course agreed, but in the event they managed to cause a ten-mile traffic jam on the A1 motorway, causing a lot of frustration and anger for people not wanting to go to the concert, several of whom had important commitments to get to. Johnny Carson, the jockey, missed his ride at York races because of the chaos.

The acts this year were Linda Lewis, Roy Harper, Captain Beefheart and his Magic Band, the Steve Miller Band and Pink Floyd – kept to just five in an attempt not to overrun the midnight curfew. Special guests were Graham Chapman, with friends from the Monty Python Show, and the compère and disc jockey John Peel.

Once again we were lucky with the weather, and it was a lovely day. David rushed round trying to sort out the traffic and other problems, while I lay on my back in the sun in the arena with the two younger children and enjoyed the music. The atmosphere was humid and the smell of large, hand-rolled cigarettes hung heavy in the air. Hundreds of colourful flags fluttered over the crowd, and there were stalls selling badges, frisbees, patchouli oil and king-size cigarette papers. A lot of people were asleep.

I wandered back to the house a few times to have a shower and a pee. Although you could still hear the music, the peace and quiet of the gardens was an extraordinary contrast to the mass of humanity in the arena. Getting back to our camp again took ages, especially with two children and quite often the dogs, stepping over bodies and trying not to stand on them or their belongings. But no one got cross, even when you fell over on top of them. It was all so relaxed and friendly.

The sun was setting by the time Pink Floyd came on, and they gave the most spectacular show I have ever seen. It opened with two Spitfires flying past and a rocket which slid down a wire from a sixty-foot mast at the back of the arena, over the heads of the audience and on to the stage, to be met with thirty rockets shooting into the sky and an orgiastic burst of sound from the group. Lights flashed; the crowd roared. The band played all of *Dark Side of the Moon*, now one of my very favourite records. A large circular projection screen was used, on which images and films were synchronised with great precision and relevance to the music. I felt stunned by the end, partly because listening to loud, and in this instance memorable, music for sixteen hours non-stop is very exhausting and partly because when the air is heavy with 'pot' you must inevitably absorb a bit even if you don't smoke yourself.

David had invited Pink Floyd back to the house after the concert so that they could miss the worst of the traffic. I had not prepared

1 Knebworth House and Park

2a Knebworth House as it was up to 1810

2b The Banqueting Hall

3a The elaborate State Drawing-Room, decorated by Edward Bulwer-Lytton

3b Edward Bulwer-Lytton in his study, painted by E. M. Ward

4a The family trying to move the barn, 1971

4b Miss Steam at the Stately Steam-Up, 1972

5a The Barnstormers' 'girl on the wing' stunt, 1972

5b Ballooning over Knebworth Park

6a 'An evening with Dickens and Bulwer', 1973.
David and Nigel Lambert as Edward Bulwer-Lytton and Charles Dickens

6b Serving wenches posing before the Dickens and Bulwer banquet
(Pattie is third from the right)

7a and **7b** A Wild West day on the steam railway

8a Rosina feeding Bambi

8b Richard and Rosina with the Tunnicliffes' lion cubs

anything and rushed back to get some drinks and ashtrays out. I did not expect many to come as there were only five in the group, so I didn't bother to open up our large Picture Gallery and prepared the small study instead – a great mistake, as I soon discovered. People poured into the house, not just the band but friends and 'liggers' as well. 'Who are you?' I would ask. 'A ligger,' came the reply as they walked in confidently and helped themselves to a drink. I eventually found someone who told me that a 'ligger' was a 'hanger-on', and there are always plenty of them around rock stars.

There was a bad moment when the police and drugs squad arrived to recap on the day's events and have a drink. David had collapsed into bed exhausted, and I ended up trying to keep the police drinking their whiskies and coffee in the kitchen, and the group and their friends (possibly rolling joints or worse) in the overcrowded study. It was a great relief when it was decided that the traffic had cleared and they could all leave. I never did discover who was who, and I don't think anyone knew who I was either, but David and I both agreed that it was the best musical experience we had ever had and, for us, nothing has surpassed it yet.

The park looked a dreadful mess for two weeks afterwards and the numbers of visitors to the house dropped quite a lot – not surprising really, as it did all look awful. There were the usual post-mortems after the event. Some of the fences had got knocked down and a few of Mr Rourke's deer had escaped into the woods, never to be seen again. Max Diamond had had a fight with a couple of fans trying to find a short cut through his stables, but only twenty arrests had been made by the police for minor offences – nothing compared to a football match. Overall it was a success. We still went on partying for a week or so, while Hal, Thump and Barry cleared up.

I then took the children down to Devon for a couple of weeks during the August summer holidays to stay with my parents. It was wonderfully relaxing teaching them how to prawn in the pools and surf in the huge Atlantic waves. My other sisters and brother, now all married, came down with their children; in all my parents have twenty grandchildren, and at Christmas there are often thirty-six staying in the Abbey. This summer holiday was a wonderful opportunity for all the cousins to get to know each other.

Back at Knebworth again, we found a vast marquee going up in the park for the August bank holiday weekend antique fair. It was the first we had had and was well attended by dealers and dabblers alike. The British public seem to relish shopping seven days a week and everything sold well: silver, jewellery, old postcards, bottles and all manner of bric-à-brac spread out on stalls. Mr Roberts, our gardener, had found the old Knebworth House rubbish dump and had had an interesting time unearthing clay pipes and antique bottles from it. I never realised there was such a market for them.

In September there was a Grand Medieval Gala in aid of Shelter, and 30,000 people were expected. Large marquees were erected in the park for the event, one for the beauty contest and the others for the catering facilities. But overnight there was torrential rain and fierce winds, and by morning the site was devastated. The marquees had collapsed and the ground was a sea of mud, so everything had to be moved into the Barns and the jousting tournament was cancelled. We managed to hold the beauty contest, which we also moved into the Barns, and some bunny girls from the Playboy Club came down from London, although I am uncertain what they were doing in a medieval gala. Terry Denton de Gray (an actor renowned for his role as Henry VIII at medieval banquets) came to judge the beauty contest; he claims to hold the world record for kissing women – 25,000 to date! News-reader Leonard Parkin compèred the fashion show, which was put on by two local Stevenage firms. As all this took place in the Barns it was just as well only 412 people turned up, but it did not help Shelter very much.

If your business is dependent on the weather and you live in England, you are going to spend a lot of time groaning and gnashing your teeth. David and I have spent hours (in the bath usually) trying to think of indoor entertainments which would not spoil the park with large expensive buildings but which would keep visitors dry and amused.

One idea of David's was to dig an enormous underground cavern, about twelve foot deep, and cover it up with a roof and returf it. The visitors would then get into a lift which would give the impression of going down for miles, then get out and be treated to a variety of shows and entertainments, such as Aladdin's Cave, Tutankhamun's tomb and a working mine – all to be seen from an underground train. However, in spite of the climate it has not happened yet!

Another idea he thought of was a 'haunted drive', which could be taken in your own car during the winter months on dark evenings. Visitors would pick up 'the Knebworth Haunted Drive' musical commentary on their car radio as they came into the park, using an inductive loop sound system, then drive the two miles around the park roads between the three avenues. Luminous skeletons would hang from the trees, ghosts would emerge from under the ground and coffins would open up, while appropriately eerie sounds would be transmitted into the car through the sound system. The drive would end with a cafeteria selling coffin-shaped buns with heart-shaped hamburgers and lots of tomato ketchup. Smiths Crisps and Heinz Spaghetti were both doing a 'haunted' series at the time, and David talked to both of them. They were interested, but not enough to back it, which was a pity. I wonder how Sam Rourke's deer would have reacted?

In 1975, 182,000 people had visited the park and 40,000 of those had been through the house; that was not counting the 80,000 who came for the rock festival, so we felt quite happy about our progress. We still hadn't made a profit, but that was because of the huge interest bill we had to pay each year to the bank for the loan. It was lucky that David had a good job in London to pay the family bills, as the business could not pay for itself, let alone support us in any way.

When the house and park closed we found ourselves back in the film business. *Trial by Combat*, a major feature film, was made almost entirely at Knebworth; the main stars were Donald Pleasance, John Mills and Peter Cushing. It was a bizarre story about a strange sect of men who dressed as knights and, fed up with the puny prison sentences doled out by the law courts in England in the 1970s, kidnapped criminal offenders and meted out their own form of punishment, challenging the prisoner to a joust and inevitably kocking him off the horse and killing him in hand-to-hand combat with swords, maces and other weapons. It involved lots of stunts, and I soon found myself with my first aid box bandaging and administering to bruised stuntmen in my kitchen. Conveniently, all the knights acting in the film came from our jousting stables. David's brother Rowland, his wife Gus and their two children were back on leave from Calcutta at the time, so it was unexpected entertainment for them.

We had yet another film crew staying that winter for a film called *How to Keep it Up Downstairs*. Diana Dors and William Rushton were the main stars, and Robert Young was the director; he arrived each morning really looking the part, dressed in a long fur coat. It was filmed in great secrecy, and no one but the cameramen and directors were allowed to watch. I saw why when it came to our local cinema with an 'X' certificate the following year – even the children's tree-house had been used for some pretty torrid scenes!

Producers like us to let them use the spare bedrooms as dressing rooms for the main actors and actresses, as it saves them money on caravans. But make-up gets spilled on the carpets, and cigarette burns and glass marks stain the furniture; so I always try and say no. Keeping the extras and hangers-on out of our private rooms is a constant problem as well. However many 'private' signs and barriers are put up, they are always 'Just having a quick look for . . . the loo . . . the telephone . . . the way out' etc. You only need to lose one or two small valuable pieces to have lost any profit you might have made on the film, and things do disappear.

Soon after we moved into the house we put in an elaborate alarm system. This is designed so that we can leave alarms on in rooms not being used, which helps a bit, but before that the house seemed to get broken into every year.

One night when we were away the burglar alarm went off and Pattie, who was alone in the house with Rosina, went down and found a window broken in the Falkland Bedroom. The silver Indian throne from the Gallery was lying on the floor. The police arrived and went round the house with alsatians looking in every room, even under Rosina's bed, and discovered that the burglar had climbed back down the magnolia tree outside the bedroom window when the alarm went off, dropping the heavy silver throne he had planned to take. The police eventually left and Pattie went back to bed. Half an hour later the alarm went off again, though another search round the house revealed nobody. To be a nanny at Knebworth House you have to have nerves of steel!

On another occasion we had left the lights on in the Picture Gallery while we went and had Sunday supper in the kitchen. David went back in afterwards and found a man standing in the Gallery with the two brass candlesticks from the mantelpiece in his hands. He shouted at Pattie and me to turn the alarms and floodlights on. We could not think why and took our time over it, but meanwhile the burglar had dropped the candlesticks and climbed back out through the window he had broken and disappeared into the night. The police came round and we searched the room to see if anything was missing, but did not notice that anything was gone. It was sheeting down with rain and the police did not stay long. The next morning we discovered an eighteenth-century French clock from the mantelpiece under a bush in the garden. A night in the rain had not done it any good at all, but luckily we still had it and our insurance cover paid for it to be repaired.

We have suffered numerous other burglaries over the years: all our valuable wedding presents which we had left in Knebworth House when we were living abroad were stolen, and on another occasion, when we were staying in the house for the weekend with Henry as a baby, we did not discover that we had been burgled until we went upstairs to bed. David's mother came rushing along to our room, saying the drawer had gone from her dressing-table with all her jewellery in it. I had no valuables with me but I looked in my purse and found all the money had gone from it. I had been upstairs quite often during the evening to check on Henry in his cot and must have narrowly missed bumping into the thief. He had taken a ladder from the garden shed and removed a leaded pane from a first-floor bedroom window in order to open it. On leaving he had put the pane back and replaced the ladder, scattering the jewellery boxes – though not the jewels – in the garden. He was never found.

People are amazed that I often sleep alone in the house, but it never bothers me. In fact I am more scared of ghosts than burglars. The Abbey where I was brought up is haunted, and I was conscious of spirits and ghosts from an early age. It was built as a monastery during the twelfth century, and the monks lived in the Abbey until 1539, when Henry VIII dissolved the monasteries and gave Hartland to my ancester William Abbot. The Abbey church is called St Nectan's. Nectan was a Welshman who had twenty-four brothers and sisters, which may account for his decision to set sail from Wales, committing himself and his voyage to the direction of the Lord. He arrived safe and sound on our beach at Hartland and settled himself in the wooded valley, living the life of a hermit and devoting himself to God.

The story goes that he was given two cows by a local landlord who was impressed by his religious fervour. One day while he was out looking for the animals, which had strayed, he was set upon and beheaded by two robbers. But, putting his head under his arm and dripping blood everywhere, he calmly set off back to his hut. The horrified thief who had beheaded him instantly went mad and clawed himself to death, and the other man, who had only held Nectan down while the deed was done, was terrified at what might befall him; finding his sight rapidly failing, he followed the dead man, trying to mop up the holy blood as he went. Nectan collapsed by his hut and the man buried him there. Many years later one of the monks in the Abbey had a dream which revealed the spot where St Nectan had been buried. They dug up his remains, which are supposed to have healing qualities, and moved them into the church. Ever since, St Nectan is reputed to walk around the Abbey park each year on 17 June, the day of his murder, with his head under his arm.

As children we used to try and stay awake to see his ghost, but the few times we managed to there always seemed to be a thick sea mist. However, the peacocks would shriek and our ponies could be heard galloping around the park; it was easy to imagine he was there. There are also chanting monks in the cloisters and a horse-drawn carriage which comes up to the front door. None of us liked going off to bed alone, and I still feel spooked when I am there, but it has never worried my parents.

Knebworth ghosts are all friendly and not very obtrusive. I have met a quiet grey lady in the Picture Gallery, and Edward Bulwer-Lytton makes his presence known to many. During his centenary in 1973, when we held the special exhibition for him in the State Drawing Room next to his study, the burglar alarm used to go off every night at exactly 2 a.m. It works by radar and should only go off when something is moving in the room, so a caretaker we had at that time sat up all one night to see what set the alarm off. He swore that the ropes around the display panels and cases moved as if someone was walking around looking at the exhibition.

Bulwer-Lytton must have been satisfied with our efforts, for the problem stopped until the very last night before we took the exhibition down, when the alarm went off at two o'clock again. We decided that it was Sir Edward having a last look around his own centenary exhibition.

The main oak staircase also has a definite aura about it, and more than one visitor has commented on it. I do not believe in looking for ghosts or stirring them up too much, but I have a great sympathy for the children when they are scared of going upstairs on their own or want to have their bedroom door open and the light on in their room. Browsing through the attic one day, I found two very plausible stories about ghosts at Knebworth. I showed them to David, but he scoffed and said they had probably been made up during a weekend houseparty as a party game in Bulwer-Lytton's time.

The first is headed 'A Narrative of occurrences touching on the haunted Chamber at Knebworth' and dated 1764. It consists of thirty pages written in longhand by an old lady, who had encountered the ghost in the Beauchamp Chamber in her youth. The other is 'The History of Jenny Spinner, the ghost of Knebworth, written by herself' in 1856. Both are intricate love stories, involving mystery and murder – not very good bedside reading for nervous house guests!

Chapter 7 | The Rolling Stones

Our 1976 season opened when we had Charlie Drake, the diminutive comedian, to stay for Easter; he was a friend of Max Diamond's and came to open the jousting tournament. On the Friday David, Max and Charlie sat up all night singing around the piano, and at the tournament Charlie and Max were a hilarious sight fighting in hand-to-hand combat – a real-life David and Goliath.

Poor Valentine, the bouncing whale, had not survived his first season very well. He was too big and ungainly and had holes everywhere, and several times the generator had not been able to puff enough air into him to compensate for the holes and he nearly collapsed, frightening the children inside. He also looked extremely grubby in spite of being hosed down regularly, so we reluctantly decided he had to go. We had had several thousand car stickers printed with 'I've had a whale of a time at Knebworth' and it was a painful business having to scrap him. His replacement was an inflatable 'Toy Town', which was the same sort of idea but was not covered over and so much safer and easier to keep inflated – luckily it was just as popular with the children.

As well as battles along the tilt, Knebworth resounds every year to the sound of cannon and musket. Two associations, the Sealed Knot (Roundheads and Cavaliers) and the Southern Skirmish Association (Confederates and Yankees) fought their respective civil wars in the park on May bank holidays that year. A rough-looking lot, they travel down in the trains from King's Cross on Friday evening from London in full costume, with muskets and pikes, causing a few raised eyebrows amongst the commuters of

Welwyn Garden City. They come from all walks of life, and from all over the country – people who enjoy fighting, men who have never grown up. Camps spring up in the park with wood fires and battle songs. The Lytton Arms does a roaring trade, and I suspect there are rather fewer rabbits around by Monday morning. The battles are earth-shaking, ear-numbing events which I fear ruin many a neighbour's quiet afternoon in the garden.

Horse events are quieter but, like the battles, are fairly unremunerative. People tend to tear up the grass with huge horse boxes and bring their own sandwiches rather than use the restaurant. Much the nicest yearly horse event is a meet of the British Driving Society. They come, dressed beautifully in Victorian or Edwardian clothes with about thirty carriages, for a drive around the park and country lanes in vehicles of every kind: landaus, governess carts, large travelling coaches. There are horse-drawn competitions and a prize-giving ceremony, then they all end up with Pimms and cucumber sandwiches on our lawn. They are popular with the tourists, and we like having them, so we pay a contribution towards their costs and give them the tea.

It was at that year's Driving Society event that we first met George Mossman, who offered to give us all a ride in his coach and four. George has the largest collection of horse-drawn vehicles in the country; he also has the horses to go with them and does the majority of all film work needing carriages in England. He invited us to go and see his collection on his farm, near Luton, so the following week we drove over to his house and he showed us around. The carriages were all piled into three huge barns – fire engines, buses, post vans, governess carts, landaus, travelling coaches, the lot. We came away thinking what a fantastic museum they would make, and tried hard to persuade him to come to Knebworth with his collection. We promised to provide a huge building for the vehicles and a house for him and his family. He thought about it, and then to our disappointment said no – they didn't want to move house. We still hope he may one day change his mind.

1976 was the long, hot summer, and for once it did not rain all the time. We held a couple of dog shows and some more car rallies that season, and found it fascinating to compare the vehicles and dogs with their owners. One weekend it could be sharp-nosed Alvises, and the next broad-shouldered, low-slung Classic Americans; yapping terriers or pug-nosed bulldogs – it is a cliché that dogs look like their owners, but it really is true. The children are always entering our overweight and scruffy dogs into the competitions. Lotta, our dalmatian, won first prize for 'the dog with the waggiest tail' one year and came back with a red rosette pinned to her collar looking very pleased with herself.

'First ever' events are always newsworthy stuff. In July we planned a 'narrow-gauge steam train rally', the first of its kind to be held in England. Ten locomotives turned up to run on our two-mile track. The largest train was an 0–4–0 tender locomotive, built by Vulkan Werke of Stettin in East Germany in 1912 and known as 'Iriving of Berlin'. The oldest was 'Lilla', built by Hunslet in 1891 for use in the Penrhyn Quarries in north Wales. Another 0–4–0 saddle tank, 'Pixie', was also on show; this was owned by the Reverend Edward Boston, who had been to Knebworth before for the Stately Steam-Up in 1972. 'Trixie' was the last engine to be built in this country, by Barber in 1974. It was a major operation getting them to Knebworth, and then rolling them down planks on to our railway tracks. But it was a fantastic sight – all ten engines steaming together, hooting noisily, their drivers all dressed for the part and enjoying every moment of it.

We were planning another rock festival for August, but finding a weekend that suited the groups and also fitted in with our booked summer events was proving difficult. Our major events are usually planned well in advance with a deposit paid, so it is embarrassing when the only day a particular rock group can manage falls on the same weekend. Other organisations are reluctant to come to the park the week before or after a concert because of the mess, but as the festivals are so much more remunerative than any other event we have to give them priority treatment. We have made ourselves very unpopular by cancelling events and returning deposits, but unfortunately business is business and we need the money.

There was great excitement when it was announced that the Rolling Stones were coming to Knebworth. Even *we* had heard of them! The usual relatives and friends started enquiring about tickets and a bed for the night. Most of our contemporaries consider themselves far too old for rock festivals and cannot understand why we don't go away for the weekend, but I was beginning to find that it was the one event of the year I really looked forward to and would not have missed for anything. In any case, 100,000 people in your garden take a bit of looking after!

The Rolling Stones went overboard with their publicity. They arranged for two people dressed as harlequins to run on to the centre court at Wimbledon between sets on the final day with a long banner saying 'Stones at Knebworth'. Unfortunately, David's father, who was Lord Chamberlain at the time, was in the Royal Box and got some very frosty looks. When he returned to Knebworth he was in a high state of fury and we had a lot of trouble persuading him that we had had nothing to do with it all, which was the truth. A large banner was also draped over the arch at Hyde Park Corner with the same message on it, and two topless girls ran on to a cricket pitch in Sussex with the same banner during a game which was being televised live.

Hal, Barry and Thump were back again to organise the festival. The concert was to be held in August and there had not been any rain for weeks. Water was going to be a real problem, and the fire brigade told us they would not promise to provide a service for us. We were very worried about the woods catching fire, so all camp fires had to be banned and we had two large communal bonfires instead. Everyone was very good and obeyed the instructions. There were water tankers carring 16,000 gallons of water standing by in case of emergencies.

The Rolling Stones came down a few times before the concert to get an idea of the place. We were in London, so Pattie looked after them and gave them tea and showed them round the house; the first time we met them was on the night before the festival when they came down for a sound check. It was a hot summer evening. There was just the band on the vast stage, and I joined the dozen or so people sitting on the grass in the evening sunshine. It was wonderful.

Unfortunately we had fifty Girl Guides camping in the park until the end of the week. Their 'Guider' was not at all pleased by the noise. She stormed up to the house and burst into a meeting that David was having with the promoter and the police. 'We booked the park until the end of the week,' she complained. 'How can we hold our camp sing-song tonight with this dreadful racket going on?' David explained that it was *the* Rolling Stones and perhaps the girls would prefer to go and listen to them? 'Certainly not. I want it stopped,' she demanded. David said she would have to go and ask Mick Jagger.

She accordingly went down to the stage, elbowed her way past the security guards and grabbed Mick Jagger by the arm. 'This noise has got to stop, young man, my girls can't hear themselves sing.' Mick's reply is unrepeatable, but he stopped – much to our disappointment and I expect that of the Girl Guides.

The Stones came up to the house afterwards. They were excited about the festival and enthused about the house and the arena in the park. Keith Richards had cut his finger and was understandably worried, so I searched around for an elastoplast for him. We all sat in the Picture Gallery talking, drinking and listening to their music on tape until 7 a.m., when they eventually left for their recording studio.

Friday night was also a write-off as far as sleep was concerned. The crowds arriving were bigger than we had ever had and the camp site soon filled up. David and Freddie Bannister had to go and wake the local farmer at one in the morning and pay him a lot of money so that we could use his fields for extra camping. At three David and I thought we would try and grab half an hour's sleep, but no sooner had we got into bed than the night was shattered by the sound of ear-splitting rock music. Someone was playing a record on the concert stage in the park at full volume.

The telephone by our bed rang instantly. First it was a neighbour in fury at being woken up, then it was the police. David leapt out of bed, jumped into the car and dashed to the stage, where he found the Rolling Stones manager in a raging temper complaining that nothing was ready and he could not find the promoter, Freddie Bannister, anywhere. The noise would continue until Freddie was found. David persuaded the manager that he knew where Freddie was and would fetch him if he stopped the music – so all was peaceful once more, and poor Freddie was roused from a quick nap in the back of his car.

The festival was called 'The Knebworth Fair' and it certainly had a light-hearted feel about it. There was a carnival atmosphere, with gaily dressed clowns wandering among the crowds, and hoopla stalls, coconut shies and sideshows. Two special stunts were performed – an Irish escapologist called Michael Blondini packed himself into a coffin with twenty-five sticks of dynamite and then proceeded to blow himself up, and a diver dropped into a small paddling pool from a great height. (Thump, at the last minute, was made responsible for finding water for the pool as there was a shortage of water because of the drought. He spied the gully cleanser lorry which had just arrived to empty another batch of lavatories and asked the driver if he had any ideas. Together they went down to the lake at the bottom of the park, sucked up a load of water into the tanker and emptied it into the pool – not very hygienic, but no one knew and the diver survived.)

The Stones came to the house during the day with friends and children and we had a house full as well, so it was very social. Our children were all at home too. Henry, aged fourteen, decided that there was good television that evening, so he never came down to the arena – he has never been allowed to forget the fact that he watched television while Mick Jagger was singing in his garden!

The other groups playing were 10cc, Hot Tuna, Lynyrd Skynyrd, Todd Rundgren's Utopia and the Don Harrison Band. The number of bands had gone up to six again, and David and I were very worried that the concert would overrun the midnight curfew. We were right, and this time there were more than the usual technical hitches because apparently someone spilt a pint of beer into the sound mixer. 10cc came on very late and the Stones, who were to follow, eventually got on stage at eleven-thirty, thirty minutes after they were supposed to finish. As a result the music did not stop until 2 a.m. The crowds were in fact amazingly patient, but they did get very fed up with all the waiting and started slow-handclapping. At times they threw beer cans and the occasional bottle towards the stage, which was a bit frightening, and once, in order to divert the crowd's attention, a naked man came on stage and danced around to the records that were being played until he fell off and broke both his ankles. I tried to get out of the middle of the arena to go to the loo before the Stones came on, and it took me an hour to climb over all the bodies in the dark to get to the exit gates. Everyone was packed so tightly together.

There were two large video screens at the back of the arena showing a simultaneous film of the Stones on stage, which helped a lot as it stopped people pushing to the front and squashing each other. The stage was in the shape of huge red lips with a tongue protruding out towards the arena; it had long wings on either side and Mick borrowed my bicycle to ride down them. He didn't use it in the end, though – I don't think the cord on his microphone was long enough. From remarks I heard the group make after the concert I don't think they were very happy with their performance, but the fans seemed pleased. David was very worried about the concert finishing late, and he felt frustrated at not being able to do anything about the delay. Luckily, British Rail held back all the special trains, but a lot of fans still missed their connections home and had nowhere to spend the night.

The Rolling Stones came back to the house after the concert, with their friends and the usual 'liggers'. This time I was prepared, and drinks and food were laid on. Everyone wanted to come in and help, in order to see the famous band. Jack Nicholson was with them and I enjoyed hearing a friend of mine asking him what he did for a living; a huge grin spread over his face and he said he was in the entertainment business. She has never been allowed to forget it. Roddy Llewellyn stays in my mind as being one of the guests because he was the only person to write a 'thank you' letter.

Keith Richards' small son Marlon, white-faced and petulant, fell in love with some baby rabbits of Rosina's and threw a tantrum when he was told he could not keep them. We tried feeding him on sausages and chips and finding other amusements to divert his attention, but to no avail. Mick eventually calmed him down, explaining that life 'on tour' was not suitable for bunnies (maybe not children either). I could see why the band were such a success. Not only is their music excellent but Mick Jagger has a very striking personality; he was interested in everything, he enjoyed the house and he was good at organising and looking after the people around him. He impressed David and me a great deal.

The party finished at 7 a.m. and there was quite a lot of clearing up to do, including one ill-looking girl who said Keith Richards had brought her to Knebworth and then left without her. She was barefoot and penniless, so I took her to the railway station and bought her a ticket to London. We collapsed into bed on Sunday evening and poor David had to go back to work in the City on Monday morning, having not been to bed for the three previous nights.

After the event we found ourselves in trouble with the local council. Our licence had been for 100,000, but the papers and the police were busy quoting figures of 250,000. The group's managers and the police always overestimate the numbers and Freddie, who put them at just over 98,000, was more likely to underestimate for one reason or another. No one will ever know for sure – the turnstiles put in for the purpose of settling the matter were out of action on the day of the festival. We had also broken the law by overrunning the music until 2 a.m. Surprisingly few people complained, however, though the noise could be heard six miles away. It was a fine hot night and I think many were in their gardens listening.

The usual clearing-up process started. Over a hundred cars were left in the park after the concert, some of which were collected over the following week, but around twenty-five had to be towed away for scrap. It turned out that most of them had been stolen just to get to the festival and then abandoned. The park was also littered with supermarket trolleys, and the local Sainsbury's and Tesco's claimed to have lost 75 per cent of all their stock. They came and picked them up by the lorry-load.

The long, hot summer seemed to go on for ever. The weather had helped us enormously, but by September we were all feeling a bit jaded. The numbers were up to 195,000, the best ever, and that was without counting the festival. In the house we had topped the record as well, with 44,000, so in a way it was an appropriate moment for Mrs Martin, our curator, to decide that it was time to retire. She had been involved with Knebworth House since the 1950s, first as tutor to Rowland Cobbold, David's younger brother, and then as curator for the house. She was going to be sadly missed.

In the autumn of 1976 we started to advertise for a new curator and had hundreds of replies. David thought we ought to have a young person with a university degree, and we eventually chose Joanne Wilkins, who came to live in a cottage in the village.

Max Diamond also decided to move on, partly because he hated the rock festivals and the way the fans would take short-cuts through his stables, but mainly because everyone in the Hertfordshire area had seen the jousting tournaments and the numbers were beginning to drop off. He moved to Chilham Castle in Kent, a wonderful backdrop for a tournament. However, Mike Horsborough, one of his knights, split from the association and kept on our stables, forming his own group of knights. He wanted to keep the tournaments going and 'David of Knebworth', now quite an accomplished knight, was naturally keen.

Max had done a lot for Knebworth. His jousting tournaments, though not to be compared with rock festivals, had made a name for themselves at Knebworth. He had made great friends and lots of enemies. The neighbours complained about the four-letter words wafting from the loudspeakers during his events, but we missed him and his horses when he left. I used to have fun at London dinner parties when strangers asked whether my husband played golf or cricket at weekends. 'No,' I was able to say, 'he jousts.'

Chapter 8 | Overseas sales

'Housewife, mother and stately home-owner Christina Lytton Cobbold will be putting her chores aside to travel 29,800 miles around the world to promote Knebworth House,' said the *Evening Post* in January 1977. It was the year of the Queen's Jubilee, and I was offered the chance by British Airways and the British Tourist Association to go to Australia and New Zealand for three months to do some tourist promotion.

I was apprehensive to start with, as I had never done anything like that on my own before. Taking off for three months, leaving David, four children and my responsibilities at Knebworth, seemed out of the question, but David encouraged me to go. He got out the maps and planned an exciting trip via India, Nepal and Hong Kong on the way to Australia and New Zealand and back via Singapore and Thailand. He promised to look after everything at home.

1977 was the centenary of the great Delhi Durbar when Queen Victoria was proclaimed Empress of India by David's great-grandfather Robert, 1st Earl of Lytton, who was Viceroy at the time. The house is full of Indian treasures and David wanted to spend the three months while I was away researching and setting up an exhibition and audio-visual presentation in the old squash court with the help of Joanne, our new curator. It was unfortunate that the squash court was the only available space, because the children had been using it as a vast play room for rainy days and were just beginning to learn how to play squash. David was going to be very busy and did not think he would have much time to miss me.

So after the children had gone back to school, in January, I flew to Delhi. It was not possible to do any promotion there, as most Indians had difficulty getting into Britain and they were only allowed to take £15 out of the country, but for me it was a good chance to see India and get ideas for our exhibition.

I arrived full of trepidation at the airport at 4 a.m., and after standing in a long queue to change my money into Indian currency I went to stand in another endless line to get a taxi. A young Indian appeared out of nowhere, put my suitcase on his head and rushed off saying 'Follow me.' He disappeared out of the airport building and down the road. I followed, thinking it was the last I would see of my new suitcase, but he had a friend round the corner in a car – I suppose it was a taxi of sorts. He bundled me in, took my tip and disappeared. The car was already full of grey, blanketed figures, their faces hidden in the darkness. After a terrifying twenty-minute journey through chickens, dogs, bicycles and red lights, they dropped me off at my hotel. I stood on the balcony of my bedroom trying to see the view. The sky was just beginning to lighten and through the haze I could see vast acres of scrub stretching out in all directions. I felt very alone and a long way from home.

I was woken by a pigeon cooing outside my window. I hired a taxi and asked the Sikh driver to show me the sights of Delhi; he took me all around the tourist route, including the government buildings designed by Sir Edwin Lutyens, David's great-uncle. He dropped me back at the hotel at six, and said he would be back at eight to take me to the *son-et-lumière* at the Red Fort.

Having always been under the false impression that the British had been the major influence on Indian civilisation, I was surprised to find that only one short sentence during the show referred to British rule in India, and to learn that the Moghuls were the leading force in their history – I had a lot to learn about India. I expected to go back to my hotel after the *son-et-lumière*, but my taxi driver left his cab, took me firmly by the arm and whisked me into the midst of old Delhi.

The streets were teeming with life. I did not see another European the whole evening and felt very conspicuous with my fair hair and western clothes. My escort (I never did discover his name) took me to visit his friends in various little shops and hurried me up and down a maze of crowded alleys. I kept thinking I might never be heard of again but he delivered me back safe and sound, if rather scared, to my hotel a few hours later.

I collapsed into bed and rang the number of a friend of a friend called Vicki Singh, who was Indian and lived in Delhi. He said he would meet me in the hotel bar in half an hour, so I staggered out of bed, dressed again and went down to the bar. By this time it was about midnight and there was not another woman in sight, just a row of men sitting up at the bar, some with turbans and some without. Thus I was fairly obvious to him and we had a drink together, though he told me he never drank at home because of his Sikh religion. He said I could not possibly stay in a hotel and must come and stay in his parent's house with him. So the next day I went round to his house, which was a lovely airy building in the middle of Delhi.

In the evening there was a birthday party for his father. About thirty people came, the ladies in beautiful saris and the gentlemen with handsome silk turbans to match their shirts. We sang 'Happy Birthday' and sat around sipping home-made ginger wine and eating chocolate birthday cake and ice-cream. I couldn't believe that I wasn't at a party in England, except for the clothes and strange voices. After everyone had left, Vicki and I sat up in his small apartment above his parents, drinking Indian whisky, and I endeavoured to learn as much about India as I could.

I left the next day for a two-day journey by bus to Jaipur, Fatehpur Sikri and Agra. It was a real Indian bus – bone-rattling – and after sixteen hours of being bumped about, plus numerous breakdowns and a nervous night in a tourist hostel, barricaded into my room against the unwelcome advances of the manager, it was lovely to get back to Delhi and the Singh family again.

After a day or two with them I spent a week in Nepal before returning to India. An architect friend of ours, John Sanday, was restoring the magnificent Nepalese temples for UNESCO – quite a change from the roofs of Knebworth House, for which he had previously been responsible. I clambered up some rickety wooden ladders on to the roofs of the temples and watched the craftsmen at work. We then flew with John's wife and two small children to 'Tiger Tops' in the Chatwan National Park for the weekend. There was a crashed aeroplane on the runway, its clock still ticking in the cockpit: a shepherd and his sheep had not got off the airstrip quickly enough the week before.

Elephants met us at the airport and we rode on howdahs on their backs to the camp, through long elephant grass and muddy rivers which came right up to the elephants' shoulders. Each morning we went out on the elephants looking for rhino, tigers and monkeys. There were lots of rhino and the elephants became very excited when they saw them; I was amazed at how fast they could move with us on their backs. One morning an unfortunate American lady was taken short and had to ask the *mahout* to stop the elephant and let her off. It was quite a palava and she could not go anywhere once she got off as the grass was too high and thick. So we all had to look the other way and I made a mental note always to wear a skirt and not trousers in the future, in case I had the same problem.

Rats chewed through the Sanday baby's powdered milk packets that night and ate most of the contents, but otherwise I thought the children survived very well, swimming naked in the river and napping under the trees. We were having dinner one night when the message came that a tiger was eating the bait (a live goat) up in the forest. We all crept up in our socks to a hide, and a spotlight was shone on to the tiger while he was eating; rather contrived, I thought, but probably the only chance of seeing the great beast in his natural habitat.

I flew from Kathmandu to Calcutta with an unscheduled stop in Patna, as the air-hostess wanted to have tea with her boyfriend. I loved the lack of time-keeping and the relaxed way in which everyone lived – it was so peaceful. I didn't see much of Calcutta as I was staying with a friend of David's brother Rowland, a Hindu called Habi de Varma. In contrast to the teetotal Singhs, there was no lack of drinking amongst his friends. Rowland's wife Gus came out from England for a few days while I was there, and we stayed up all night; dinner was served at 1 a.m. most nights, long after I had finished feeling hungry. The others slept all day and I did not feel like venturing out into the streets on my own.

My host did get up early one day, however, and took me on a sightseeing trip of the market and the Victoria Memorial. He was horrified by the fact that, as I was European, we were followed everywhere by beggars and never left alone for a second. He did not make another attempt!

One morning I met up with Derry Moore, who was taking photographs for an exhibition in Sydney, and Jocelyn Dimbleby, who was writing a book on Indian cooking, and we all went round Government House together. It seemed strange to think of David's mother living there as a child and of his great-grandfather, Robert, as Viceroy.

My next stop was Hong Kong. This was officially the start of my promotional tour and I had some work to do. Rowland worked for British Airways and had given me introductions to the British Airways people in Calcutta, where he had worked for two years, though he and Gus were now living back in England. So I was given a seat in the first-class section and the captain invited me to sit in the cockpit for the landing at Hong Kong, which we made literally through the washing. Shortly afterwards I had my first newspaper interview, with the *South China Morning Post*. It went off very well, and they gave me a good spread plus a picture of the house and family. At last I had something to show for my trip.

I stayed with a Swiss bachelor friend of ours called Nicholas Kessler, who was a health fanatic. On my first morning in Hong Kong he took me over to one of the islands for an eight-mile trek up a mountain. He was not impressed by my performance; sweating Indian whisky from every pore, I never made it to the top and I was so stiff and sore as a result of the experience that I could only hobble painfully around Hong Kong for the next few days, visiting one or two travel agencies before flying on to Sydney.

Sydney was wonderful after the wet and drizzle of Hong Kong – everyone looked so tanned and healthy and the men went to work in shorts and long socks, which looked very strange. I had a full programme booked for me, but my first radio interview did not go very well; the interviewer asked me a lot of stupid questions about the English aristocracy. The second one went better, though, and I also did several newspaper interviews and talked to the travel trade. I found that without David to turn to I became more confident all the time and even rather enjoyed it.

The people I stayed with in Sydney took me to a pub one

evening. It amused me to see how the men all stayed talking on one side of the room and the girls on the other. One man came over and asked if I would go to bed with him, but I said I would not sleep with someone I didn't know. He obviously didn't think it was worth the effort as he went back to the men's side again! My estimation of Australian men went down quite a bit. The segregation of women really annoyed me. Women were not allowed in the surf club or the men's bars or to play darts in the pubs. I am amazed they put up with it.

I disliked Melbourne after the beaches, hills and harbours of Sydney. I took an instant dislike to the hotel I was booked into and for the first time felt homesick. I dared not ring David up as I thought it would make me feel even worse, so I wrote long letters instead. I had my first television interview in Melbourne, and the show went out live, which was a bit nerve-racking – no room for mistakes. The best thing about it was that no one else knew more about the subject than I did.

The only person I knew in Australia was David Brown, who had become disillusioned with Stevenage and returned home for some sunshine and surfing. I decided to give myself a week off and flew to Mount Gambier in an aeroplane that felt as if it was tied together with string. David met me and we drove to Port Macdonnel on the coast, where he had been working as a fisherman. His landlady, Janice, worked in a lobster-tinning factory, and when she discovered I liked lobster, she gave it to me for every meal three times a day. It was delicious but they never ate it themselves. We drove back along the coast to Melbourne, from where I flew on to New Zealand.

Arriving in Auckland at customs I was sent for a body search, I suppose because I had come from India and Nepal. The idea shook me quite a bit but luckily I managed to talk myself out of it. I showed the large customs lady a brochure of my stately home and told her I was late for a radio show, where I was talking about my ancestors and Britain's tourist industry. I did in fact have to rush to the radio interview, even running up three flights of stairs straight into the studio and on to the air. It was called the Barry Holland Show. We had had no chance to discuss the interview before, but luckily – owing entirely to his experience and the fact that I had not had time to get nervous – it went off very well.

Once more staying with friends of friends, I spent a wonderful weekend sailing off North Island and then flew down to friends of theirs in Wellington. The Queen and Prince Philip had just arrived, so the newspapers were not very interested in me. However, the *New Zealand Herald* did a good splash and the New Zealand *Woman's Weekly* did a long article with lots of pictures. I was given a haunted room in Wellington, although I wasn't told that, and I spent most of the night trying to work out what was going on in the room – I knew something was happening but couldn't work out what. At moments it felt almost like an earthquake. It was a very strange sensation. When I told my hosts at breakfast, they all laughed and said others had had similar experiences in that room, but they refused to tell me why.

A very hospitable lady, Marjorie Jackson, who was a courier for upmarket tours from New Zealand, had me to stay in her house on Lake Taupo. We zoomed around the lake in her speedboat, fished for huge trout and swam in the freezing water.

Adelaide was the next stop, so it was back to Australia. The vice consul met me, took me to my hotel and then accompanied me to a Cornish evening that British Airways were holding. We drank cider and ate Cornish pasties, and British Airways offered to distribute my brochures to the travel trade for me, which was a great help. It meant that I was able to take off for a few days to a farm outside Adelaide, to stay with some people called Throsby whom I had never met before, though we had mutual friends. They bred racehorses and took me to Adelaide races; I believe that he subsequently called one of his racehorses 'Knebworth'.

In Perth I stayed in a scruffy hotel called The Forest Lodge. The temperature was in the nineties and it was a public holiday, so I got on a bus saying 'Beach' and, after half an hour of wondering where I would end up, arrived at a huge and very crowded beach. I had a lonely swim and somehow managed to find a bus going back in the right direction. The hotel was full of Aborigines, which was interesting, if noisy – their children ran up and down the corridors shouting all night and never seemed to go to bed.

British Airways had asked fourteen travel agents to lunch to meet me, and organised two newspaper and television interviews, so I did lots of business. There I met a PR man from the Dorchester Hotel, London, who was giving a cocktail party for the travel trade and journalists in his motel and invited me to go along. He obviously felt he had done me a favour by including me in his party, and I had to make a hasty exit via the lavatory and the back stairs of the hotel to avoid him. I spent the rest of the evening in the cinema hoping he wouldn't find me.

Singapore was quite different. Tom Rendall, a friend of David's whom I had known since Cambridge days, and his family were now living in Singapore and I went and stayed with them. Hal Christensen, who had helped with our concerts, was now married to Sally Dimbleby and they were also living in Singapore; but Sally was in England and Hal was away on business, so they sent some friends with garlands of flowers to the airport to greet me. The British Airways representative was not interested in me at all so I had a lovely week exploring Singapore on the buses.

Bangkok was my last port of call. I had one lecture to give in a huge hotel, to the South Wind Rotary Club on UK tourism. I had been told that my audience would be Thai and a mixture of men and women, so I worked out my talk accordingly, including bits of medieval English history, the rules of jousting, etc. In fact they turned out to be all Europeans and all men, and knew far more about English history than I did. So after showing a few slides and giving rather a tame talk for about ten minutes I dried up. I was supposed to have spoken for twenty minutes and no one seemed to know what to do with the spare ten minutes – it was very embarrassing.

I was grateful to get out and take the next bus to the seaside town of Pattaya with an American friend and five American sailor friends of his. They managed to restore my self-esteem and even persuaded me to go parascending on the end of a very long rope out at sea behind a motor boat – a great act of courage on my part as I am terrified of heights!

Two days later I was back in the wind and rain of the English spring. Both David and I found it hard to adjust to married life again, as we had both got used to being on our own. And going back to caring for the family once more was quite an effort. It is difficult to tell how many people came to Knebworth as a result of my trip, but I like to think that all those Australian names and addresses in our visitors' book are a direct result.

Meanwhile, Joanne and David had made a spectacular Indian Exhibition in the squash court, which is still there today. A young artist called Robin Kimmins had decorated the inside of the court in Indian style, and Derek had built showcases down both sides of the room, which David had filled with photographs, letters and artefacts from Lord Lytton's viceregal time in India. Two huge blown-up photographs of him dressed in full splendour with his Indian servants behind him were hung on the walls, and two viceregal robes were loaned by Buckingham Palace. A screen for the audio-visual show at the far end of the room is flanked by portraits of Lord and Lady Lytton. A couple of small annexes were partitioned off, one for the 2nd Earl of Lytton, who was born in Simla and was Governor of Bengal in the 1920s. In 1925 Lord Reading, who was the Viceroy, went home on leave for four months and left Victor Lytton as acting Viceroy in Delhi; Pamela, his wife, was in England, so Hermione at the age of nineteen acted as Vicereine, quite an experience for a girl of that age. We have a lot of Indian letters and photographs from that time.

The other annexe is full of earlier Indian ornaments, weapons and pictures. The centrepiece of the exhibition is the magnificent silver throne, a present from the Maharajah of Mysore, that was almost stolen the year before. It is a smaller replica of his throne, with a silver canopy and red plush cushions. Beside it is an attractive silver Ganges boat, the cabin of which is a casket containing a proclamation about sewers, of all things. My favourite exhibit is sixteen beautifully coloured enamel animals about two inches high from Rajasthan; they include elephants, camels, peacocks and tigers, and we put them on the table at Christmas for decoration.

The audio-visual show, which David had written and produced, gives an account of the Delhi Durbar and the political and social problems that Lord Lytton had to deal with in India. The proclamation of Queen Victoria as Empress of India at Delhi on 1 January 1877 signified in an extravagant gesture the supremacy of British rule in India. Twenty years on from the Mutiny the country was in a sufficiently stable and settled condition to make the occasion a peaceful and happy celebration.

It fell to Lord Lytton to organise the actual proclamation which was to take place at the Durbar, a traditional form of assembly used by the Indian princes to celebrate important occasions. Delhi, the old Moghul capital, was chosen as the site, and arrangements were made to accommodate over 60,000 guests in a camp outside the city. Geoffrey Lee re-created the spectacular nature of the event in a centenary article in *Country Life*:

> Lytton arrived at Delhi station on December 23, 1876. Waiting for him were gorgeously caparisoned elephants and the soldiers of the Rajpoot chiefs. The procession was led by the Deputy-Assistant Quartermaster-General, followed by the 11th Hussars, a battery of the Royal Horse Artillery, a regiment of Bombay Cavalry magnificent in blue and silver, the personal escort of the Viceroy in scarlet uniforms, with the aides-de-camp on elephants, two abreast.
>
> Then came the Chief Herald, Major Barnes, who was to read the proclamation and was reputedly chosen for the job because he was the biggest officer in the army. Twelve trumpeters were in attendance, followed by the Body Guard – the flower of the native cavalry. Immediately behind came the Viceroy and Lady Lytton. They were seated in an elaborate howdah on the back of a magnificent tusker elephant. A gilt umbrella was held over their heads with an attendant seated behind waving off imaginary flies with a brush made from a yak's tail.
>
> The next elephant carried the Viceroy's daughters. Then came the remainder of the Body Guard, a squadron of the 10th Hussars, three Lieutenant-Governors (each on an elephant), their staff, members of the Council, secretaries to the Government and chief justices. Following them were the native chiefs, with their elephants painted in all the colours of the rainbow and sparkling with jewel-studded gold and silver trappings.

Lining the street were more soldiers, some in chain mail and mounted on magnificent war elephants. One great attraction was the six-pounder guns of Baroda made in solid silver and gold and drawn by oxen whose horns had been dipped in gold . . .

Once in camp Lord Lytton received the chiefs and princes and presented as gifts banners which Rudyard Kipling's parents had been involved in making – one in the design work and the other in the embroidering. The Viceroy also returned visits, gave state banquets, and generally made himself agreeable to the dignitaries present.

The day of the proclamation, like those of the preceding week, was blessed with perfect weather. The scene of the ceremonial presentation was a turf-covered plain about four miles from Delhi. Its centrepiece was the graceful blue, red and gold Throne Pavilion for the Viceroy. A hexagon with each side 40ft long, it stood on a solid masonry base 10ft from the ground surmounted by a gilded railing. The upper part was a canopy supported on 12 slender shafts. At the top the Imperial Crown rested upon a cushion beneath which was a drapery of red cloth embroidered with gold.

In front of the Pavilion was the Amphitheatre, 800ft long and painted blue, white and gold. This housed the 63 ruling chiefs with their retainers, and senior government officials. The exotic costumes of the princes in satin, velvet and cloth of gold mixed with the European officials in their red and dark blue uniforms to make a colourful spectacle. In the centre of the Amphitheatre were the three boy princes of India – the Nizam of Hyderabad, the Gaekwar of Baroda and the Maharaja of Mysore. On the other side of the Throne Pavilion were stands for representatives of foreign governments and spectators. British troops were drawn up on a plateau to the north of the plain, native retainers to the south. Guards of Honour were in place on either side of the Throne Pavilion and at the entrances to the Amphitheatre.

> At noon the Viceroy, in his robes as Grand Master of the Order of the Star of India, arrived. The military bands played and Major Barnes read the proclamation of the assumption of the Imperial Title by the Queen. The 12 trumpeters sounded a fanfare. The Foreign Secretary then read the proclamation in Urdu. A salvo of 101 shots was fired, nearly causing an elephant stampede. The band played the national anthem followed by the march from *Tannhäuser*. Lord Lytton made a speech and several of the princes attempted replies, but the noise from the excited crowd drowned their efforts.
>
> The celebrations concluded with entertainments, races, athletics, displays of fireworks and other amusements, which went on for several days. On January 4 Lytton gave a farewell reception to the chiefs, and on the 5th, the last day, a general review was held with some 14,000 troops taking part. A few days after the celebrations were over and the visitors had departed a deluge of rain turned the camp site into a quagmire. But by then the Viceroy was safely back in Calcutta.

Apart from the Durbar, it was a difficult time socially and politically in India and Lord Lytton must have been relieved when he returned home to Knebworth three years later.

The audio-visual continues with the story of his son Victor as Governor of Bengal. The present Winston Churchill talks about his grandfather's meeeting with Pamela Plowden (later Lady Lytton) in India and their relationship. The show finishes with Lady Cobbold, David's mother, describing her memories of India and the holidays they took in the Himalayas.

We had a big opening in April. Actress Sneh Gupta, who was Miss Anglia that year, came to the party; she is Kenyan Asian rather than Indian, but made a pretty addition to the proceedings. The exhibition has been a great success and we would like eventually to build a special Indian Museum to house the collection, but by that time I expect we will be too old to play squash and the children will have left home.

Chapter 9 Knightshirts and skateboards

By this stage, living at Knebworth House was having an effect on our relationship with each other and with the children. I had found earlier in our marriage – and listening to friends I think we were not alone – that we had little to say to each other in the evenings: I could relate stories about the children and my day, and David would try and interest me in his banking affairs. But now we had so much to discuss that we would find our bathtime board meetings were taking one or two hours at a time, and Pattie would get very fed up waiting for us to come down to dinner. I think the quality of our relationship improved a lot.

On the other hand, I was so busy that I think the children were probably rather neglected. I could never start a game with them without an interruption of some sort, but I used to try and take them out for the day once a week (even to visit other stately homes) in order to have an uninterrupted day together. Of course they benefited in a lot of ways as well. Living in a large house is marvellous for children – there's room to make a mess, run around, play sardines or witches and play their record-players at full blast. And it is not every child who has an adventure playground in his garden with a thirty-foot astroglide, or a narrow-gauge steam railway. The park is perfect for under-age motor scrambling, go-karting or learning to drive a car as soon as you can reach the pedals.

With our different events at weekends they had opportunities for parascending, hot-air ballooning, riding in horse-drawn carriages, driving our steam train or listening to the world's major rock groups. When they were at local schools, their friends' birthday parties were usually held in the park. It was hard for them not to become big-headed about living in 'the Big House', but boarding school soon put a stop to that.

Henry was at Eton by this time and had begun bringing home Danny and Harry, two Ugandan boys who were at school with him. Their parents were divorced and both lived abroad, so we made a home for them during their holidays and half-terms. They have become part of the family since. I had always wanted six children, but because of the difficulty I had in having babies this was the ideal solution – so I now have five boys and a girl.

Henry by this time had a guitar and full disco equipment, Peter had a drum kit, Danny and Harry both sing very well, Richard was learning the saxophone and Rosina strummed on the Bechstein grand piano – they could all play or sing at once without disturbing anyone. There can be a party of 300 people at one end of the house and you would not know there was anyone in the house from the other end. The fact that the house is open and that visitors are wandering around is hardly noticed by any of us any more, as we are all so used to it and have never known it otherwise.

Rosina and her friends from school were always getting into mischief. They would hide under the four-poster beds and giggle as the visitors went round the house. One day I found them rolling down the drive on skateboards with no knickers on 'flashing' at the surprised visitors. Skateboards were all the rage in 1977 and Peter had been nagging at us for months to build a skateboard park. He and his friends skidded around the house between the furniture, knocking into the grandfather clock and tripping up over the valuable chairs. So when a firm called Skateopia, who had made a fortune from selling skateboards, said they were looking for somewhere to build an £80,000 skate park, we jumped at the idea. Knebworth was to become Britain's first Stately Skate Park. It would be ready for the 1978 season and would, we felt, make up for the loss of the Bird Garden, which we knew would have to close by the end of the year.

Sadly, the Tunnicliffes could not make enough money to keep it going. We tried to help them by not charging any rent and giving them free accommodation, but the feeding, heating and vets' bills for the delicate tropical birds all winter with no money coming in was too much for them. They packed it all up and went back to the circus. We still miss the squawks and colourful plumage of the macaws around the garden.

By this time Mr Roberts the gardener could not cope with the main garden any more, and he certainly did not have time to do the vegetable garden, so I started to do it myself. I bought myself a rotavator as I am not good at digging. I sowed, weeded and picked whenever I had a moment and found it a marvellous way to relax. It was always private and peaceful and I could work in my bikini in the walled garden, unseen by visitors and mostly undisturbed.

I love sunbathing and sometimes, desperate for a quiet roast, I would go up on the roof and strip naked. But even there I am not safe. I was once surprised by our bald bachelor architect, who blushed from his cheeks right over to the back of his neck . . . and still does every time he sees me now! There is also the risk of low-flying aircraft.

We built a wall around a small area of the garden at the south end of the house soon after we moved in, just in order to have some privacy for family meals outside and sunbathing. It is also somewhere to put the dogs. My dogs never understand that people have paid to come in, and they are particularly aggressive towards small dogs on leads. I have had to pay quite a few vets' bills for stitching up badly bitten ears etc. The dogs also find it hard to understand that the open part of the house, full of strange people, is also part of home and that house-training still applies. There have been many embarrassing moments when visitors have had to take care where they stepped and both valuable old and expensive new carpets have suffered.

By the spring of 1977 Mrs Roberts, the gardener's wife, and I had made quite a lot of things for the house. Mrs Roberts, as well as being very good at making all the costumes for the theatricals, was also able to upholster. She used my wedding dress to cover an eighteenth-century chair and stool, appliquéing the tapestry back on to the satin. Everyone who went round the house admired it. She also re-covered the Banqueting Hall chairs in red velvet with gold braid; they had last been done in 1910 and were in a very tatty condition. She re-covered the Library chairs and our dining room chairs and made quite a few loose covers. I kept to the curtains and cushions, which were not so complicated. So it was with heavy hearts that we had to suggest to Mr Roberts that it was time for him to retire, as we needed a younger and more energetic gardener to cope with the problems in the garden. We gave him and his family a cottage in the village to move into, but he became very ill and died shortly afterwards, and Mrs Roberts had to work full-time in Stevenage, so I lost her as well.

We had no rock festival during the summer of 1977, as Freddie Bannister said he could not find any groups willing to play a large outdoor venue. In some ways it was just as well to give everyone a rest after the huge Rolling Stones concert the year before, and we had two major films made in the house, which made up for it a bit financially.

The first one was in August – *Sir Henry at Rawlinson End* with Trevor Howard. It was the most amusing film I have ever watched being made. It was a low-budget black and white film, with a wonderfully quick dialogue which even during the short scenes that they do at a time kept you laughing. A diving board was erected outside Peter's third-floor bedroom window and a stuntman dived off it into a pile of cardboard boxes on the ground. He had a rope attached to his ankles which stopped him actually hitting the ground, but it all looked very dangerous. Quite a few of our staff were extras in the film, including the dog.

We went to see the film at the old Paris Pullman cinema in Drayton Gardens; it was a great success and moved to Leicester Square for a while. I saw it twice but the story was quite incomprehensible to me.

In September we had the remake of Raymond Chandler's *The Big Sleep*, starring James Stewart, Robert Mitchum, John Mills, Sarah Miles and Candy Clarke and directed by Michael Winner. It was three weeks of fairly good hell. We had to waive our rule of 'no smoking' in the house; Michael Winner smoked cigars continuously and had a young boy one step behind him holding an ashtray all day long. He also had to have his own dining room and cook. He seemed to live on smoked salmon and red jelly from the glimpses we got of the dishes going in and out; we hoped for some smoked salmon leftovers but all we ever got was red jelly. We let him use our dining room while we ate in the kitchen, and the final straw came when we were told to put the lights out

9a Deer in the twilight

9b The family in 1974

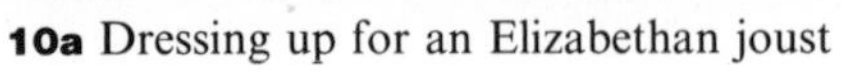

10a Dressing up for an Elizabethan joust

10b 'David of Knebworth'

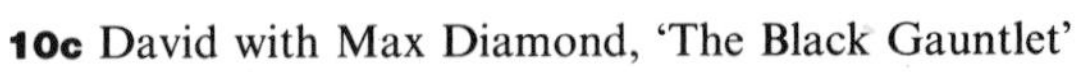

10c David with Max Diamond, 'The Black Gauntlet'

11a Bouncing inside Valentine's tummy

11b The skateboard park

12a The Rolling Stones concert, 1976

12b Led Zeppelin fans in front of the house, 1979

13a
Setting up the Indian exhibition, 1977

13b
Robert, 1st Earl of Lytton, Viceroy of India in 1877

14a Putting the finishing touches to the knightshirts

14b Planting vegetables for banquets

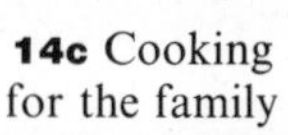

14c Cooking for the family

14d Preparing for an Elizabethan banquet

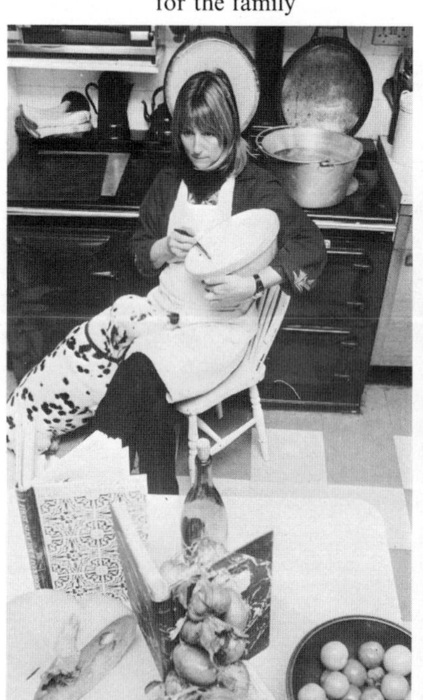

15 June Mendoza's portrait of the children, 1980

16a The family with Lord and Lady Cobbold

16b The end of the day

in the kitchen where we were eating dinner, as the lights were disturbing the filming.

Although the house was closed to the public, the front door was left open because of the filming. I found two people in my bedroom one morning, and when I crossly asked them what they were doing they said, 'The house is open to the public, isn't it?' They were just having a look around. I was very suspicious of them as my bedroom is on the top floor and quite difficult to get to, so I took their driving licence number and made quite a fuss. They could not understand why I was so cross, but I think it was the blatant cheek of it that annoyed me so much.

Sarah Miles brought her young son Thomas with her. He soon became bored with watching the filming and came and joined in with my children. He tried hard to impress them by pouring tomato ketchup over his ice-cream at lunchtime. He was a restless, bored child and I felt sorry for him.

Our next project that winter of 1977–8 was 'Knightshirts'. David, if he wears anything in bed, prefers nightshirts to pyjamas and I had difficulty finding comfortable cotton ones for him. So we thought, why not go into the nightshirt business? We could sell them in the gift shop and perhaps some of the big London stores would take them. We would call them 'Knebworth Knightshirts' and they could be designed like a knight's tabard with chainmail sleeves and white front and back with different coats of arms printed on them. We could even do a damsels' version as a Knightie and a shorter Page's Tunic for children.

I found a fashion designer, Mary Brown, who did some drawings and patterns, and together we went round the rag trade in London looking for 100 per cent white knitted cotton material, printers and a factory to make them up. It was a new world to me and fun to learn about. We already sold 'Knebworth' T-shirts in our shop, so we used the same printers in the end, and a factory in Harrow Road made the shirts.

I traipsed round the major stores asking if they would like to sell our Knightshirts, a wearisome business which I hate. So I was relieved when Selfridges said they were having a special Historic House Association and British Tourist Authority exhibition called 'Noble Heritage' for four months in the summer, and if they could have the exclusive rights to the garments for the summer we could have a stall and sell the shirts ourselves.

Pattie and I spent hours packaging the Knightshirts into plastic bags and sorting out colours and sizes. The exhibition was on the top floor of Selfridges, and manning it was a big problem. Neither Pattie nor I wanted to do it all the time and we could not afford to pay someone else to, so we took turns, half a day each. It was very time-consuming and I did not enjoy it at all. I hated the stuffy shop atmosphere, and the customers could be very tiresome as well. The male ones were more interested in taking us out to lunch than buying the shirts, and I wished I was back in my garden at Knebworth.

The Knightshirts were good publicity, though. *Country Life* came down to Knebworth and took some photographs and did an article. David and I dressed up in the Knightwear, and Mike Horsborough came round dressed as a knight on one of his jousting horses, and we posed for pictures with him and also in the Elizabethan four-poster bed.

In the spring of 1978 the dollar was $2.40 to the pound. David said it would never be so good again, and we had better go to the States. We had always longed to take the children to Disney World, and it seemed an ideal opportunity to try and sell the Knightshirts as well. So, missing our Easter opening at Knebworth, we flew to New York. The first evening in New York we went to see *The Big Sleep*, which had not opened in England yet. It was a very strange feeling coming straight from England, as the film starts off with a car driving off the motorway into our drive and up our park, through the main gate and up to the front door. The bell is rung and Gordon Jackson, the butler, opens it and the camera moves on into the Banqueting Hall. Almost the entire film was shot in and around the house and there were loud stage whispers in the cinema of 'There's my bedroom' or 'Look, there's the cat' from the children.

CBS television were interested in filming our Knightwear, and thought that Belvedere Fort in Central Park would be the nearest thing to a castle for the setting. So we all met up there on a chilly spring afternoon. We had a suitcase full of Knightshirts, but changing into them was a bit of a problem. Eventually each member of the family went behind a tree to change, and the Central Park muggers and joggers watched in amazement as we stripped off and donned our cotton Knightshirts. The children wore page's shirts, I wore the long damsel gown and David the tabard. The interview went well, but it was cold and the children and I got fed up long before the interviewers did.

We then went off to Bloomingdale's to try and sell them, but discovered that the USA charges 100 per cent tax on cotton imports, which would have made them ridiculously expensive, and the $2.40 pound was working against us; so we had to give that idea up. The children were delighted not to be dragged round any more stores. We hired a car and drove down the east coast to Florida, staying in motels on the way.

The Americans were suspicious. Why were the children not at school, we were asked all the time – apparently American children do not have four-week Easter holidays. The day before we got to Disney World we discovered a four-lane water slide; in scorching sun David and the children spent all afternoon sliding down it. David was hooked on it and of course wanted one for Knebworth. The following morning, however, Rosina had sunstroke with a temperature of 104 and Peter's face and back had come up in purple sun blisters. We just managed to get round Disney World before putting them to bed in a hotel. Only in America would one find a television set in the bedroom which showed the hotel pool on its screen; it meant we could leave them for an occasional swim and they could watch us from their beds.

We then discovered that Richard had worms, so we spent quite a lot of precious time sitting in the doctor's waiting room. Having all been dosed as a precaution against the worms, and Rosina's temperature having subsided, we set off again, through the Nasa Space Centre and the Okefenoke Alligator Farm, and on up to Alabama and Virginia to stay with friends. Sadly, the bears were still in hibernation in the Smokey Blue Ridge mountains. But in Washington we were given a private tour of the White House by the curator and, as the President was not there, we were allowed into the Oval office, which was a great treat for everyone.

Wherever we went I could feel David itching to visit travel agencies and do some Knebworth House promotion; but I felt this was a holiday primarily for the children, except for the 'Knightshirts', and I kept him away from them as much as I could.

We got back to Kennedy Airport in New York on Saturday evening and went to check in on Iran Airways, with whom we were flying. At the check-in counter, the man said he was sorry, but no passengers were being taken on that flight; we would have to go the following evening on their next flight. David was furious. He had to be at work in the City on Monday morning, and he always worries when he is away from his office in case someone else might be in his seat when he gets back! He argued and pleaded with the officials and refused to leave.

We sat on our luggage with the children, looking like refugees. In the end they gave in and said we could go after all, and it turned out that we had the entire jumbo to ourselves, except for a few official-looking Iranians. We lay flat out on four aisle seats each and had a really good night's sleep. In London we discovered that our luggage was not on the plane, but they promised to send it on to Knebworth when it did arrive. It was all very mysterious and I can only hazard a guess that maybe the plane was loaded up with gold, or some other very heavy cargo, which prevented them taking passengers and even our small amount of luggage.

We got back to find the 1978 summer season had got off to a good start. We had opened with a big jousting tournament and about 6000 people had come over the four-day Easter weekend. The skate park was not due to open until May, but was beginning to look very exciting. They had put in a concrete free-style area, a 350-foot snake run and bowl, a clover leaf and 150 feet of half-piping rides. Apparently it was the biggest in the country, and at £80,000 it should have been.

By Whitsun it was ready. It was opened by former Arsenal and Scotland goalkeeper Bob Wilson, and some of the country's champion skateboarders came to try it out and give their verdict. It had its own pro-shop, tuition, first aid equipment and refreshment facilities. We just hoped there would not be too many accidents. It is a dangerous sport and there are a lot of accidents; Peter concussed himself badly falling on his head in the early days and we spent a worrying forty-eight hours with him in hospital. It was a continual battle to get children to wear helmets and safety pads.

Skateboarding was not the only dangerous thing going on in

the park that summer. A local garage, G. E. Harper, staged a large promotion for 5000 car dealers in June, and as part of the entertainment Eddie Kid, a motorcycle ace who had just broken a world record by jumping eighteen double-decker buses, one for each year of his life, performed for them. But because of a sprained wrist he only ventured jumping six brand new cars that day. The dealers were impressed and he was besieged by fans for his autograph, not easy for him with a sprained right wrist. His big ambition, he said, was to jump the Grand Canyon in a couple of years' time! The same event featured 'Tomorrow's World' presenter Raymond Baxter, who joined in the cabaret of African limbo dancers, but the general opinion was that he needed to practise his performance.

Two films were made during that summer: *Beauty and the Beast* with George C. Scott and Tricia Van De Vere, his wife, and *Ike* with Robert Duvall as Eisenhower and Lee Remick as his English chauffeur. *Beauty and the Beast* was responsible for giving Rosina nightmares for ages. George's make-up as the Beast took two hours to put on every morning, and it also prevented him from smoking, which had a bad effect on his temper and made him quite unapproachable. He was a frightening sight for an impressionable child of seven.

Only a small part of the six-hour TV film *Ike* was filmed at Knebworth – a meeting in England during the war between Eisenhower, Monty and Churchill, and for which they used the Banqueting Hall and Library. There is a painting of the Banqueting Hall by Winston Churchill hanging in the Hall where it was painted, and the director made a point of making sure that it was visible in the background during a scene when Churchill is talking to Eisenhower.

Once again the highlight of the season was the rock festival. As if to make up for the lack of a concert in 1977, we held two in 1978. Freddie Bannister was very guarded over who was playing and rumours were rife; there were headlines in the music press saying things like 'Dylan and Clapton to play Knebworth?' The first concert was held in mid-June and called 'A midsummer night's dream'; the big names were Genesis and Jefferson Starship. The second was in September with Frank Zappa and The Tubes. Neither expected to pull in more than 50,000 people, which was just as well as the Stevenage Carnival was on the same Saturday in June.

Members of the Jefferson Starship group were skateboard enthusiasts and we wondered if they would want to use our new park. Craig Chapuico, the band's leader, had his own motorised skateboard, which went at thirty-five miles per hour; he had just made a film called *Skateboard* and had broken his arm shortly after, falling off it. Peter Sears of the band had managed to break his leg and their publicity lady had broken her arm, all on skateboards. But luckily they were fit by 24 June. Their enthusiasm for skateboarding must have cooled by then as they did not seem keen to try out our park.

The Genesis concert was a relatively low-key affair. The fans were an average age of thirty-plus and came with picnics, dogs and children and enjoyed the sunshine and atmosphere. There were no problems and only one arrest. David was photographed lying in the middle of the rock crowd reading the *Financial Times*, and it was published in quite a few magazines and newspapers.

The September festival had a younger audience and was very 'punk'. The Boomtown Rats, with Bob Geldof, were chart favourites and went on just before the controversial Frank Zappa. He came to the house with his bodyguard, a huge bald black man, before going on stage; he had a neurosis about strangers being around him and we had to keep everyone out of the rooms he went into – quite a difficult task in our house. We showed him around and he commented that our Picture Gallery could be quite a nice room if we got rid of all the pictures; he was interested in a child's musical chair we have in the nursery and remarked, 'No wonder the English are so strange, being brought up with music coming up through their arses!' On the whole he was thoroughly disagreeable. He spat out the coffee I gave him and said he wished he'd brought his own, and when we got back to the Picture Gallery, we discovered that his bodyguard had consumed a whole box of David's favourite Swiss chocolates, which a friend had given him as a present. So we were relieved when they left for the arena. He has a big following, though, and fans seem to enjoy his abrasive remarks.

We had our usual camp down by the stage and it was a beautiful September day. The fans sitting behind us were handing round magic mushrooms and flapjacks. The mushrooms were small with long stalks and hooded tops with small nipples on the ends; I had never seen any like them before, so decided not to risk taking any and to opt for the flapjacks instead, which looked somehow safer. I could never be sure I would not be needed to help with the organisation during the day and it would not do to be incapacitated.

Sure enough, just as I had finished my flapjack David came through the crowd and asked if I would come and help move some illicit traders who were selling cans of coke from the car park. It took about an hour, by which time I was beginning to feel very strange and only just made it back to our pitch. I will never know what was in those flapjacks, but the clouds turned into animals chasing each other across the sky. I found it difficult to focus, so I tried shutting my eyes, but the colours in my head were so chaotic that it was better with them open. I couldn't move. I do not like not being in control of myself, so I did not care for the experience much and I kept praying it would soon wear off and no one would ask me to do something before it had. The young girl next to me had taken two flapjacks and I looked at her to see how she was faring; she had fallen asleep and was still asleep when the concert finished – we had to wake her up to go home. She was very annoyed at missing it all.

The Tubes came on last and gave a very theatrical performance, with good special effects. One song called 'Smoke' involved half a dozen people dressed as ten-foot cigarettes staggering around the stage; the stage filled with smoke and they all fell on top of the lead singer, Fee Waybill. Waybill was dressed in a sequined suit and twelve-inch high-heeled boots, and by this time forty people were on stage. Keith Moon of the Who had died the week before, so they ended with a tribute to him, playing some Who numbers. Then a firework display ended the festival. No one came back to the house afterwards, which was probably just as well as I was feeling rather jaded.

The following morning, however, an amazing female singer from the Tubes band, called Ree, arrived at the front door with a friend and asked if they could see round the house. David offered them vodka and took them on a tour. Ree was already over the top when she arrived but David caught up with her quite quickly. She fell in love with everything, including the icebucket, which David gave her and she promptly dropped on the floor and broke. He ended up getting into the chauffeur-driven Rolls with her and disappearing down the drive, but luckily she turned him out at the gates. By the time he had walked back he had sobered up a bit.

The concert had not attracted as many people as Freddie had hoped, and some of the voluntary services working on the day complained that they had not been paid this time. But the park meanwhile had to be cleaned up and life had to go on as normal.

It had been a busy summer, starting with our trip to the States in April with the Knightshirts, and followed by the opening of the skate park, two films, two rock festivals and numerous smaller events of which the most successful was the Custom Car rally. Another car rally, named 'The Wonderful World of Wheels', with over 200 veteran cars, steam organs and steel bands, was well attended, and the Capital Radio Fun Bus came down one weekend with DJ Adrian Love and some Fun Girls, who added to the spirit of things by running about amongst the crowd (which unfortunately only numbered around sixty) handing out badges, stickers and photographs.

It was a relief to us all to close the house and park. The staff could take their much deserved holidays and, having got the older children off to boarding school, I could concentrate on getting the house straight once again.

The winter was uneventful, except for Rosina's decision to become a Brownie. I encouraged her; as I was president of the local Girl Guides, it seemed appropriate. The uniform was quite expensive, so when she was due to go and be enrolled on the first day she changed her mind about being a Brownie, I got quite cross. In the end she agreed to go if I came too. So I sat on a small hard chair at the back of the Guide hut with Rosina sitting firmly on my lap throughout.

The following week she was no keener to be a Brownie, and neither was I, but we had to get some use out of the uniform so we both trooped off and sat in the draughty hall again. Brown Owl was very disapproving. No other child needed her mother and she said I should slip away and she would occupy Rosina. I did eventually, and Brown Owl and two helpers held on to a screaming and kicking Rosina while I made my escape.

I sat outside in the car blinking back the tears and stayed there for the rest of the meeting, just in case I was needed. At the end of the evening my Brownie came skipping out with two other Brownies – she had had a wonderful time, next week they were going to make biscuits and could she buy some smarties to take with her? She had already set her heart on going to boarding school the following autumn, and I just could not believe she would be ready to leave home when the time came.

After one busy season the skateboarding craze, which brought with it a multi-million pound industry, had all but burnt itself out. Around two million skateboards had been sold the previous year, but now companies were wondering what to do with them; firms were making bonfires out of them and adapting the urethane wheels to make trolleys for their warehouses. Skateopia, who ran our park, were no exception. They could not take the concrete with them, and we were hardly going to pay them for it. However, we did give them something towards it, and have continued to use it ever since. There are still some enthusiasts around, and when BMX bikes came into fashion a few years later they shared the concrete bowls with the few remaining skateboarders.

Chapter 10 A record year

Walking through the main hall at the *Daily Mail* Ideal Home Exhibition in Olympia in March 1979, I saw a sign saying 'Knebworth House'. The building behind the sign was a modern, red-brick, two-storey house with three up and three down. 'Ideal home for practical, comfortable living,' said the advertisement. I went up to the sales desk and said 'I thought I lived in Knebworth House.' The man looked at me blankly. 'Why do you call that house Knebworth?' I asked. 'Oh it's just a name, we give all our houses names, it helps to sell them,' he said. My brain ticked over for a few moments. 'There must be some publicity in this for both of us,' I suggested. 'Let's give a big Knebworth key from our house to the first person who buys one of your houses.' The salesmen thought this was a great idea; we could have an official handing-over of the keys to the new owners and invite the press.

I went home to find a key and he waited for a buyer. Unfortunately, we had never thought of removing the large decorative keys from the locks in the house when we opened to the public and they have all been pinched, even the front door key. But I did manage eventually to find something suitable in a box in the butler's pantry. The ceremony took place in the Olympia Hall a few weeks later. The new owners of a modern 'Knebworth House' were presented with an old key from the original Knebworth House. A gimmick, yes – but good publicity.

1978 had been another record year for us and 195,000 people had visited the park, not counting the 80,000 who had come to the two festivals. Our regular festival friends had dispersed by now. Thump had gone to work in Kenya, Hal and Sally were in

Singapore and Barry had gone back to Bristol to his wife, boat-building and deep-sea diving.

Fed up with the English winter and having itchy feet, I thought I would go out to Africa and visit Thump. I had felt a great affinity with the country as a teenager, and I longed to visit it again. Thump had just started a new government job for the Agriculture Information Services in Nairobi and I knew he would be busy, so I joined a club called 'Wexas' and took a package tour for a fortnight before meeting up with him.

There were only four of us, all female, on the package – one was a spinster and the other two widows. We had to pair up for bedrooms so I shared with one of the widows, called Chris, as neither of us smoked. She was a good-looking woman in her fifties and had lost two husbands. The other two, Connie and Sheila, were in their sixties. None of them had been to Africa before and I don't think they chose the best tour to start out on.

Our first night was spent in wooden huts on a scrub hill overlooking Lake Naivasha. There was a full moon over the lake and the night was rich with African noises. It was magical – I felt immensely happy to be alive and in such a beautiful place, and sat outside drinking it all in. Not so my three companions, who were terrified and miserable. They tried to find someone to complain to; they had never expected to be left out alone in the bush with no male protector. The loo was a smelly affair, a plank over a pit with no light, and the huts had no glass on the windows and were open to mosquitoes or anyone else who wanted to come in. The two Africans who had cooked our dinner could not help them, and went back to their village. A manager did appear eventually from Naivasha to see how we were getting on; he calmed the ladies down and promised, if they were still nervous the next day, that he would move them, but there was nothing he could do that evening.

I went off for a walk to get away from the sound of their voices, and when I got back I found they had sensibly opened up their duty free and were well away, drowning their fears in vermouth.

Next day we were moved down to the Lake Naivasha Hotel, a lovely place, but I was sad to leave the wildness of the hills. It rained all day, so I was glad I had brought a mackintosh. After a comfortable night in the lake-side hotel and a boat trip to see the birds and hippos, we went on to the Masai Mara Game Reserve. The shock-absorbers went on the minibus, so it took all day by the time we had found a garage. When we passed one tented camp our driver, Ben, commented, 'Very dangerous camp, all washed away last year in floods.' We carried on and soon came to the Kichwa Tembo camp, where we were supposed to be staying. The manager came out looking worried. 'I'm very sorry, we're full up,' he said. 'You'll have to go back to the other camp.' So back we went to the 'very dangerous' one, the Mara Sara. It had been completely rebuilt but was still right on the river. A thunderstorm was raging, the rain was sheeting down and the river looked very brown and full, but the camp was lovely inside with large bamboo huts to sleep in and all mod cons.

The dinner was delicious and we soon collapsed exhausted into bed, only to find that there was no way of turning out the naked electric bulb in the middle of the room. There was one main switch for the camp and that went off at midnight. So I covered my head with my coat and went to sleep to the sound of rain and frogs.

My room companion woke me at six every morning. It took her two hours to dress for breakfast and she liked to discuss politics at the same time. I have trouble being civil before breakfast, but we had to live together for a fortnight so I did my best. On the second evening the generator broke down, so there were no lights to keep us awake and we got to sleep early, which helped. I loved every minute out in the wild looking at the animals and birds, and was sad when it was time to go back to Nairobi and fly on to Mombasa.

The four of us were to stay for a week in Diani Beachalets, a small resort about an hour south of Mombasa on the Indian ocean. It was hot and humid on the coast after the altitude of the plains, and our taxi driver did not know the way. It was dark, too, which did not help. We stopped at a few smart-looking hotels before eventually arriving at the chalets.

We knocked on the door of the manager's house. He and his wife were having dinner, and were not expecting us until the next morning. The chalets were all full and they even had a couple in their spare room that evening, so the four of us slept in their children's room. I slept under the window and there was a big thunderstorm during the night. One of the ladies kept smoking and turning the lights on, then Chris started getting up at six as usual, so it was a short night. There was an argument over breakfast as to who should sleep in the air-conditioned spare room for the rest of the week. I escaped to the beach for a swim and when I got back I found that Chris and I were in the children's room, which suited me as I hate air-conditioning.

Harold and Jean Barker, the owner-managers, could not have been kinder and we were treated as house guests. They had lived in Uganda all their lives, so I told them about our two Ugandan boys, Danny and Harry. They were stunned. Harold had worked for their father in Obote's government and knew them well. He was Harry's godfather and Harry had been called after him. They produced their photograph album and there was a picture of Danny and Harry as toddlers with their mother. They had not heard anything of them since they left the country when Idi Amin came to power. We all made friends and they promised to come and visit us at Knebworth when they came to England.

I hired an old combi van from them to go up to the Ocean Sports Hotel, about a three-hour journey away, to visit David's parents who were on holiday there. Frances, a girl in her twenties who was staying in one of the Barkers' chalets, offered to come with me. She had finished a dentistry course in Bristol and had gone out to the north of Kenya to work as a dentist. She was quite interesting on the subject of teeth, and said that the Africans' teeth were ruined by all the sweet canned drinks they had nowadays. The area she was working in was well known for lockjaw, and as a precaution the country people automatically removed their front teeth so they could still be fed and therefore possibly survive if they caught the infection. However, when they went into the towns to work people laughed at them for being country folk and having no front teeth, so Frances's job was mainly fixing false front teeth for these people.

She had waist-long bright red hair and, when she first arrived, had had the unnerving experience of people sidling up to her with knives and scissors; someone explained to her that they thought her red hair was a sign she had been to Mecca and they all wanted a piece of it. After that she tied it firmly up in a bun and kept a sharp eye around her when she went out. She had had malaria very badly and been invalided down to the coast to recover, and was still very weak. But it was wonderful to have her company, especially as she spoke Swahili, which proved to be very useful.

We got lost on the way north; the Kilifi 'bypass' sounded like a good idea but took us on a three-hour detour, instead of a ten-minute journey on the ferry. Frances collected butterflies, and every time we ran into one we had to stop the car and scrape it off the windscreen. She was also suffering from dysentery and had to find a bush every fifteen minutes – not difficult but there was usually a group of giggling children behind it too. So it took us five hours to get to Ocean Sports.

Ocean Sports is a smart hotel and we felt naked in our bikinis and kangas, the only clothing we had brought with us. But Kim and Hermione seemed pleased to see us and gave us lunch. On the way back the police stopped us: two white women on their own were worth having a go at. I was thankful for Frances's Swahili. She talked her way around the policemen and they waved us on, but the old van would not start again and in the end the police had to push to get us going. It was a good outing and I liked Frances.

At the end of the week a car came to take us back to the airport. It was late and we had a terrifying journey as the driver only overtook on corners, steep hills or when he could see something coming. The airport was packed, everyone hoping to go to Nairobi that evening. I did a quick head count and decided that a lot of passengers were going to be left behind, so I made sure I was first on to the plane. I was right, a lot of angry people did not make it.

Thump met me in Nairobi. He was at work during the day so I met up with an American girl called Hazel who had two small children, and we spent a few days exploring together. Then Thump and I set off on a safari, first to Nara Moru, a lovely fishing lodge at the base of Mount Kenya, Nanyuki, then to Samburu Park. We reached Buffalo Springs Camp at 6.20 p.m., but it was full up and they suggested we drove on to Shada Camp, seventeen kilometres away. It was dark, no one was supposed to be in the park after six-thirty, we were in a Ford Cortina that was quite unsuitable for the rough tracks we were driving along, and we thought we would never find the camp.

I imagined a chilly night in the car, with animals all around us, but somehow we did find it. It was completely deserted at first glance, but then the African manager appeared, and we discovered that there were two complaining Britishers staying as well. We could not see much but could hear a roaring river; huge bats were flying around and a lot of mosquitoes.

The next day, after a big breakfast, we set out to explore. It was very hot and with relief we found a lovely deep spring and settled down to eat our picnic and have a swim. We had not been there long when suddenly two huge overlander trucks appeared; people poured out of them and started jumping into the water, swimming, washing their clothes and eating their lunches. They then jumped back into the trucks and disappeared as quickly as they had come. A few empty beer cans lay around, otherwise all was peaceful again except for the bugs.

We spent another night at Nara Moru on the way back. The chalets have log fires in them, and one certainly needed them as it was bitterly cold at night. The rooms had no lights, so I couldn't find my socks to keep my feet warm, and what with the mosquitoes and the rats running around I did not get a lot of sleep that night. We got back to Nairobi the following day, eager to explore some more, so we set off again with Hazel and the children to Lake Magadi, a huge soda lake. It was unbelievably hot, and when we found a swimming pool which had just closed it was like finding a glass of water in the desert that turned out to be only a mirage. Luckily the attendant was still around, so for 20 shillings he opened it up again, which was a life-saver.

All good things come to an end, and I flew home on a crowded jumbo sitting next to the lavatories. One man took his shoes off and never found them again; I have seen three people lose their shoes on aeroplanes, and they have all had to walk out in slipper-socks provided for first-class passengers. I can't imagine anyone wanting to pinch old shoes, so it's a mystery where they disappear to.

David was at the airport to meet me; full of news about Knebworth and plans for the summer. He had once more become involved in politics; the first-ever elections for the European Parliament were to be held in June and, as an ardent European,

David was keen to stand. To me the idea of living in Strasbourg was rather daunting.

He was accepted as the Liberal candidate for Hertfordshire, so at least we could do it from home. He was a good candidate; he has had experience of working in Europe and speaks French, German and a little Spanish and Italian, and in order to stand in the election he had left his job as group treasurer for a London-based investment company. We canvassed night and day. Labour were reluctant participants in the election, but the Tories were very well organised and it was infuriating to see how much money they had to spend. We had to find our own funds, which meant a lot of it coming out of our own pockets, but various fund-raising events were held and we had posters stuck all over our orange minibus and cars, and 'David Cobbold for Europe' T-shirts for all the workers and family.

We printed an eight-page newspaper called *Focus Europe* and put it through thousands of letter-boxes. There was a picture of David and me on the front, and David had had it printed without showing me. I hated the picture of me with such passion that I could hardly bear to put it through people's letter-boxes – very childish, I suppose, but I really minded everyone seeing me looking so dreadful. David liked it, but it was a good picture of him!

We went out at night and fly-posted all over the countryside. A lot of our Conservative neighbouring landowners were furious when they found their trees and fences covered with Liberal posters with David's picture on them. Not being a Liberal myself, I found I was always apologising to people and I am not sure how loyal I was to David, politically anyway.

We opened our 1979 season with another jousting tournament, and David was asked if he was issuing a challenge to his Conservative and Labour opponents. 'No,' he said, 'I think it would be unchivalrous to deprive the other parties of their candidates so soon before the election.' Perhaps he should not have been so gallant. As the *Financial Times* pointed out in an article about David standing as Liberal candidate, he really had little chance.

The seven Westminster constituencies that made up the Hertfordshire Euro constituency mustered only 59,626 Liberal votes between them in the May 1979 general election, 14.3 per cent of the total vote. A month later only 37 per cent of the electorate bothered to vote in the European elections on 7 June and Derek Prag, the Conservative, got in with 97,174 votes and Labour came second with 49,619, just beating David into third place with 46,575 votes or 24 per cent. It was a triumph in a way, constituting a 9 per cent swing to the Liberals. David's Liberal vote was the fourth highest in the country and, if there had been proportional representation, the Liberals would have sent ten MPs to Europe and David would have been one of them.

David was not the only member of the family to be in the news that spring. I was asked by Mary Parkinson of 'Afternoon Plus', Thames Television, to do a programme on opening the house. It was a twenty-minute film and was shown along with an antique collectors' programme filmed in the Barns Restaurant and an interview with Lord Bath, David Hicks and David talking about the problems of stately homes. I spent two days with Mary, dressing up in various Elizabethan and Victorian costumes and describing the rooms in the house and our life at Knebworth. It was fun to do and I thought the programme was quite good when it came out. I even got paid £100 for my efforts!

I was surprised after the programme was shown at how many newspapers rang up and wanted to do an article on me and the house; it was all very good publicity. *Women's World* did a big spread which forced me to look up some statistics: £3500 for the heating that year, £2000 for cleaning the house, £8000 to keep the gardens going, £120 for window-cleaning every year – and that is only the glass that can be cleaned safely, for a lot of the lattice panes are too delicate to touch.

Antique expert John Bly, with Anglia Television personality Jane Probyn, came down and did a programme on 'Anglia Heirlooms' soon after the 'Afternoon Plus' programme. We then had a break-in. A tramp broke a window in the drawing room, but the alarms went off and the police caught him. He was taken to court and stated: 'I went in to see if there was any security and "case" the place, then the alarm went off. I only went in to check valuables.' He was jailed for six months. Publicity about one's belongings is not always a good thing.

More publicity came in May, when Walt Disney's film *The Spaceman and King Arthur* was filmed in the house, and I was dragged out of my office by the press to have my photograph taken sitting on Kenneth More's lap at an enormous round table in our courtyard. I felt incredibly silly sitting on Kenneth's lap in the pouring rain, and refused to look at the pictures in the local newspapers the following week.

We also had a nerve-racking day with a British Airways commercial in June, when Robert Morley had to be lowered from the roof in a balloon basket; it was difficult to find anything stable and firm enough on the roof to attach the basket to – it had quite a weight to support. Robert Morley was not easy to talk to as he is so deaf, but he was happy to do all the talking himself and was very amusing and full of anecdotes about his family.

By June the local papers were full of nothing but the next rock festival. After the usual rumours that bands such as Wings or the Eagles were playing, Led Zeppelin were finally announced. They had not played in England for four years and the excitement was great. Tickets sold out so quickly that a second concert a week later was planned. People slept out in the streets in order to get tickets from the record companies as soon as they came in; around 120,000 were sold for the first concert, and 80,000 for the second.

The hall at the bottom of our drive was turned into a factory to make wooden lavatories, the old tin ones having finally become too sordid. I knew quite a few of the carpenters from previous concerts, so they used to come up to the house for a swim in the evening after work. After they had finished building the 500-plus wooden-seaters for the festival they made me a wooden boat with 'Christina' written on the side for the swimming pool. I hoped the lavatories were stronger than the boat, which sank immediately.

The atmosphere became tenser the nearer the concert date came – it was obviously going to be a big one. Freddie was nervous because Peter Grant, Led Zeppelin's manager, was an overpowering character. Huge, with long black hair and dressed in flowing robes, he caused Freddie a lot of anxiety. The crowds were so big the night before the concert that we needed Land-rovers and police with dogs to keep the fans from breaking the fence down before the arena staff were ready to let them in at 3 a.m.

The second concert a week later was smaller and therefore more pleasant, except for the fact that one had to sit on broken glass from the previous one. Captain Ollie was once again responsible for clearing up the festival litter and this year he tried a hoover-like machine, but it kept getting clogged up with grass. There is yet to be invented a machine that can do the job properly. It is important to pick it all up as quickly as possible, otherwise it blows all over the park and into the most inaccessible places. The unpleasant smell of burning plastic lingers for days after a festival.

Considering the size of the two Led Zeppelin events, approximately 200,000 people in all, there were no major problems from the fans; the only noteworthy events were that a baby was born and a couple got married in the park church during the first concert. But officially it did not go well. The newspapers and the police quoted figures of 250,000 people attending the first concert, and Peter Grant did not believe Freddie Bannister's figures of 93,794; as Led Zeppelin were on a percentage he was not happy. So for the second concert he sent his own men in and as far as I can gather they took over the organisation. Freddie's company, Tedoar Ltd, was unable to pay all the bills, and went into liquidation. He owed us quite a lot as well – our final cheque arrived on Friday afternoon and bounced on Monday morning!

The police bill was the biggest debt, but then it was totally unreasonable at £50,000 anyway. But as a result of these money problems it was obvious that we would never get another licence with Freddie as the promoter. We were sad as we liked Freddie and his wife, Wendy; we had enjoyed the concerts and they had done a lot for Knebworth. In September a full-page advertisement was taken in the *New Musical Express* by Freddie, stating how helpful Led Zeppelin had been over the concert expenses, and how it would be a privilege and honour for him to work with them again – all of which I found rather hard to believe.

The North Herts Council had a lot of discussions after the festival. Some councillors suggested that the Council should run the next Knebworth festival and make lots of money for the county. But as Councillor Gordon Dumelow, chairman of the Licencing Committee, commented, 'If seasoned promoters regularly go into liquidation after putting on concerts, the likelihood of novices being able to make a profit is minimal and who would pay the bills if they made a loss?' David was taken to court for breach of the licence, which is always granted to him personally, as the concerts had overrun their allotted time. He was fined £150. It took quite a while to clear up after the two events, and a barley field and a corn field had been flattened and the crops destroyed; one had been needed for extra camping and the other had been trampled over.

By 1979 the National Association of Custom Car Clubs (or hot rods, as we used to call them) had taken to holding their annual August bank holiday rally in the park, and 3000 members camp with their cars in the park. They come in cowboy hats, tight jeans and rude T-shirts, and most sport large beer tummies. CB radios crackle with good-buddy chatter. They are an easy-going lot, heavy drinkers and rowdy. The cars are amazing conversions, painted with colourful stardust paint; the chop-top cabins have blackened windows, chain-link steering wheels and naughty murals airbrushed on the back windows. Sheepskin rugs, chandeliers, pictures and televisions furnish the interiors. One is done up as Dracula's hearse, with the fanged Count in his coffin, and even some of the engines are velvet-lined!

They hold various competitions during the weekend and put on a 'Show-n-Shine' for the public on Sunday to show off the cars, which is very popular. Their favourite occupation is roaring around our concrete two-mile park drive day and night, revving their engines, doing wheelies and leaving black tyre-marks everywhere. On Saturday and Sunday nights they hold a disco in a huge marquee, large quantities of drink are consumed and by midnight the party is usually well out of hand. The wet T-shirt competition is followed by the sexiest knickers, and so on. *Men Only* magazine was invited to the event one year to write an article about the cars. They did an article, with photographs, but it was not about the cars, and there were some angry red-faced girls around afterwards.

They always assured me that their parties were quiet, orderly affairs, so I enjoyed confronting them with the naughty pictures at the meeting the following year. We have had various disagreements with them in the past and they have gone off trying to find another site to hold their event, but they have a reputation as an unruly bunch and up to now have never found a site as long-suffering as Knebworth.

Sharing the park with all these events were Sam Rourke's deer, which had now grown to over 300 head. Sam exported a lot to Germany – a stag shipped abroad for breeding purposes was worth up to £1000 – and, wondering how they managed to catch and load the wild stags without damaging them, I went down to watch one day with the children. It was November and the deer willingly ate the drugged food put out for them. As soon as they ate it, they fell down on the ground and a couple of fork-lift trucks picked them up and lifted them into the waiting horse-boxes. Wocko, who looks after the deer, then sawed their antlers off so they would not harm each other in transit. In five minutes they were standing up again and seemed quite happy. Each truck held quite a few deer, and I was surprised they did not panic.

Sam was finding that the events upset his deer and the park was not big enough for both, so he decided to move and take the deer with him up to Yorkshire, which suited us all. We bought a few deer from him and have subsequently built up a smaller and more manageable herd of our own.

All these years the office staff had been growing. David Condy was still managing the estate and commercial side of things, and he had an assistant, two secretaries, a public relations lady and two or three people in the accounts department. The accounts were a continual problem; they were always at least a year behind and we found it increasingly difficult to run a business with no up-to-date figures.

Poor David was spending most of his precious weekends from the City, which he had now returned to, trying to sort things out. I am fairly efficient at running the house, catering and office work, but I am hopeless at figures and they bore me. David decided to get a mini-computer to help, and to cut down on the accounts staff. Our office is in a small gardener's cottage, and in order to get the computer into the accounts room on the first floor we had to get a fork-lift truck and take the whole window frame out. Everyone came out to watch and not much work was done that day.

We had to make one of the accountants redundant; his wife ran the gift shop so unfortunately she left as well and we now needed a new gift shop manager. Pattie was keen to take on the job. Rosina had been pestering me for months that she wanted to go to boarding school like the boys. She found it boring on her own at home and thought dormitory life would be fun. It was true that she hated sleeping alone, but at seven years she seemed very young and she still wet her bed; leaving home would, I feared, be a lot more traumatic than joining the Brownies six months previously. But we went and looked at a school, Maltman's Green in Berkshire, which had 290 children with 90 boarders aged from seven to thirteen, and they were prepared to take her that autumn. I liked the headmistress and the children looked cheerful, so with some trepidation I agreed she could go. This meant that Pattie had no children left to look after, so we put her in charge of the gift shop with Jan, Wocko's wife, who was a friend of hers.

Buying Rosina's school uniforms with her was fun, and packing the school trunk was okay, but driving her to the new school was a silent affair and leaving her there was agony for me. Rosina has a lot of hidden strength; she will scream, rant and rave about ridiculously small problems but when something is inevitable she accepts it stoically. She gave me a goodbye kiss and said, 'I think you'd better go now, Mummy, see you in three weeks' time.' Which for a child who had refused to spend a night away from us or even to stay with friends before was quite brave. I did not feel at all brave and drove home in a mist of tears.

When you are busy you do not have time to be miserable, however, and now I did not have Pattie to help in the house there was always plenty to do. I had also planned another trip to Kenya after Christmas. Thump had married his long-standing girlfriend Leslie in the New Year; he had also organised six Warwickshire farming friends of his to go out for a safari, and suggested I came with them.

It had been such fun the year before that I persuaded David I needed a holiday, so in January 1980 I went to London Airport to meet up with the Warwickshire farmers. I searched around the Terminal 3 departure lounge but could not see what I imagined six farmers to look like anywhere. I searched for Sudan Airways as well and could not find them either. Their fare was £100 cheaper than any other airline, and as my ticket had only arrived the day before, I worried that perhaps the whole thing was a con. But I eventually found Sudan Airways in a far corner of the airport building.

I boarded the aircraft with still no sign of the farmers. There was a twenty-minute wait and at what seemed like the last minute a bus drove up to the aeroplane's steps. The captain started revving the engines of the plane, the unmistakable Warwickshire farmers clambered aboard clutching their duty-free gin and cigarettes, and we were off.

I introduced myself to Steve, Simon, Richard, Peter, Bay and David, but it took me two weeks to get their names right. A couple of them had not flown before and headed up the aisle in search of a bar. They were very put out when they found the queue was for the lavatories. As it was a Muslim airline, there was no drink on the plane in any case, and they eventually settled down to cards and chess and the duty-free.

Khartoum was hot and smelt of Africa. For no good reason I could see, we were all made to get out and the luggage was taken off on trolleys while they changed the flight number. Then we all got back on board again, hopefully with the right luggage, but not before Richard had nearly ended up in a Sudanese prison for taking photographs of the airport. I made the mistake of going to the airport 'Ladies', the floor of which was covered with large sleeping bodies which groaned and stared at me balefully as I stepped over them. There was the sound of someone being sick coming from the 'Gents'.

We arrived in Nairobi at 5.30 a.m. The immigration officer looked wearily at our upside-down passports, stamped them and various other medical forms generously and waved us through. Thump and Leslie were there to meet us with a minibus.

After twenty-four hours of rest, queuing to change our money and buying tickets for the onward journey, we took the overnight train to Mombasa, a 'must' for anyone travelling from Nairobi to Mombasa – so long as you go first class. An old steam train, now converted to diesel, it creaked, banged and jolted its way through the African bush. Unfortunately it was too dark to see much through the windows of the panelled dining car with its old bracket lights and red plush curtains, but they produced a good dinner. Too late I found I should have paid the 15 shillings for proper bed linen, as the sleeping bag Thump had lent me was stiff with grease and smelt.

Hal and Sally Christensen, who had left Singapore and now

lived in Mombasa, came to meet us in a couple of cars and put us up on their floor for the night. Hal now had a job as captain of a tug boat which went down to Zanzibar every other week doing seisinic runs for an oil company. The next day we headed up to Malindi and then to tiny Lamu Island, which has no roads and does not import much, so we had to take things like coffee, sugar and powdered milk with us, and of course booze. Fresh fish was brought to the door every day, and we went into the town one day and bought a couple of live chickens for supper. I was glad I had so many farmers with me as we had to carry the birds back on the boat under our arms to our self-catering house, and then they had to be killed and plucked before we could cook them.

After a week on the coast we went back to Nairobi and Thump took us on a safari, first to Lake Naivasha for some fishing and then on to the Masai Mara game reserve. As Thump and the farmers packed up the Landrover ready for the journey, I complained about the amount of beer that was being put in. 'How about some "7-up" for me?' I said (it is a popular soft drink in Kenya). 'You'll get seven up before you've finished with us,' they laughingly replied and grudgingly put a few cans in. The trip was named 'the 7-up safari' after that.

It was a fantastic holiday – I didn't have to do a thing. The seven of them put the tents up, collected the water and firewood, cooked the meals and even washed up afterwards; I have never been so well looked after before. After years of camping holidays with the children, where I have had to do everything with no one lifting a finger to help, this was bliss. But I have to admit that I did find it frightening camping out in the bush with only the canvas tent between me and the elephants and buffalo. We did not have a gun, only a *panga* (a knife used for cutting grass), which I kept by my side in the tent at night.

The worst experience was towards the end of the safari. We had set up camp in the evening by a river just outside the main Masai Mara park and had a big fire going, when a Landrover bumped its way over to us. 'You're crazy if you spend the night here,' said one of the two men inside. 'Of course it's up to you, but I wouldn't do it. Some Masai held up a family a few weeks ago at knife-point and took all their belongings, even the clothes they stood up in.' They drove off again shouting, 'You have no protection out here.' We looked at each other. No one could face packing up the camp, so we stayed.

We had been travelling for five days and the cool box was not as cold as it had been earlier on in the expedition; the steak that we had for dinner had a distinctly greenish hue about it, and as a result I was ill all night. I had to rush from the tent in my long white nightie about six times and find a bush that was far enough away from the camp. I could hear the hippos in the river below and I was scared of what I might bump into, but I was lucky – I did not even get bitten by an ant.

The following day we moved on to the Tanzanian border and camped by a shallow stream that we could swim in without fear of being caught by a crocodile or hippo. Then it was back to civilisation, if that is what it is – Nairobi and then London again. I was beginning to depend on these yearly trips for my health and my sanity. Knebworth is so completely absorbing when you are there and everything tends to get on top of me. Also I hate the English winter and have been prone to bronchitis ever since my damp Devon childhood. Going right away to a completely new environment refreshes me and makes me able to face the problems of the year ahead, so many of which repeat themselves year after year.

I am lucky to have a long-suffering and broad-minded husband, who does not mind if I go off on my own. As long as he has someone to look after him, he is as happy to have a break as I am; it enables him to work into the small hours of the night and at weekends without feeling guilty about his neglected and complaining wife! We are also all the more pleased to see each other when I return. I sometimes say to him, 'What if I don't come back?' He says it would be a challenge to come and look for me.

Chapter 11 | Events galore

During the winter we had the children painted. They stood on the main staircase in the house, dressed in blue jeans and T-shirts, and we hung the portrait on the stairs – a period piece amongst the ancestors in the fashionable clothes of their day. The artist, June Mendoza, had also painted David and me a few years earlier. My father had given David £500 and said, 'This is to have Chryssie painted – by the time you can afford it she won't be worth painting.' So we had gone off to the Royal Portrait Painters exhibition in the Mall and each chosen the three artists we thought best. We both came up with the same first and second choices. Our first was June, an Australian artist, and she painted me wearing a long green skirt and white blouse. Was I ever that thin? We loved the portrait but my uncle, who is a judge, says I look as if it's Monday morning and I have woken up with a curse pain! A few years later June painted David sitting in the Banqueting Hall in his slippers.

By the beginning of 1980 the church bells had been silent for some time. Normally there is bell-ringing practice every Thursday night and I do not care for the sound much. 'The tower is falling down,' David said. 'It's going to cost around £60,000 to repair, we'd better do some fund-raising.' I had long since learnt not to look for work so I kept quiet, but before long letters started arriving on my desk from the church supporters. With a sigh, I agreed to an Edwardian Garden Party to be held in our garden in July in aid of the church. It was to include croquet on the lawn and cucumber sandwiches for tea. Rain poured down all day but luckily cleared up by the time the guests arrived – I could never have fitted everyone into the house. A group of amateur actors put on *The Importance of Being Ernest*, and there were other attractions, including bowling for a pig.

A few weeks later we held a craft show in the park, organised by my mother-in-law, at which my only contribution was to sit and cane a chair as one of the exhibits. I was surprised how many people came up to me and asked if I would repair their chairs for them. Unfortunately I do not have the time, but it was nice to know I could make a living out of caning if necessary. I had taught myself from a book in desperation, when I discovered we could not possibly afford to have all the chairs in the house mended. It is peaceful work, though hard on the fingers, and I can do it while watching television in the evenings.

In the winter months fund-raising took the form of wine and cheese evenings in the house. As well as supporting repairs to the church tower, we were also having to raise money for the European Liberal account which was still in the red, and as David is president of the local Multiple Sclerosis Society branch, and his secretary, Vi Sykes, was a keen supporter, we held some functions for them too. In the winter it means heating the place, which at £5 an hour is not economical, but it is difficult to do evening functions in the summer months as it means putting the Banqueting Hall table and all the china and chairs away after closing the house at 6 p.m., and getting everything clean and straight again before opening at 11 a.m. the next day. Organisations are forever wanting to 'borrow' the house for charitable fund-raising events, and it is very hard to know what to do. It seems petty and mean to say no when it is not being used, but on the other hand it means a lot of wear and tear on the house and an invasion of privacy. They always want to use my kitchen or pantry and borrow plates, ashtrays, table cloths, etc., and I have to put all our personal things away each time. The house smells like a pub for days afterwards and the floors take a lot of cleaning to get the food and drink stains off them, not to mention the occasional cigarette burn. As the years go by I get less inclined to let the house out in the evenings at all, and for all the above reasons do not allow private parties except for close friends.

One exception was for rock singer Kim Wilde, who celebrated her twenty-first birthday in the house that winter. Henry had met her a few times and she had asked him if she could put on a surprise party for her parents. She had told them she was asking a few friends to a small local venue, and invited them to come along too. They were amazed when their car drove them up to Knebworth House, where 300 guests in medieval gear were waiting to greet them. The party lasted all night, while David and I roamed around worrying about the furniture and the house burning down, but it was a great success and no damage was done. A few years later her father, Marty Wilde, laid on a surprise party for his wife in the house to celebrate their silver wedding anniversary. The highlight of the evening was a big firework display, but unfortunately dinner took such a long time, with lots of speeches, that it was midnight before the fireworks went off. The explosions were ear-splitting in the quiet of the countryside and we had quite a few complaints from the neighbours.

We were beginning to feel that charity should begin at home and we ought to be raising money for ourselves. What glimpses we did get of the way-out-of-date accounts did not look encouraging, but the bank managers went on allowing our overdrafts to increase, holding everything David possessed as security, and it worried us a lot.

In spite of the large numbers coming into the park and house, opening the estate did not seem to pay. Keeping the office going twelve months a year with money coming in for only six months of it made it impossible ever to catch up with the expenses. We had to keep a lot of permanent staff on throughout the year; there were the accounting, budget preparations and plans for the following year to work out; advertising brochures and leaflets to be printed; event lists, menus and mailing shots to organise; the souvenir gift shop to stock up. There were conferences to be attended, such as the AGM of the Historic Houses Association (our union) and the Thames and Chiltern Tourist Board meetings, and trade fairs to have stands in, as well as staff yearly holidays to be fitted in before the next season started. There was also the estate side of the business to attend to, rents to review, roads to be mended, forestry plans to be looked at – every day brought new problems. So when people remark what a relief it must be for us not to be so busy during the winter months, I cannot really agree with them!

We replanted the 150-year-old chestnut avenue in January 1980 with 98 young trees. We did not want to cut down the old avenue, so planted the new trees among the old ones and hoped the old ones would not fall on top and crush them; they were becoming very unsafe and large branches had broken off them. We gathered together as many family members as we could find for a tree-planting ceremony, and any estate staff who wished to plant one came as well. It was a cold frosty morning and the local press were there to capture the event. We hoped the rock fans would not use the saplings as firewood the following summer.

After Mr Roberts had left we had a series of head gardeners, none of whom seemed able to cope with the Knebworth House gardens, and we eventually hired Michael Calnan as head gardener in 1979. He had just finished at Wye Horticultural College and was only twenty-five years old, but he was very keen and full of ideas. With a couple of other gardeners and some 'work experience' boys to help him, he set to and during the next five years transformed the gardens.

At the beginning of the century Sir Edwin Lutyens had stripped out much of Edward Bulwer-Lytton's Victorian decoration inside the house and completely redesigned the gardens. Before the last war there used to be fourteen gardeners, but since 1940 the wilderness had gradually encroached as a result of staff cuts. Lutyens's garden had lost most of its original layout, grass now covered the red-brick paths and many of the flower beds had disappeared. The 'wilderness' part of the garden was laid out in 1887 by the 1st Earl of Lytton using seven acres of meadowland, and it was planted out originally with twenty-seven varieties of hawthorn and numerous specimen trees. After the last war it was never kept up and the entire area became an impenetrable jungle of bramble, elder and sycamore, but Michael cleared it and it is now a mass of daffodils in spring and foxgloves and wild flowers during the summer.

In 1891 the *Gardeners' Chronicle* said:

> The Knebworth Wilderness is in fact one which ladies could pass through in their ordinary costume without being stung and torn; and who would care for a garden in which the fair successors of mother Eve were

> excluded, through its rude disorder, and the growth of nature's most unlovely specimens of vegetable life, foul toadstools, slimy fungiode and deleterious Agarics.

We were proud that it was once more restored to something approaching its former glory.

Mike Calnan discovered plans for a herb garden that Gertrude Jekyll designed specially for Knebworth in 1907, but which had never been built. He persuaded us to let him do it now. The intricate red-brick designs and variety of plants have already brought many garden enthusiasts to Knebworth and earned us quite a few mentions in garden books, and as a result of the herb garden I was made Patron of the Letchworth Homeopathic and Alternative Medicine Society for a while. My larder is full of drying herbs, and my friends now get given feverfew sandwiches for their headaches instead of aspirin!

The fountains are also working again, but the maze planted in Victorian times and burnt down accidently in the 1950s has been a problem. We tried cutting the overgrown trees right back in the hope that they would recover again, but it has not worked and we have had to demolish it. We very much hope to be able to replace it eventually, but the new design will have to be capable of coping with thousands of visitors, not just the family.

Unfortunately, now that we have so much enthusiasm in the main gardens my walled vegetable garden is no longer so peaceful. It is full of potted plants and things being grown for the big borders and garden shop. I have to fight to keep my patch and it is getting smaller all the time.

By January 1980 Penelope Bennet (known as Nem) was running the house-opening side, as Joanne Wilkins had left after a year. Nem had been a guide in the house for many years and lived in Knebworth village, so she was the ideal person to take over as curator. She has to find the thirty-five guides and room wardens needed for the house-opening and to care for the house. During the winter months she keeps an eye on film companies and functions. She organises and helps with cleaning and polishing, washing the chandeliers and laundering the lacy Edwardian nursery clothes, and she dusts the books in the Library and makes sure there are no gaps. She reframes prints, renews the roping and signs and paints the woodwork with Rentokil, as well as coping with archive enquiries.

I am always being asked how we keep the house clean. In former times there would have been scores of servants working full-time in the house, but nowadays it would cost a fortune. For a time we had 'contract' cleaners for the part of the house open to the public, and I had Mrs Waldock. She and her husband Stan have worked for the family for over forty years. He worked in the gardens first for my in-laws, and for the last few years for me in my vegetable garden. They are both invaluable to me and I dread the moment they decide to retire as I will never be able to replace them. After we gave up the contract cleaners I took on another lady, Pam White, and between them she and Mrs Waldock, both coming in for around three hours each morning, somehow manage against all odds to keep the whole house looking respectable.

Before the beginning of the season, in April, we used to run an Education Week especially for schoolchildren. Schools from Hertfordshire, Essex and Bedfordshire would bring parties to look around the house; it was supposed to encourage the local children to study their environment and local history. It was quite an effort to try and open up the house early and it was always freezing cold. Nem suggested we gave it up and hoped the school parties would come during May or June instead, which they seem to do.

The previous autumn, we had held an office meeting with all the heads of departments to think of some new attractions for the 1980 summer season. The rock festivals and big car rallies were the crowd-pullers and financially good business, but the numerous smaller rallies, although popular, were not money-spinners. Staging our own events was risky, as we might spend a lot of money on an attraction and then it would pour with rain all day and no one would come. It was safer to hire out the park for events and be sure of one's money.

But we had managed to come up with a couple of new ideas for the 1980 season. We had been introduced to Jack Waldock, a retired employee of British Rail, by Tom Hill, a director of Pleasure Rail who owned our steam trains. Jack had collected defunct railway memorabilia for years, and kept it all in his garden in Hertford. At the top of his house he had a wonderful electric model railway with an intricate layout of lines with tunnels and stations, and we spent a fascinating afternoon with him looking at his collection. He also had records of steam engines puffing along, and he could identify them all by the sound they made. We thought this would make a great museum to go with our railway in the park.

We had built a new piece of railway line, so the train now went round a complete circle to the adventure playground and back through the park to the Barns Restaurant. It was not easy finding engine drivers for our steam train, so we were very pleased when Jack said he loved driving trains and would bring his collection to Knebworth Park. Signal boxes, points, station names, signs – they all came over. I was anxious at first that he would miss having them in his garden, but instead he comes over seven days a week all year round, has his lunch in a signal box and keeps an eye on his collection. When the weather is fine his wife comes too and sits in their car knitting.

The second idea I did not really approve of, but I was out-voted. It consisted of a miniature golf course together with some fibre-glass gaily painted animals, into which one feeds 5p and they bounce up and down. The former meant someone doling out clubs and balls and taking money, and the latter were hideous.

Anyway, by Easter the new additions to the park were completed, and we had a press conference to publicise them. The railway museum was a bit static for press photographs so Jack Waldock and Stewart Madgin, our railway manager, stoked up the steam train and Felicity, our public relations lady, and I took it in turns to be tied to the railway line while the train steamed up to us, stopping just in time. The photos were good, but I can think of more enjoyable ways of spending the afternoon!

Lotta, our dalmatian, produced ten illegitimate puppies over Easter, and we held a family polo bicycle match in our skate park for the neighbours. So it was a busy time.

During the first May bank holiday weekend 3000 Boy Scouts arrived to camp and they held a giant jamboree which doubled on Sunday when 3000 Cubs arrived. A non-stop programme of events was organised, including boating on the lake and assault courses, and the weekend ended with the Chief Scout, Sir William Gladstone (grandson of the famous prime minister) spending a day at the camp and presenting the Chief Scout awards. The organisers of events are often far more trouble than the event itself or the people who come to it, because they're always complaining, and our main problem was providing enough water and lavatories for them. No camp fires were allowed because of the risk of fire, so they all had to cook on primus stoves and camping gas, which I thought was very boring and probably just as hazardous.

May 1980 must have been one of the busiest months we have ever had. We managed to pack in the Scouts camp, a classic car auction, a couple of jousting tournaments, a junior motorbike weekend and a National Soul Day for 15,000 disco dancers. To top it all, our new fibreglass towers and gargoyles arrived.

We had been given a Historic Buildings Council grant to spend on the roof, to restore the intricate turrets, chimneys and pinnacles. It involved replacing four of the copper domes and gargoyles around them with fibreglass substitutes. The domes were made of green fibreglass, the same colour as the remaining copper ones, and were then covered over with new copper, the idea being that when the copper eventually falls off again, the fibreglass underneath will carry on. No one knows how long they will last, but they look very good at the moment. The total cost was £50,000, and we had to find £15,000. It was the first time that the Historic Buildings Council had ever grant-aided the use of non-traditional materials, but I am sure Bulwer-Lytton would have used fibreglass if it had been available at the time.

Simon Scott, a close friend of mine since I was thirteen who was now living in Durham with his family and farming, had started a company involving small 50 cc motorbikes. He travelled around the country to different showgrounds with the bikes, setting up tracks and hiring out the bikes to children to ride round on. He came to Knebworth for the first time in May, we made a straw-edged arena for the bikes and children queued all day to ride around the track. The bicycles were aimed at the 6–15-year-olds, but as long as their feet touched the ground any child could ride them. A four-year-old was the youngest I saw. By this time my boys were bike-mad, and I had already splurged out and bought Henry and Peter a Beta 50 cc to share and Richard, who was eleven, a smaller Puch 50 cc. Of course they were not allowed on the roads but they roared around the park on them and set up tracks through the woods, with jumps and water splashes. My mother sounded disapproving: 'You spoil them,' she complained. I pointed out that she would not have said anything if I had bought them ponies with bridles and saddles, and they would have cost far more to buy and maintain, and in my view they are equally dangerous. I hoped they might learn something about mechanics as the bikes were always breaking down, but being true Cobbolds they did not and I spent a lot of time taking them back to the shop in Welwyn Garden City.

The National Soul Day event was held in a huge circus tent provided by a Mr Fossett. It was organised by 'Show Stopper Promotions', tickets cost £8 and dancing was continuous for eleven hours. I was not very well versed in soul bands, and Eddie Grant and Lonnie Liston Smith were the only ones I had heard of before. The event was so popular that the tent proved to be too small and the catering was totally inadequate. The result was rather unpleasant.

It was impossible to move inside the marquee, and there was certainly no room to dance. Ten neck injuries were caused by fans having their gold chains or necklaces ripped off them by muggers, the caterers lost control of the queues for food and drink, and the punters got so fed up waiting that they turned the entire catering unit over on its side and helped themselves. I took Rosina and Richard down to see what was going on and we were chased by a group of drunks. I drove the car off at full speed as they threw empty bottles at us; it was quite frightening. The St John's Ambulance people who were on duty were not at all happy and said they would not attend another function at Knebworth Park without police there to protect them. But it was not all bad. A lot of people enjoyed themselves and at least it finished on time!

In June we had the annual Classic American Car Club rally, a popular event which had been held there ever since we opened the park. Their star attractions are one of the three remaining 1934 Packard V.12s in existence, a number of early model-T Fords, a selection of rare Chryslers, Packards and Ford V.8s, pre-war Harley Davidson motorbikes, Indian 4-cylinder motorbikes, a very rare Henderson 4-cylinder and a bike used by the New

York police department in 1926. The Jaguar day included, as well as a vast range of Jaguar XKs, Ferraris, Maseratis and a Ford G.T.40 which had won the Le Mans 24-hour race.

Another fairly chaotic day in June was the Liberal Fun Day. It was held in the park and was to be the largest ever fund-raising event organised by the Liberal party. As it was the Year of the Disabled, the Spastics Society joined in and 10 per cent of the proceeds were to go to them. David Steel was put through his paces. First he was expected to go parascending, which involved being towed along on the end of a parachute behind a car all round the park, and then David dressed him up as a knight in armour, sat him on a horse and took him off jousting. Eric Morecambe came too and made everyone laugh. But despite all the effort, the day was not very successful financially – not nearly enough people turned up.

The biggest excitement of the summer was once again the yearly festival. We had hoped that Harvey Goldsmith, the best promoter in the business, would take over the running of our rock festivals, but he was put off by the high police costs. We were beginning to think that there would not be any more concerts, so we were pleased when Capital Radio, Allied Breweries and Andy Hudson joined forces and wanted to do one. Andy Hudson was the promoter, Allied Breweries were interested in the catering side and Capital Radio wanted the music and publicity. When we requested a licence for 100,000, despite some strong local objections, we got it; the Council were impressed by the new consortium's presentation. After Led Zeppelin it was generally expected to be an easy concert to organise, as the Beach Boys, Santana, Elkie Brooks, Lindisfarne, Mike Oldfield and the Blues Band all appealed to the more mature fans, or 'ageing hippies' as the papers bluntly put it.

As usual we had a big party in the house for the concert. Thump and Leslie came back from Nairobi; Hal from Mombasa; five of the farmers from Warwickshire; and Carolyn Allen, who had sung at our Dickens and Bulwer Evenings and was now a West End star, came with Paul Jones. He was playing with his newly formed Blues Band in the festival. Simon Scott also came down, not with his bikes this time but with his camera – he has photographed all the concerts we have held.

I was up at the house when Carlos Santana came in to have a look around, so I gave him a tour of the state rooms. We finished up in the Picture Gallery, where he spotted my guitar. Picking it up, he put Rosina on the sofa next to him and played to us. It was magic – I could have listened all day. The guitar had cost me £19 in Boots the year before, but it now became a treasured possession.

I went up on stage while Santana were playing and, spying me, Carlos tried to get me to come to the front of the stage and join him. I refused, so he dedicated a song to me. I felt very flattered. The Beach Boys also came to the house for something to eat and drink before going on stage; they were all very friendly and we promised to call on them if we ever went to California. Brian Wilson, who wrote most of their lyrics, devoured a whole chocolate cake I had made for the children and then went to sleep on the sofa; we had a difficult time waking him when it was time to get them all down to the arena. In spite of the wet weather the entire audience danced throughout the Beach Boys set – it was an unforgettable sight.

Sadly, however, the concert lost money. Instead of the expected 100,000, only 40,000 turned up, the main problem being that most of the bands – including the Beach Boys – had played in London in the weeks previously, so a lot of people had already seen them. It did not seem likely that Capital Radio would be back next year.

August bank holiday took some organising that year, as we had a jousting tournament in one corner of the park; a huge marquee for the Antique Collectors' Fair, which had been coming for six years now, in front of the Barns; and the National Street Rod's custom car rally, with over a thousand cars, in another part of the park. Action, culture or noise – you could take your pick over the long weekend.

A week later, in order to give the skate park a bit of a boost, we turned the free-style area into an 'ice rink' for the day. It was covered in plastic sheeting, and water and glycerine were sprayed over it to make synthetic ice. It was not a great success, however. The temperature was in the seventies and it did not seem right somehow to be skating in the middle of the summer. The other attraction that day was the Driving Society, who had been regular attenders at Knebworth and were a colourful sight, with sixteen horse-drawn carriages.

It never fails to amaze me what people do in order to enjoy themselves at weekends. All I ever want to do is lie in bed and read the papers during the winter, and lie on a long chair in the garden and read the papers in the summer. It would be purgatory to me to have to get into a car and 'go' somewhere, but luckily for us the crowds kept coming, and overall it was a good summer.

In the autumn of 1980, Richard became a royal page to the Queen. Kim, his grandfather, had retired from his job as Lord Chamberlain and, doubtless because of this, Richard was offered the job as page. It was a tremendous honour and he was very excited, as much by the fact that it meant extra days off school as anything. Previously, pages had been about fourteen or fifteen years old when they took the position, so the other pages were all much bigger than Richard. It was explained to us that it was a bit of an experiment having a younger one, and Richard was naturally expected to be on his best behaviour. Luckily, it is possible to borrow the uniform and sword nowadays, otherwise it would be very expensive. We set off to Ravenscroft and Ede, the court tailors, to have him fitted up. They had a problem as Richard was a small eleven-year-old and everything was too big for him; the black pumps with silver buckles had to have cotton wool stuffed down the toes, and huge tucks were taken in his shirt and jacket.

His first assignment was the State Opening of Parliament in November. A royal car came to pick him up in the morning, and David and I were invited to the ceremony. Richard has always been the sort of child you can take anywhere, he would never let one down and he took it all in his stride. It was me who was shaking like a leaf in case he stood on the Queen's train or fell up the steps. He looked so small, compared to the other three boys.

The following summer he was needed to hold the Queen's train for the Garter Ceremony at Windsor Castle. Kim Cobbold is a Knight of the Garter, so they did it together, which was great fun for both of them. There was a huge banquet in the Great Hall in Windsor Castle before the parade and church service, and as it was always a struggle to get Richard to eat anything but fish fingers and ice cream at home, I wondered how he would fare with an elaborate banquet to get through. But he said the champagne had helped wash down the prawn cocktail! He had also had a chat with Lady Diana, which made his father very jealous, but sadly he was not needed for Prince Charles and Lady Diana's wedding. The job is only a two-year appointment, and when he retired at thirteen he was presented with some gold cufflinks with 'E.R.' on them.

Towards the end of the year, the Muppets made a film at Knebworth called *The Great Muppet Caper*. All the filming took place at night, and mostly on the roof of the house. It sounded noisy, so we arranged to stay in London for the week, but David then heard that Diana Rigg was in the film and, being a fan of hers, decided to go down on the last evening. He came back full of remorse that he had not been there longer. It had been fascinating to see how it was done, and I would have loved it too, he said; the puppets were all played by good-looking young Americans who were very friendly and great fun.

Around the same time, the Monty Python team made part of the film *The Meaning of Life* in our private courtyard. They turned it into a medieval village with horses, goats, geese, ducks, chickens, straw and stalls adorned with rotting meat and plastic fish and vegetables. I had to manoeuvre my way through all this chaos every time I wanted to go out of the house to the office or my car, and we were not allowed to move in or out of the house when they were actually filming. The only ones to enjoy it all were the dogs and the cat, who loved all the unusual activity and smells in their courtyard. They chased the chickens and sniffed with puzzlement and then disgust at all the plastic food.

Chapter 12 | Sink or swim

By 1981, I was exhausted. I no longer felt the same enthusiasm about opening the house and park that I had once had, maybe because it had all become rather monotonous – the same problems and same annoyances recurred each year and the family were demanding a lot more of my time. The children were at five different boarding establishments: Danny was at Oxford, Henry at Kent University in Canterbury, Harry and Peter at Eton, Richard at Wellesley House and Rosina at Maltman's Green School. It was always someone's half term or exeat, sports day or school play. I could have done with Pattie's help, but she was busy with the gift shop for most of the year.

When I find I cannot cope with a situation, I switch off emotionally and carry on with what has to be done with no feeling for what I am doing. It was in very much this frame of mind that I started off the year and David, aware of the problem, suggested that we might go to Africa together. We were coming up to our twentieth wedding anniversary, and I was longing to go somewhere. He had always been wary of going to Africa as he does not care for 'creepy-crawlies', as he calls them, but I persuaded him that there weren't any, and that the food was delicious, so he agreed to come. Thump and I organised the trip, which included a week on the beach and a safari in the Aberdare Hills and on Lake Baringo. The holiday was a great success, and he promised that we would go again for our silver wedding anniversary.

I came back from our holiday in a slightly better frame of mind, but was still not looking forward to the season. The first major event was an Alliance Ball in June, which took place in a huge marquee in the gardens. The dance was fairly heavy-going in more than one way. It had poured with rain all day and the rush matting on the floor was sodden; the water kept soaking up the hem of my long dress until it was so heavy I had to go and change, but after this had happened twice I gave up and wore a short one. Danny and Harry joined in as part of the cabaret. It was early days in their singing career, the sound system was appalling and they had had too much to drink, so it was fairly disastrous. But they are now a very proficient cabaret act under the name of 'Black Tie' and are in great demand, especially at university balls. David and Debbie Owen and David and Judy Steel stayed in the house for the weekend. They said it was the first time they had met and talked informally, and I found it interesting listening to their comments on the Sunday papers over breakfast.

Since Henry was fifteen he had worked in the park during the summer holidays earning himself enough pocket money to pay for his own holidays. Peter had never been interested, but when he was offered a job with Capital Radio as a 'fencer' for their Jazz Festival in London, he became very keen. The year before, Alexandra Palace had burnt down just before the Jazz Festival was due to start, so this year they were planning to hold it on Clapham Common.

I had injured myself carrying too many crates of drinks and boxes of food for David's annual birthday party and had been rushed to hospital on the morning of the party for ten days. I lay in bed, bored stiff, and worried about Peter in London on his own at the age of sixteen working on the Festival, although everyone assured me he would be all right. The next thing I heard was that, because of the risk of riots in south London, the Metropolitan Police were not happy about the Jazz Festival taking place in Clapham, so the show was to be cancelled and Peter had apparently suggested to the organisers that they move the Festival to Knebworth.

Capital Radio thought it a good idea: they knew Knebworth Park from the previous year's Beach Boys concert, the musicians would be over here anyway, and Capital needed a venue to be able to record the music for their programmes. So I came out of hospital to find an arena, a stage, fencing and lavatories in the park. Everything had been transferred from London, literally in five days, and Peter was very pleased with himself as the instigator of it all.

Lambeth Council were not so pleased. They had been very involved all year in setting up the event with Capital Radio and did not want to lose it, but the police were adamant; there were apparently definite plots being hatched to disrupt the Festival were it to be held in London.

We had a major international Girl Guide camp in the park the same weekend as the Jazz Festival – 1500 Girl Guides from all over the world. The Chief Commissioner, Lady Baden-Powell, was opening the event and there were quite a few angry Guide parents. They were horrified that the festival was being held in the same park where their children were camping, and some parents even stopped their children from coming. Quite ridiculous really, as the two events were at opposite ends of the park and jazz fans did not seem to me to be the types that would go raiding Girl Guides' camps, especially as there was no overnight camping for the music fans. They were only there for the day and were paying a large sum of money for a ticket to listen to the music.

As if the Girl Guides were not enough of a headache, we also had a family wedding in the house that weekend. A cousin of David's was being married in our park church, Rosina was a bridesmaid and the reception was in Knebworth House. Just out of hospital and feeling very weak, I had to put the finishing touches to Rosina's dress, which luckily I had made the week before I was taken ill, sort out the reception for the wedding and calm the ruffled parents of the Girl Guides, who were constantly on the telephone complaining.

I escaped to the peace of the jazz arena as soon as I was able to. All the top jazz musicians seemed to be there: Ella Fitzgerald, Chuck Berry, Sara Vaughan, and blues singer Muddy Waters, amongst many others. Paul Jones and Carolyn Allen, both jazz enthusiasts, came and stayed at the house, and some of the wedding guests, still dressed in their tail coats and top hats, came down to hear Ella Fitzgerald. David, a great fan of hers, gave her tea in the house and she signed an album he had had since before we were married. The children rescued her teacup from the tray and hung it up in the dining room, where it remains four years later, with her lipstick still on the rim!

Amazingly, the weekend went off without a hitch. Capital Radio did not get as many fans as they would have done in London, no Girl Guides were ravished – although someone stole their pennant – and the bride and groom were delighted by the musical accompaniment.

During that summer of 1981 we began to feel the crunch economically, more forcibly than ever before. We had to face up to the fact that we had lost a lot of money in opening up to the public – it had become a nonsense. It began to look as if we would have no option but to close down the business, sell up the house and move elsewhere. We discussed it with the children, who begged us to struggle on. They loved the house – Henry in particular, who hoped to inherit the house one day – and we must not sell it whatever happened.

David went and discussed the problem with the Council. He made the point that Knebworth Park was an important leisure amenity for the local population and there would be an outcry if we closed down and ploughed up the parkland for agriculture, and that Knebworth House was an important part of the local heritage and the Council would very probably find themselves having to take it on if we were forced to give up. The estate at Knebworth is all in the 'green belt' area, and as agricultural land was worth about £1500 per acre David suggested a deal to the Council. If they were prepared to bend the rules and grant us a few acres of planning permission, he would put the land in question into a private charitable trust. The money raised could then be used only for the preservation and maintenance of Knebworth House in the public interest. Furthermore, the Council could act as one of the trustees of the charity.

The Council, although sympathetic, doubted our chances of success but nevertheless recommended that we put in an application and see what happened. In the event, we put in three applications for outline planning consent. One was for a 4½-acre residential site on the outskirts of the new Knebworth village, a mile and a half from the house, that has grown up around the railway station. It was a site which would inevitably be developed at some stage in the future, and half of it was a huge infilled dell, so of little agricultural value. The second was a 14-acre derelict orchard in the old village of Knebworth, which is a conservation area. The village is rather spread out and has no village green or focal point, and we therefore suggested a special development of only fifteen houses, all different, surrounding a new village green.

These two applications, if granted, would provide the funds to endow the charitable trust, which would cover essential repairs and restoration. David also argued that, in order to survive, Knebworth needed further commercial activities to contribute towards annual running costs and maintenance. The third application was therefore for a hotel and conference centre to be built at the entrance of the park from the A1 motorway in Stevenage.

The applications went to the Council in the autumn of 1981 and were turned down flat. We were bitterly disappointed but resolved to have another go. Then began a series of negotiations and meetings of numerous Council committees that was to last three years until September 1984, but more of that anon.

The economy drive meant drastic staff cuts in the office – not a nice thing to have to do, especially with people who had worked for us for a long time. David Condy had been with us ten years; he had worked hard running the office, often seven days a week, and from his point of view Knebworth had perhaps already passed its peak and it was time he made a change, but it is never easy moving jobs – especially when one has a family, a wife with local friends and interests and children settled at school. Luckily, he soon found another job running Hagley Hall in the Midlands: managers with 'stately home' experience are not that easy to find.

We also made redundant the assistant manager, the public relations lady and the receptionist. The office was now down to a bare minimum – we still had Vi Sykes as secretary and two ladies doing the accounts – and we took on a consultant manager, John Wilkinson, who came three days a week but retired to a farm in Wales nine months later. The burden looked like falling on me, but luckily I had Henry to help; he was now eighteen and had been making a valuable contribution to the park organisation during his long vacations from university. We decided that the winter should be kept as low-key as possible.

I had an opportunity to go to the States in October. Sir Humphrey Wakefield had set up a business with Baker, Knapp and Tubbs, a large furniture wholesaler from Chicago. He chose pieces of furniture from 'stately homes', took the measurements and some photographs of them and Baker had them reproduced in their North Carolina workshops. Humphrey had been looking particularly for eighteenth-century furniture, but we have little from that period except for our Banqueting Hall table. It is made from rosewood, with a satinwood and ebony border. David was sceptical that any money would come from this project (we had had similar propositions before that came to nothing) so Humphrey bought the rights to our table. Other owners would get a percentage based on sales of their particular item.

There was a big promotion to launch the finished furniture, and the various house-owners were invited to the States as guests of Baker, Knapp and Tubbs to help sell the furniture. David was now working for British Petroleum in the City and had used up his holiday allowance for the year, so I went alone. I looked at the guest list: Lord and Lady Thynne from Longleat – I had met Antonia years ago in London; Lord and Lady Mexborough – I knew Johnny, who had been a friend of my sister; Lady Middleton from Wollaton Hall in Yorkshire; Lord De L'Isle from Penshurst, Kent; the Duke and Duchess of Hamilton from Lennoxlove in Scotland; Lord and Lady Clifford of Chudleigh from Ugbrook in Devon; Lord Eliot from Port Eliot, Cornwall; and Lord and Lady Astor. Only the first two couples meant anything to me, and I hoped everyone would be friendly. I did not much like the idea of going on my own.

We all met up in the VIP's lounge at London airport, except for Lord Eliot of whom there was no sign. We were travelling first class, which I had never done before, but that was just for starters. We were to be dined and wined and put up in the best hotels wherever we went – we felt like royalty. Peregrine Eliot was already on the aeroplane when we boarded; he was about my age, alone and looked a possible kindred spirit. The man sitting next to me was very busy sorting out his papers for a meeting he was going to in Chicago; I helped hold some for him and he said I could help him if I liked by reading some of his notes to him. I looked at the sheets in my hand and said, 'Oh, how interesting – you work for Shell. My husband works for BP.' He quickly grabbed the papers out of my hand and shoved them back in his briefcase. He did not talk much after that.

We stayed in the Drake Hotel in Chicago for two nights. I had a suite of rooms with a huge bay window overlooking the lake and two bathrooms. I could have held a party for fifty people in the sitting room. Two high-class ladies were assigned to look after us: Mary Jane Poole, former editor of *House and Garden*, and Letitia Baldrige, who had been Jacqueline Kennedy's public relations lady. We nicknamed them our 'nannies', and they told us what to do and what to wear. We were 'on show' from 9 a.m. until midnight most days, so it was quite hard work. Philip Kelly, the president of Baker, Knapp and Tubbs, and his wife Rowena were our hosts.

I was right about Peregrine; he came and sat next to me on the coach the first morning and asked me about our rock festivals. He had started up his own festival in his park at Port Eliot in south Cornwall which he called 'The Elephant Fayre' and he was great fun to talk to. I need not have been nervous about going on this trip without David – everyone was very friendly. We flew to North Carolina and then travelled everywhere in a smart bus, which had a bar and a loo, and was known as 'the Dukemobile'. The bar was put to good use, Angus Hamilton played his bagpipes and Christopher Thynne regaled us with funny stories, while Peregrine and I played silly paper games. We spent hours on the bus travelling through the spectacular fall colours, and all got to know each other very well by the end.

In Charleston we were entertained in some of the old plantation houses. We had tea at Middleton Place, lunch at the Medway Plantation and so on; it was a non-stop programme. I managed to swap my first-class ticket from Chicago back to England for a seat on Concorde from New York, so I flew up to New York with Christopher, Antonia and Peregrine and spent a couple of days there before flying back on Concorde. The whole trip had been rather unreal and dreamlike, and it was difficult coming back to reality again – Tesco's, school runs and Knebworth problems.

Peregrine and I had parted with promises to meet up in England when we got back. But I was surprised all the same when, a week or so later, he rang up and asked me to come and stay at Port Eliot the next weekend. David was busy working on Knebworth budgets and was happy for me to go. It took four hours to drive down to Cornwall and I became more apprehensive the nearer I got – people you meet abroad are not always the same when they get home. By the time I reached the village of St Germans, I was so nervous that I managed to miss the front gates of Port Eliot altogether and ended up driving through the garden and up onto the lawn on the south side of the house. At first glance it looked exactly like Hartland and, like Hartland, it had been built as a monastery and dissolved by Henry VIII. The Eliot family had bought it in the sixteenth century. I managed to find my way round to the front door and found a note pinned to the heavy oak door, welcoming me to his fairyland. I walked through the huge hall and, following the directions, found Peregrine in a dark red room with a log fire blazing and the smell of joss sticks burning.

Peregrine is one of the few people I know who lives his life exactly as he pleases. He lives alone most of the time, and is well looked after by John, the butler, and Joan, the housekeeper. He has a friend called Jasper Heathcote Williams, a brilliant sculptor and writer, living in a part of the house, and they meet maybe once a week. Peregrine claims to do nothing and in *Who's Who* lists his recreations as 'mucking about', but he actually runs his estate very efficiently and has no intention of opening his house to the public. The signs on the lodge gates saying 'Please do not intrude' mean exactly what they say, a sentiment with which at that moment of my life I sympathised. He had just designed and built brick paths for a maze in his gardens, and we went down and planted the first trees to form the hedges.

Over the next few years Port Eliot became for me a haven of peace and quiet, a place I could escape to from the pressures of Knebworth. Peregrine does live in a fairyland, and of course fairylands are very tempting, but most of us have to live in reality and luckily my life is full and fun and Knebworth does not only consist of chores.

Snow fell heavily during December of that year, and Knebworth House sparkled in the sunshine like a wedding cake covered in white icing sugar. We got out the skis and put snowchains on the minibus wheels, with a rope behind it, and skied around the park. We had two Swedish girls staying with us, both of whom had been au pairs with us some years before, and Santa Lucia day on the 13th was celebrated by them arriving in our bedroom at 5 a.m. with a sleepy Rosina, all with flowers in their hair, holding candles and singing Swedish hymns. They produced cups of tea and cinnamon cake.

It was a Knebworth Christmas again; the lake was frozen hard so we made a big bonfire on the ice and had Boxing Day lunch around it. The shooting syndicate were shooting that day and for one drive the guns all stood on one side of the lake, while we curled and skated on the other. It was a happy end to an eventful year.

Chapter 13 | Jazz and the blues

1982 was not an easy year – I was beginning to find the lack of privacy really irksome. I am a very private sort of person and fairly anti-social by nature and there was always some reason for office and other staff to have to walk through the house at all times of the day; they were very good at searching me out when they wanted me – even going as far as banging on my bedroom door. I was becoming rather neurotic. Every weekend was taken up with events of some sort and our office was short-staffed. When John Wilkinson left in June it was too far on in the season to find anyone else, so Henry, Vi, and my abilities were really put to the test.

Henry was in his second year at university. He was doing a degree in film studies, but only went to Canterbury for his lectures; he said that having been sent away to boarding school from an early age, he now meant to spend as much time as his studies would allow at home. I didn't complain – I couldn't have managed without his help. He organised two 'alternative music festivals' in the park that year, made up of local Hertfordshire young bands with names like The Vicious Hampsters, Anzok Chant and Onslaught. The fans were a colourful lot of punks with Mohican hairstyles. The first festival was on Whit bank holiday Monday, the same weekend as the Sealed Knot members were fighting a civil war battle in the park. We thought the park was big enough to take both events, but we were wrong. Both parties complained bitterly about the other group's noise and at one moment it nearly became a battle between the Cromwellians and the Punks: a lot of tact had to be used to keep the peace.

The next big event was held in the middle of June: the John Lewis Gala, or 'open day'. They had been coming for a couple of years now, and about 3000 John Lewis and Peter Jones employees would turn up in coaches and cars on a Sunday in June. They have a huge marquee and catering facilities, and various competitions and entertainments go on during the day. David and I usually judge the fancy dress competition, which with so many designers and shopfitters involved is of a very high standard. The first two years they came it poured with rain and the day was a wash-out, but they kept coming. I shop a lot in John Lewis – in Oxford Street, Brent Cross or Welwyn Garden City – and it surprises me how many assistants connect the name and address on my account card with their annual outing. It produces much better service and I usually get taken off to see the photographs from the previous year's event at Knebworth. I have asked for a discount but haven't got one yet!

A large Classic Car rally was held at the beginning of July, and 13,000 people turned up for it. John Wilkinson came back from Wales to manage it and Henry helped, so I did not have to get involved with it that year, but it caused us unbelievable problems over the next two years.

Capital Radio decided to come back to Knebworth again in July, and in conjunction with Chiltern Radio they put on two weekends of jazz. Andy Hudson was once more the promoter and site manager, and Peter, Danny and Harry helped to put up the wooden fencing and set up the arena and lavatories. Richard was given a job as a 'gofer'. We had the house full of friends, which meant anything between twenty and thirty people staying for both weekends.

Once again all the best musicians came to Knebworth: B. B. King, Dizzy Gillespie, Ray Charles, Lionel Hampton, Benny Goodman, Dave Brubeck and the Modern Jazz Quartet to name only a few. Crowds of up to 15,000 were expected on the four days, but unfortunately they were affected by a train strike and only on the first Sunday, when the Crusaders were playing, did they top the 15,000 mark. But it was an enjoyable event. The fans came with deckchairs, picnic hampers and bottles of wine, and their ages ranged from babies in arms to grandparents. There were some minor problems, such as when the Modern Jazz

Quartet came straight from the airport and their suitcases arrived without the keys, which had gone to their hotel in London. They refused to go on stage without their special clothes. I searched the house for keys and came up with about a hundred odd ones, but none fitted the locks. They were due to go on stage at any minute, and we were all getting fairly desperate, when Richard suddenly managed to make one of the keys work, and all was saved.

Benny Goodman refused to have any amplification, so only the first six rows could hear his music and there were soon shouts of 'Can't hear you' from the crowd. He took no notice and some people went and asked for their money back. I sympathised with him – jazz is best played in a smaller indoor venue, but as we were outside he should have realised that no one was going to be able to hear him and there were bound to be complaints.

My favourite blues singer is B. B. King. I pushed my way right up to the front of the stage when he was on, and after he had finished his set I ran backstage and asked for his autograph. Lionel Hampton was a big showman too; he must be over seventy but insisted on dancing and singing up and down the stage. I was sitting in a corner on stage listening to him, and his manager was very nervous, expecting him to fall off the stage at any moment. 'Sit down, you silly old fool,' he kept shouting at him. But Lionel took no notice. The musicians were all having a good time too, and the atmosphere on stage was far more relaxed than with a rock concert. Rock musicians are all megastars and tend to be very tense and uptight.

After Whit weekend, I suppose we should have realised that the Custom Car Club rally and the Green Belt Festival were not going to be the ideal pair of events to stage together in the park over the August bank holiday either. The Green Belt Festival, held in aid of the Deo Gloria Trust, was a Christian event which had been running for eight years and had become so large that it had grown out of the field they had held it in previously. We agreed to have them at Knebworth. They did not expect more than 15,000 people each day and, as they were good Christians, we did not expect any problems with the local community. The rector was delighted and our parish church was opened up for recitals and extra church services.

We put them in the Mausoleum Park well away from where the Custom Car Club were camping. They built a huge tented village with a main stage in the middle and stalls running up one side; the marquees were used for seminars, cinema shows and theatre. That side of the event was quite impressive, but Jonathan Cook, the Green Belt promoter, was not easy to deal with and hid every time he saw me coming. I presume he thought I was going to complain about something, and he was right – I was. The camping and car park manager had no vehicle to get around in and was therefore quite incapable of controlling the traffic, and by 1 a.m. on Friday, Henry and I found ourselves trying to sort out the shambles in the park and prevent a build-up of cars on the motorway.

Most of the Green Belt helpers were giving their services for free, with the result that they came and went when they felt like it and did not seem to communicate with each other. Tents and cars were everywhere, and there were no fire lanes for emergencies – even the park drive was blocked with cars left on the verges. They were very concerned that the Custom Car fraternity might come and infiltrate their show. The hot-rodders viewed the Christians with suspicion and gave them a wide berth, but (in spite of strict instructions from us) they could not resist doing a few wheelies and rev-ups along the park road by the Green Belt camp, though how they managed to find a spare bit of road to do it on surprises me. But overall it could have been worse.

Henry ran his second alternative music festival in September, the same weekend as the Railway Gala, but without the problems we had experienced on the other two occasions. He advertised the event by inviting the press to a painting session, and he was photographed painting 'Knebworth Festival Returns 4 September' on to the back of an attractive, naked young lady; body-painting was to be one of the attractions of the festival. The papers liked it and did a couple of articles on him.

With his long plaited hair, black and white clothes and make-up, Henry had become quite a distinctive character in the area. He was popular with the staff and his social life was made up of the friends he had working for him in the park during the summer. Occasionally an angry visitor would appear at the office with some complaint and demand to see the manager. If I was not there,

Henry would appear and they would ask again to see the manager. He would say, 'I am the manager' and they would take one look at him, shrug their shoulders and walk away without even bothering to voice the complaint. It was quite useful. He manages to keep wonderfully calm through all the pressures during the summer and was invaluable to me during the two years that I had no manager.

Our events seemed to be getting noisier, and there had been more complaints about them than usual. Henry and I took it in turns to go and placate the neighbours; we did try not to disturb the local residents, but it was not easy. There were so many events which involved a lot of noise from loudspeakers, gun battles, cannon shots, revving car engines, motorbikes, hooting trains and even aeroplanes and, noisiest of the lot, microlight planes. Our neighbours seemed to fall into three categories: the ones who put up with all the noise and enjoyed the events in the park, the estate employees who knew it was no good complaining as it was their livelihood, and the complainers – but luckily there were not many of them. They were mostly newcomers to the village who had moved to Knebworth to get away from the noise of London, only to discover, too late, what was on their doorstep! Thanks to our entrance off the motorway the village was not affected by extra cars or people coming to the park, except for large events such as the rock festivals, and the Lytton Arms on the edge of the park does good business, especially from event organisers and their teams of workers who use it as their works canteen.

We try to redeem our popularity stakes locally by allowing charity organisations to use the park free of charge on Mondays during the summer, when we would normally be shut. They man the gates and we let them use the adventure playground, and they can often raise £2–300 during the day. It is no trouble for us and it means that the park is open seven days a week, so there are no disappointed visitors who may have come a long way.

I managed to get away one weekend during the summer to the Glastonbury CND Festival. David was disapproving, and said if I had my photograph taken in front of a CND poster and it got into the press he would never speak to me again. But I was not interested in the political side of the event – I wanted to see the festival, as I had only ever been to ours and I was interested to see how other people ran theirs. The Elephant Fayre from Port Eliot were running a huge cabaret marquee there as well.

Peter came with me and we took two vans to sleep in. David Brown and Jessica, his new wife, and a crowd from Stevenage came as well. There was a long queue waiting to get on to the site on the Friday when I arrived, and a policeman who was directing the traffic came over and chatted. 'What is someone like you doing going to a festival like this?' he asked. 'I wouldn't go if I were you, filthy dirty people, drugs, all sorts of unpleasantness.' I thought, what a pity – the police have such a jaundiced view of life!

Michael Eavis, who runs the festivals, has been holding them on his farm since the early seventies and they have grown from a couple of thousand people to over 40,000 that year. I was introduced to Michael and we had a chat about the various problems connected with festivals. I was impressed by the good-natured behaviour of everyone, and there was not a policeman in sight; Michael said he did not allow them on to the farm. I wondered how he managed to get away with it. He also allows camping anywhere on the site. His farmhouse is the centre of the festival – a hive of activity, catering for welfare, information, first aid, telephones and so on.

I think it is more fun than a one-day festival. It goes on for three days and nights, and there is a main stage with loud music, but also numerous other marquees with theatre, cinema, and smaller bands playing all the time. Peregrine had been many times before and knew a lot of the regulars, and when he was not organising his cabaret tent we wandered through the crowds visiting the other marquees and chatting with old friends. The Elephant Fayre marquee put on various entertainments including jugglers, clowns, comics, story-tellers, skits and musical reviews from noon until the small hours of the morning. Everything closed down at 3 a.m. and started up again at 11 a.m., and the atmosphere was marvellous.

On the first evening I lay in my minibus listening to the music. Another van drove up and parked next door, and a man got out, took all his clothes off and proceeded to spend about half an hour fixing a loincloth around his middle. He then frizzed his hair out, put on some make-up, surveyed himself in a mirror until he was finally satisfied with his appearance, and then set off into the crowd. I caught glimpses of him over the weekend; and at one point he seemed to have discarded the loincloth altogether – but then the weather was quite hot. At seven o'clock on Monday morning, I was woken by a banging noise on the van next door, and a voice shouting, 'Dad, Dad, wake up, Dad. I've got to go to school.' 'Fuck off,' came the reply. 'But Dad, I'll be late, and you've got to go to work.' I peered through the curtains of my van and saw a boy of about eleven banging on the loincloth man's window. 'Okay, okay, I'm coming,' he grumbled and five minutes later he emerged wearing trousers, shirt, tie and jacket, ready for work and the school run!

The night before, one of the big latrine pits had filled up and they had moved the twenty-seater cubicle block over to an empty pit. Unfortunately, they had forgotten to put anything over the full one and in the dark a luckless lady had fallen headlong into it. She had swum around for a while before they managed to drag her out. She was, not unnaturally, hysterical and had to be taken backstage to be hosed down and given a change of clothing.

I met Rikki Stein, one of the organisers, over the weekend, and he told me he was looking for a festival site to raise money for Earth Life, an organisation that is trying to save the equatorial rain forests of the world. I thought it sounded a good cause and he agreed to come to Knebworth to have a talk about it. In spite of four days in a bus, with little sleep, I felt exceedingly well by the end of the weekend. I had even managed to wash my hair in a bucket, though I was glad I had brought my own water as there was a definite shortage and long queues for the taps. It was encouraging to find other people had the same sort of problems. I arrived home refreshed and ready to cope with anything, which was just as well considering all there was to be done.

I now had two offices, my usual one in the house and my managerial one over in the estate office. I had a cordless telephone so I could take calls from wherever I was in the park or gardens, and I spent from nine in the morning until seven at night in the estate office. The part of the day I enjoyed most was opening the post, as I liked dealing with enquiries, making dates for meetings with event organisers, working out contracts with them and so on. Most of the events were car club rallies and the organisers would come into my office and say, 'Oh no! not a woman.' I don't think they expected me to be very sympathetic to their cause, but sorting out the money side of things is like a game – trying to get the best deal possible without giving away too much. One does not ultimately want to lose the event by over pricing, but on the other hand, they are dab hands at pleading great poverty for their clubs.

Pattie was still working in the gift shop but would come over and help out occasionally when she had a moment, and everyone tried to make life as easy as possible for me. Derek Spencer was invaluable, especially over the summer events. He would do all the signs, roping and plumbing and take organisers around the park if I did not have time. Vi had to hold the fort for me when I was out of the office and we often ran two meetings simultaneously. I knew nothing about estate management, so Humberts, our agents, sent one of their special experts over once a week. However, he often did not turn up and I would have to try and keep agitated tenants or people with estate enquiries happy until he did arrive. There was little chance of being able to escape abroad this year.

During term-time, with the children away at school or university, I could just about fit everything in. I went up to London every evening during the week and spent the night with David, who was working in the finance department of BP and putting in long hours. He found commuting impossible so we had bought a tiny two-roomed flat in Marylebone. As I never had time to shop, we usually ate out at a local restaurant, though sometimes David would bring food back from the delicatessen on his way from the underground and we took it in turns to cook. David left for work at seven-fifteen in the morning, and I was back in my office at Knebworth by quarter to nine. We even managed to squeeze into our small London bath for the evening board meetings, though David complained a lot about getting the end with the taps!

But school holidays were a different matter. I had no one to help with the shopping, cooking and laundry and I was literally run off my feet. Having six children, plus all their friends, means that we never sit down to a meal during the holidays with fewer than twelve people. Their friends all congregate here as we have the most room. I know many people manage to run a home and have a full-time job, but their offices are usually well away from their homes and they must be better organised than me. I found myself tearing back over to the house between meetings to put the laundry into the washing-machine or hang it out. I would rush back at about one-fifteen and find a row of hungry reproachful faces sitting in the kitchen, wondering when they were going to get lunch, if at all. There was never anything in the larder or fridge, as I was always far too busy to go shopping, and I usually ended up taking them to McDonald's in Letchworth ten miles away for a take-away. The children got used to having to fend for themselves and to their clothes never being ironed. I never had time to do anything with them and had a continual guilty conscience.

By the autumn of 1982 our planning applications were still with the Council; the sub-committee had deferred its decision while they sought more information. A financial report on the merits of the scheme had been requested from the Hertfordshire County Treasurer's Department, it had taken them a year to complete the report and it was now being considered by the North Hertfordshire Councillors. The district-planning chief, Vernon Roberts, said the applications were beyond any previous experience he had had, owing to the importance of Knebworth House and Park, and the effect our financial straits would have on them. Our problems did not look like being solved for a while.

Chapter 14 | At the helm

I was now busier than ever before. As a result of our cuts, I had only Vi and two accountants in the office and occasionally Dave Gordon (Henry was in his final year at university and studying hard for his degree). Dave was a man of large proportions with a beard. He had come to the park the year before and set up a parascending school, and had persuaded John Wilkinson to take him on as a public relations officer. I did not much care for the caravan he had set up in the park and seemed to be living in, but I was grateful for any help at that moment.

Dave, as my new public relations officer, wanted to make sure he had plenty of things to tell the press about for the 1983 summer season, so he organised numerous rather doubtful events, starting off with an Egg-citing Easter, which involved someone dressed as a giant Humpty-Dumpty wandering around the park for a week. The costume was hired from a fancy-dress company, who were supposed to come and collect it, but they never came and it sat in the reception room of our office for weeks. We had to climb over it to get into or out of the office.

One weekend, we 'legged it' for charity – sixty-one people roped together in a sixty-two-legged race. We managed thirty paces before falling in a heap and apparently should have earned ourselves a place in the *Guinness Book of Records*; £210 was raised for a cystic fibrosis victim as a result. We also held a Wild West weekend. The Indians sat dolefully in their wigwams in the pouring rain, while the cowboys cantered around the park disturbing the neighbours with the occasional 'shoot-out'. Not many people came to watch.

One of the better days was 'D-Day Remembered at Knebworth', a mock battle and display of Second World War army vehicles. It was organised by the Military Vehicle Conservation Group and about 5000 people came, but it was not enough to make a profit from the show. I think the participants enjoyed themselves more than the audience – it is difficult nowadays to compete with television.

The aerobics marathon or 'Stately Shape-Up' was quite a sight. The idea was to raise money for the Variety Club of Great Britain (and for us of course), and a small stage was built in the park on which the aerobics teachers did two-hourly stints from midday until 8 p.m. The participants arrived clad in leotards and clutching their exercise mats. They jogged, twisted, stretched and kicked to the music for as long as they could keep going, sponsored by their friends, who came to watch and shout encouragement. Financially this was not a great success either and we had to give our share of the money to the charity. But we ended up with enough crates of Ashbourne fizzy water to keep us going for a year.

On another occasion, two naked Stevenage housewives did a streak in front of the house. I cannot remember why, but I did not think much of the picture of their fat white bottoms in the newspapers the next day. We were beginning to get tired of Mr Gordon and his ideas.

Meanwhile Vi and I were trying to cope with the Classic Car rally, which wanted to come back for a second year. It was organised by Peter Ellis, who worked for a motoring magazine, and they said they were not interested in the money side, only in the publicity for their magazine. So we were to run the finance and set up the arena, extra loos etc., and pay them a percentage of the gate money. Vi and I took Peter Ellis and another member of the magazine out to lunch before the event to sort out the details. I had heard from Henry, who had dealt with him the year before, that he was a very difficult man, so we were not looking forward to it much, but I never expected him to be as rude and as disagreeable as he was. I said nothing back and eventually he turned on me and complained, 'Why the hell don't you get angry and answer me back? You just sit there looking cool and calm, it's infuriating.' I laughed and said it was too much effort to get cross and if he wanted to be rude about last year's arrangements – go ahead. He went off muttering, 'It had better be more organised than last year – or else.'

The rally was in July, and the organisation for it was immense, as arenas had to be marked out for the classes of the National Classic Car concours, in which about 250 cars took part. There was an auto jumble, indispensable for the do-it-yourselfer hunting that elusive spare part, and a treasure house of motoring magazines, brochures, mascots and other memorabilia. Members of more than thirty clubs showed off their cars, and there was a classic car mart for those wanting to trade in their vehicles and/or acquire another on the spot. We had to have six pay-gates in operation from about seven in the morning, as the cars taking part in the event, the stall-holders and the visitors all had different-coloured labels on their cars and had to go through different gates and then be parked in the correct areas. Hundreds of wooden stakes had to go in the day before to mark out the area, and catering facilities and extra lavatories were set up.

The event was bigger than ever before – 16,000 people came, and with all the vehicles as well the park was fairly full. As we have to bring in a lot of extra untrained staff for events of this size things can get rather out of control, but I didn't think it went too badly. Peter Ellis, however, managed to have a groan about there not being enough toilets, the grass not being short enough, and the catering not good enough.

In July 1983, we held a big party for Henry's twenty-first and Peter's eighteenth birthdays. We put a marquee up over our private courtyard and had some fairground attractions in the garden; we could not use the house, unfortunately, because it was the middle of the busy summer season. About 400 guests came, and the party was a mixture of people from all professions and of all ages. One nice thing about the stately home business is the variety of people we meet and make friends with – it makes life so much more interesting. Peter was presented with a 'fencing' trophy by his festival friends, and a rock group made up of Henry's friends played for a while between the disco and the band. I was not on very good form, though. It was hard work organising the party on top of everything else that summer, and I suppose I was feeling my age . . .

In August, leaving Henry and Vi in charge, David and I took the younger children to France for a much-needed holiday, but it did not really work out that way. We had bought a dilapidated farmhouse in the Dordogne as a place to escape to. It needed a lot doing to it and we had just about got the place furnished; I had made the curtains and we had sent a vanload of furniture out. David's parents and his brother Rowland, plus family, had rented a small house near ours at the same time, and I made the big mistake of having no one to help me. As they all wanted to see our new house everyone was inclined to congregate there, and the washing, shopping, cooking and washing-up were worse than at home. I felt tired and had a continual migraine.

We got home in time to sort out the August bank holiday. The Custom Cars were coming again and the Green Belt Festival too. It was their tenth anniversary and Cliff Richard was heading the bill. We had to get a special licence for the Saturday, as they expected large crowds for Cliff, and we had to change the festival site as there would not be enough room in the part of the park they had used the year before. The new site was right next door to the Custom Cars and both parties were worried.

Because of the car-parking shambles the year before I insisted on them having a professional firm to deal with the camping and cars this year. But Jonathan Cook, the promoter, was being his usual elusive self and the manager of the car-parking firm, realising he had lost control of the parking by Friday evening, simply left the site!

The proceedings were not supposed to start until Friday afternoon, but there were so many people in the park by Thursday that in the evening Jonathan decided to put on an impromptu concert in one of the marquees. My telephone started ringing immediately, as the neighbours were not expecting any noise until Friday. I rang Jonathan's site office with no success, so eventually I went down to the arena in my nightie and wellington boots and searched until I found him. He was reluctant to stop the music and we had an argument about it. He did eventually stop it, but not before annoying a lot of people.

The Frampton family who started up the Deo Gloria Trust and the festivals are very well-meaning religious people and keen to make the event a very special and good time for everyone. They were shocked by the troubles we had on Thursday, and the money that was taken from the unscheduled concert went to our parish church. This calmed me down a bit.

The atmosphere is completely different from a rock festival; although the age group is the same, the people are quite different. There was certainly no drunkenness or drugs and everyone was well behaved, but then so they are, as a general rule, at a rock festival, and David and I found the arena with the religious seminars going on all around somehow rather spooky. A theological challenge was put forward at the weekend in the form of a pamphlet called *Pop Goes the Gospel*, a highly critical examination by three Christian evangelists of Christian involvement with rock culture. They suggested that using musical entertainment for evangelistic purposes goes against biblical principles and should be stopped. I find it hard to believe that it matters.

On Saturday night, while the crowds were flocking in to hear him, Cliff Richard came to the house and we showed him round and gave him and his manager a cup of tea. We asked him what he thought of *Pop Goes the Gospel*, and of course after twenty-five years of being in the rock music business, a lot of it Christian-orientated, he could not possibly agree with the three theologians and said it was an amazingly immature thought. His own life and career proved the pamphlet totally wrong.

We impressed on Cliff's manager how important it was to finish the concert by midnight, otherwise we would be taken to court and fined for breach of our concert licence. But for one reason or another the programme was running late and, instead of cutting out one of the groups before, Cliff ended up coming on stage at eleven-thirty. He had only thirty minutes in which to play and a lot of disappointed fans, who had had to catch the last train home, missed him altogether.

By Sunday morning we had run out of water. The weekend was hot and sunny and the Christians needed flush loos and water for washing themselves and their pots and pans – not to mention the babies' nappies, which hung on lines strung between tent poles to dry. Water tankers worked night and day to keep them supplied and our huge water tank, although supplied by the mains, was empty. The pig farmer who gets his water after us was desperate.

There were a lot of complaints all round and not much we could do about it.

An outdoor church service held for around 10,000 people was the spiritual highlight of the weekend. On Sundays our music and dancing licence finishes at 10.30 p.m., so in the evening David and I went down to the main stage to make sure that the entertainment finished on time. There was a religious musical play going on and it did not look a bit like finishing. We searched around for the stage manager, who said that owing to an electrical fault they were running late, but he could not possibly stop it and refused to do so. Luckily, no licensing officers were around or we would have been in trouble.

By Monday night we were all exhausted with the non-stop noise. The sound system was of poor quality and seemed unreasonably loud, even to us who were used to noise. But attempts to get them to turn it down were fruitless. After midnight on the Monday night a rock band struck up at full blast in one of the marquees and, fed up with the continual telephone complaints and tired out himself, David went down in his nightshirt and pulled the plug on them. The residents of Knebworth were allowed a few hours of peace before going to work on Tuesday morning.

The Custom Car rally had not been exactly quiet either, but at least that had only lasted for two nights. Our popularity stakes locally were nil, and we had to do something to redeem our reputation. We promised that we would never have another four-day festival, we would have no more battles for a year or so and we gave notice to quit to the autocross club and the motorbike scrambling club. We told all the microlight aeroplanes to go somewhere else and we swore that we would keep noise at a minimum from then on.

One of my lowest moments during that summer was when David was away on business for two weeks with BP. The bank manager rang up to say our overdraft had risen to such proportions that he was going to bounce any further cheques we wrote out, and where was I going to find the money to pay him back? He read out over the telephone a couple of cheques owing, including a bill from France. 'How you can ever dream of going on holiday in your financial straits I cannot imagine,' he remonstrated. I explained that David was abroad and that the staff wages had to be paid on Friday, but he said that was my problem, not his. I had to ring David's accountants and solicitors and get them to help sort the problem out until David got back. Luckily, I had a couple of family allowance cheques owing, so we could buy some food. An arrangement was made with the bank for the staff wages, to tide us over, and I emptied the telephone moneybox, my drawers, and all my old handbags in search of the odd pound note to keep the household going. For over a month we could not write out a cheque, and it seemed ridiculous to be living in a place like Knebworth and yet be virtually penniless as far as ready cash went. As it was, we had been selling at least one estate house or cottage every year to keep our heads above water, and the family gold plate and quite a few pictures had gone. But even selling things takes time.

The North Hertfordshire planners were still stalling. By the autumn of 1983 the full Council had approved the plans, but had then referred them to the Department of the Environment for consideration. We kept our fingers crossed.

By the end of the season I was totally exhausted – I felt the business was suffering and so was I, not to mention the family. On top of everything, my father died in September. We are a very close family and it was a tremendous shock, even though he had been ill for two years. My hair started falling out and I did not have a period for six months; it was clear that I needed to slow down a bit. The number of visitors had dropped to 120,000, and only 24,000 had visited the house that year. This was partly due to the recession – there was a lot of local unemployment and money was short and kept for necessities. Another reason was that a lot more historic houses had opened up over the last few years, so there was more competition. Most of the people living around us had already been to Knebworth – some many times – so they went elsewhere. Weather is an important factor too, and we had had a run of wet summers.

The park no longer looked as fresh as it had when we started. It needs a sharp eye and a lot of persuasion to keep the place looking smart: signs become tatty very quickly, they need repairing every year and the grass needs cutting regularly, and the verges take a hammering, especially during events which involve big lorries or horse boxes. So maybe we were getting rather slack and needed to make more of an effort. We had of course cut the expenses substantially – I was doing three people's work in the office, and without being paid. It couldn't go on indefinitely.

At one of our board meetings we decided we would have to get someone on the management level to help me. We were not yet in a position to pay a lot and the future was far from secure, so we advertised for a general assistant with public relations experience (Dave Gordon had left by this time). We also closed down the gift shop. It just about paid Pattie's and Jan's wages but generated a lot of work for the accounts department, which had now dwindled to one. The accountant had left in August to have an operation and gave in her notice at the same time. Her assistant had made a valiant effort to cope for the rest of the season but did not have the experience, let alone the time, to run the accounts office by herself, and the accounts were even further behind than usual. Ticket control and counting and banking the takings is a full-time job during the summer, so the book work tends to be deferred to the winter months, when it is too far behind to catch up with.

So we looked for an accountant as well as an assistant for me, and Pattie came back to help in the house. Perhaps I would be able to cope after all and maybe even do some much-needed jobs in the house as well.

One of the first tasks I wanted to tackle was in the attic. This is full of trunks, boxes, damp books, old letters and stacks of old clothes. It gets raided by the children looking for dressing-up clothes or penny black stamps, and my mother-in-law occasionally searches for letters or photographs. The children never put anything back, so it gets dreadfully untidy. I had given David Brown's brother Nick a job when he had been over in England from Australia during the summer, cleaning and tidying out the attic for me. I had not been up there since, so now I went up to check Nick's work. Everything was put away and neatly stacked, and labelled, but when I took a second glance I realised he had stuck labels on all the boxes and trunks describing the contents. The first one I read said 'Fucking boring books' on it in large letters – thank goodness I had looked! I had to go through the lot, censoring them all. What my mother-in-law or some other unsuspecting person would have thought if they had found them I dread to think.

In the attic were two large wooden boxes full of old film reels. Film people, on their way through the attic to the roof, were always horrified to see these nitrate film rolls lying around. Apparently they are like an unexploded bomb, and could go off at any moment. I had always meant to do something about them, but had never got round to it. Then a Japanese television company wrote to my mother-in-law asking if we had any films on Lord Lytton's visit to Manchuria in 1931. They were doing a documentary on Japanese history and they had discovered that Lord Lytton had lead the Commission to Manchuria when the Japanese had invaded China in the early thirties. We had a look and found quite a few large reels marked 'Manchuria', so we rang up the British Film Institute and asked them if it would be possible to have a look at them on their projector, as the projectors in the attic looked as if they were beyond repair. The Film Institute were interested in all the films, so we took them up to London, feeling rather nervous and expecting them to explode at any moment.

The British Film Institute were very helpful and said that some of the films were in too bad a condition to do anything with, but others were of great interest and we arranged a day to go through them all. My parents-in-law and Henry came too, and we spent most of the day in the Institute looking at the films. There were some from Calcutta in the twenties when Lord Lytton was Governor of Bengal, and my mother-in-law, her sister and brothers were in them as teenagers; we saw them at the races and at garden parties, and inspecting the troops. There was a film of Lord Lytton roller-skating in Darjeeling, and another of Antony Knebworth boxing on ice skates in St Moritz in the early thirties. One was a 'talkie', with Antony explaining a charity boxing match to be held in the Albert Hall. He was killed in a flying accident soon after the film was taken, and Hermione must have felt very strange hearing his voice and seeing him and her father walking around on film after such a long time. It was a moving experience.

Mr Whitney, the man at the BFI, wanted to know who everyone was in the films, as they were interested in keeping copies and records of most of them. One that interested him particularly was a cricket week held at J. M. Barrie's house in 1921. It was a yearly event, and Barrie invited a house party of about sixteen young friends, the boys coming mostly from Eton or, when they were older, Oxford and Cambridge. Hermione was one of the girls invited this particular year, and Antony Knebworth and their mother Pamela Lytton were also there. Barrie had made up and directed a story for them to act, with a written dialogue between shots, and it was great fun to watch. My brother-in-law Charles Worthington's father was one of the boys. He was killed during the Second World War, and I couldn't wait to show Charles the film; he could hardly have remembered what his father looked like.

The BFI promised to put on to tape for us the ones they were interested in and wanted to keep, and the rest, which are mostly Indian and skiing holidays in the twenties and thirties, we are going to get taped ourselves. One day I mean to put on a skiing exhibition. The Lyttons were some of the first people to ski for fun, and they went out to Wengen and Murren every year and helped form the Kandahar Ski Club. There is a cupboard full of old skis, sticks and clothes in the attic, and they also kept a log book on the ski runs – a record of each day's activities on the mountains. With the films as well, I could put on an audio-visual show and make an interesting display for school children, so many of whom go on ski trips nowadays. But finding the time to do it is the problem.

Chapter 15 Escape to India

Death, intrigue and a lot of shooting went on at Knebworth House between November 1982 and the New Year. Geoffrey Reeves and Jeremy Saunders made a film called *The Shooting Party* from the novel by Isobel Colegate. The entire film was shot at Knebworth, in the house and woods, except for a couple of days in Berkshire. When the director and assistant producer, Peter Dalman, came down to discuss the filming, I asked them to go and have a talk to my in-laws at Lake House, as a fair amount of the film was to be shot in the woods behind their house.

They came back very agitated about the attitude of Lord Cobbold. When they explained the story of the film, which ends up with one of the beaters getting shot and dying, my father-in-law had been adamant – no one was going to be shot in his woods. What were they to do? I advised them to wait and see what happened, as he might on reflection change his mind – which of course he did. However, as it happened they did film that sequence somewhere else – in fact they did everything they could to keep us quiet and happy.

A man named Bert was responsible for moving things around in the house. Every room was turned upside down, the pictures removed and carpets taken up, and one room was even repapered. He and I managed to maintain a fairly good rapport, considering the nature of his job, although I did blow my top occasionally.

Paul Scofield was supposed to be the leading actor, playing the part of Sir Randolf of Nettleby Hall (Knebworth House), but unfortunately on the first day of filming there was an accident. The scene included a coach and horses, and something scared the horses, which bolted; the front of the carriage broke away and the whole thing turned over. Paul broke a leg and two other actors, Edward Fox and Robert Hardy, were also injured. This meant that the film was delayed two weeks while another actor was found to take Paul Scofield's part. James Mason was filming in Geneva at the time, but only at night, so he agreed to take on *The Shooting Party* as well. He had to fly backwards and forwards in order to film at Knebworth during the day and Geneva at night; it was a logistical nightmare of helicopters and private jets. No wonder he looked so exhausted; and he died the following August. But his performance is magnificent, and I think he makes the film outstanding.

Henry, who had obtained his degree in film studies and graduated successfully from Kent University that summer, launched his film career with *The Shooting Party*. He was given a job as a 'gofer', which he loved. It meant doing all the dirty work, from breaking the ice on the lake in the morning to pacifying his mother about the props manager's next bright idea. He learnt a lot and was popular with the crew. Richard and Rosina had walk-on parts as village children, though two days of hanging around in the rain and cold dressed in itchy costumes waiting to be called for has certainly put them off being film actors. But at least they are in the film and not on the cutting-room floor, although it is a case of 'if you blink at the wrong moment' you miss them.

My mother-in-law had a lovely conversation with Jeremy Saunders. She asked him how the film was progressing. 'Very well,' said Jeremy. 'We are very pleased with the rushes.' 'Oh, I'm so glad you like my rushes,' she said, thinking he meant the rushes in the lake outside her house. Jeremy looked uncertain whether he should explain that he was talking about the film takes or whether he should discuss the virtues of Knebworth lake. He chose the lake.

It was our turn again to have Christmas at Knebworth with all the relations to stay, and I could not believe that the house would be back to normal in time. Then the director announced that, as the schedule was running over time, they would continue to film over Christmas week. I threw a fit, but luckily the crew and actors objected as well, so they eventually packed up and left the evening before Christmas Eve. I just managed to get the Christmas tree up and decorated, the beds made and the table laid in time for the arrival of the twenty-eight guests and family who were expected for Christmas. One bonus was the billiard table they left behind in the Library, which we were able to use over the holiday.

They were back again in the New Year to finish off the filming, but there was snow on the ground which spoilt the continuity, so they ended up having to go to Berkshire where there was no snow. We had a family shoot on Boxing Day and shot a record number of birds, which was another bonus from the film. They had let loose hundreds in our woods during the shooting scenes – particularly since Henry, who was in charge of letting them out of the boxes at the right moment, released the first lot before anyone was ready, so another batch had to be brought in!

The children were invited to a special preview of the film at Pinewood Studios, which was a great treat, and when it eventually came out it ran at the Curzon Cinema in London and was hailed as a great success.

Jane Granlund, whom we had chosen as my new assistant, and Shirley Miller, our new accountant, arrived in the middle of all the filming (we had had over two hundred replies to our advertisement for an assistant, and only three for the accountant's job!). The estate offices had been taken over by the film company, so they did not have a very easy start – it was difficult to find a desk and chair for them to sit on. I was delighted to have someone to help me; Jane seemed very efficient, so I soon felt I was hardly needed in the office at all and I escaped to India in March 1984.

A friend of mine, Ginny Fass, who had been instrumental in bringing *The Shooting Party* to Knebworth and was now doing a photographic book on the forts of India, wanted someone to accompany her around India while she took the photographs. I had to be back for the children's holidays, which meant I had three and a half weeks, and I flew out to Delhi and met Ginny there. She had previously published a book on Indian palaces and had stayed with many of the Maharajahs at their palaces while taking the photographs, so she had many friends in India.

On our first morning in Delhi, Ginny arranged for us to meet a guru. We lunched in the Taj Hotel with one of the directors and he recommended that we should consult his holy man, so we went back to Nasib's office after lunch and he introduced us to the guru. I was apprehensive. I had never even been to a fortune-teller before, and was far from sure I wanted to know what the future held for me. Actually he proved surprisingly accurate on my past history, but I was rather more sceptical about his predictions for the future. 'You will inherit many oxen cart' meant, I hoped, that a porsche or two were on the way!

We then flew down to Madras, where Hazel, my American friend from Nairobi, was now living with her husband Brad and children. She came with us to visit the first fort the next day – Gingee, about three and a half hours south of Madras. It was a steep hot walk up to the fort. Ginny is not very good at climbing and Hazel suddenly announced that she was in the middle of a nervous breakdown and her doctor had told her not to leave Madras, but they both survived the day.

As most Indian forts are on top of steep hills and we seldom reached them before midday (getting up in the morning not being one of Ginny's strong points), there were many hot climbs. Ginny would then take photographs until the light failed, and we would drive on to the next town and hope to find somewhere to spend the night. The drivers hated being out at night, especially with two women, as they were scared of bandits. They would scramble around the fort after Ginny, imploring her to stop photographing and get back into the car, so we could reach a place to stay before nightfall. She never took any notice of them, so I would try and calm the drivers down, then give up and sit on a cannon or battlement and gaze out over the misty plains, wondering about the lives of the armies who had defended the forts, or the people who lived on the plains below. It is such a vast, hard country, and life is difficult. For most, only their religious faith must make their existence bearable.

As I sat in Madras airport at the end of of our stay there, waiting for a flight to Hyderabad, a man came and sat next to me and started asking questions. I found this informal approach quite disconcerting, but it is apparently a form of politeness – although when it involves a man and a woman it is inclined to become more than that if you are not careful. You have to judge the moment when the encounter starts to take rather too personal a turn and stop it quickly. This gentleman was very friendly and said he had a close acquaintance in Hyderabad who would be honoured to look after us there. His friend turned out to be the chief of police in Hyderabad. I would never have contacted him if I had been alone, but Ginny thought he might be able to help with a car for us as we had some forts quite a distance away to visit. She rang him when we arrived and he came round the next morning and offered us a police car and driver for the two days we were there. He could not have been more helpful.

So we drove around Hyderabad in great style with an official police flag on the front of the car. I liked the city. The streets teemed with people and the traffic was usually at a standstill; there was a wonderful three-lane bridge, with one lane for pedestrians, one for bikes, rickshaws and bullock carts, and one for cars and buses. They were all three packed solid and there was a lot of horn-blowing. The day after we arrived we visited Golkonda fort, a few miles outside the town. Its walls are seven miles around and the fort inside is a jumble of ruins, alleyways, tunnels and rooms, easy to get lost in and rather spooky. You never knew who you were going to meet round the next corner – an ash-covered holy man, a group of jeering youths or a horribly deformed beggar.

We then drove across the Deccan plain to Habli, visiting Bidar, Gulbarga, Bijapur, Hampi and Vijayanaga on the way. Ginny caused quite a stir in Bijapur. She was wearing pink trousers which had a large split across the bottom, and when she bent down to photograph something a large expanse of knickers appeared. We were always the cause of great curiosity anyway, but the Indians could not get over these trousers. 'Give them something to giggle about,' said Ginny and went on photographing. Ginny is nothing if not dedicated when she is working and I don't think she noticed the commotion she was causing.

One morning I was sitting in the car writing a letter to David, while Ginny was taking pictures of some battlements. A large group formed around the car staring at me through the windows and giggling and chattering away. I wrote in my letter, 'There are about fifty pairs of large brown eyes watching me as I write this letter,' but at that moment a man put his head through the window and tapped me on the shoulder. 'No, no, lady, not fifty people here, only about twenty,' he corrected me. He was the local schoolmaster and spoke English, but we did not meet many people who could converse in English out in the country.

That night we arrived very late in a village, and the driver flatly refused to drive another yard. There was no hotel, so we stood in the square and waited. The crowd grew larger and larger around us. 'Anyone speak English?' we asked. No one did. Eventually an Inspector (I never discovered of what), who was visiting the village, took us to spend the night in the Inspector's Bungalow on the outskirts of the village, which was something of a relief. There was a bed with a rather holey mosquito net over it and a bed roll on the floor. Ginny gallantly said she would not mind sleeping on the floor and, having spied the two-inch-long red cockroaches which crawled all over the floor of what called itself 'the facilities' next door, I was very grateful to her. My camping experience from Kenya came in useful here. I never travel without a bed sheet, soap, towel, torch and my sleeping pills, and as there were no lights and no one could find a candle the torch was fairly essential.

Food and drink were always a problem, and bananas and oranges were the safest and easiest thing thing to eat. Ginny was braver than me and drank sweet sugarcane juice off street stalls; the plastic mugs and straws were used time and time again, picked up off the dusty ground. Bottled drinks were impossible to find except in the towns, and we gave up worrying about the water in the end – we would have died of thirst if we hadn't drunk it.

To get from Habli to Poona we had to go by the local overnight bus. We were the only women travelling and had to fight our way on to the bus with our heavy suitcases. Oaths and elbows were flung at us and we had to leave the cases in the aisle as there was no room anywhere else. During the night I heard a commotion and found a man having an epileptic fit on top of my luggage; he had wet himself and was frothing at the mouth. I tried to get someone to lift him off and help him, but only got hostile stares from the neighbouring seats. Eventually a soldier came up from the front of the bus and began pulling the unfortunate man's toes and puffing smoke from his cigarette into his mouth. This strange remedy seemed to work, for the man got up and sat back in his seat and peace was restored. But I was unhappy about my damp, squashed suitcase.

We arrived next morning at Poona, very much the worse for wear. I told Ginny I had had enough of travelling and forts for a while, and she would have to go and do them on her own. Ginny is indefatigable and went off alone, except for a driver and a guide, for the next two days, leaving in the early morning and coming back at nine the following evening, tired and dusty but with rolls of film.

By the third day I began to recover and joined her on a trip to Sinhagad Fort, twenty-six kilometres from Poona, which stood on top of a huge mountain with spectacular views. We then made a long day's journey to Janjira, a marvellous sea fort on the west coast. It was the most frightening drive I have ever experienced. The road down to the plains from the Poona hills is very narrow, with terrifying corners and nose-to-tail with heavy lorries belching diesel fumes. Everyone overtakes everyone else, disregarding the double white lines, and glancing over the side of the mountain I could see scattered burnt-out lorries and buses lying on their sides, which did nothing to help my confidence. When we asked our driver to slow down a bit he replied that our future was already written – if we were destined to be killed, there was nothing he could do to prevent it. We argued that in Europe we at least made an effort to keep ourselves alive, and did not take unnecessary risks, but he was not convinced.

We reached the coast at last, and found a dhow to take us over to the island fort. Ginny wanted to photograph it from all angles from the boat before landing; it was quite rough, and difficult to keep the boat steady, and she got very cross with the boatmen and nearly fell in a couple of times, but the boatmen were quite unmoved. The fort was beautiful, completely deserted and like an enchanted secret garden. Creepers and shrubs covered the ruins of the old barracks and king's palace, and the large water tanks were thick with green slime. The only sign of life was a few goats and two sacred cows.

We did not feel like driving the six hours back, but there was nowhere to spend the night. However, we were not destined to die and made it safely back up the hill to Poona.

We were looking forward to our stay in the comfortable Lake Palace Hotel in Udaipur, and were very disappointed when we got there to be told there was no room, although we had booked from Delhi a few weeks before. Eventually they arranged for us to stay in the Shikar Badi Hotel, which had been one of the Maharajah's shooting lodges and was out in the country; it was very peaceful, with horses, deer and waterhogs grazing outside the window at a water hole. There were lots of birds, especially peacocks, which cried during the night and made me dream I was at Hartland in Devon. We stayed in a guest bungalow – a long, low, wooden building covered with bougainvillea, with a pool in the garden. In the morning the managers of both hotels suddenly cottoned on to the fact that Ginny was the authoress of *Palaces of India*, and there was a lot of back-pedalling. The Lake Palace Hotel suddenly found it did have room for us after all, but the Shikar Badi did not want us to leave. We felt very popular all of a sudden, and Arvind and Bhuti Singh of Mewar, who live in the Shivniva's Palace in Udaipur, invited us to dinner in their palace. It was a fascinating evening; they were charming and showed us all around the palace.

Jaipur was our next stop. The Maharajah, a friend of Ginny's, had apparently invited us to stay, but no one met us at the airport and the guards at the palace were not at all keen on letting us in. However, Ginny talked her way into the ADC's office and someone eventually recognised her.

The Maharajah and his wife were away, but we were given a suite of rooms with the largest bathroom I have ever seen and were well looked after.

The next day Ginny left for the north and more forts, and I had to fly home for the children's holidays. The journey was fairly horrific as the Indian jumbo jet was overbooked, and I refused to budge from my seat, although two other people had the same seat number as me. Once back at Knebworth, it did not take long to wash away the dust and head lice I had picked up, but rather longer to recover completely from the trip. It had been an unforgettable experience. India is completely different from Africa, and I was fascinated by the contrast. India, where animals are allowed to go anywhere they wish, is like a giant farmyard – not helped by the fact that it is unclean to notice uncleanliness – but it has a rich history and magnificent buildings. Africa, on the other hand, has the most wonderful countryside and wildlife in the world, and is comparatively very clean, but lacks the monuments and obvious past. I longed to visit both again as soon as I was able.

While I had been away, Pattie had won a Smirnoff Vodka competition. She had had to write down 'her dream of a lifetime' and had put down 'to paint the *Queen Elizabeth II*'. She was asked to go for an interview in London and had explained that after painting Knebworth House, the *Queen Elizabeth II* was her next ambition. They were obviously impressed and took her out to Hong Kong for a week, as that was where the ship was anchored at the time. They lowered her over the side of the liner on a platform, dressed in Smirnoff overalls, with a paintbrush and a pot of paint, to repaint the letters on the side of the ship and the anchor. She was photographed from every angle. At one point one of the winches slipped and the platform tilted on its side; she had to grab hold of the sides in order not to be tipped into Hong Kong harbour, way below. She said it was a terrifying experience, but they gave her a fantastic week in Hong Kong before flying her home.

Henry was in Dartmouth working on a film, Agatha Christie's *Ordeal by Innocence*, starring Donald Sutherland, so we did not see much of him that spring. Peter had taken a year off between school and university, and had gone to Africa for six months and India for three months, alone – at the age of seventeen – with a knapsack on his back. He had been saving for years to be able to do the trip and, although I was nervous while he was away, I was pleased he was getting the experience. But when I got a letter from Kampala on 14 December, saying that he was lying in a brothel, had been ill and unable to eat anything for three days, and that bombs were going off outside in the street, I did begin to panic – especially when we didn't hear another word for three weeks. But eventually he telephoned us from Dar Es Salaam and wished us a happy New Year.

We had promised to take Richard and Rosina skiing in the Easter holidays, so I went off again almost immediately, leaving poor Jane, our new assistant, in charge of the office. She hadn't been there long, but generally seemed to have the place under control, and I was delighted to have help in the office – my responsibilities had definitely been getting me down.

Chapter 16 Rescued

I did get down eventually to doing some work at Knebworth that spring. We hosted North Hertfordshire's biggest ever athletics event in May, when thousands of runners, spectators and officials gathered for the Women's National Cross-country Championships. It was quite a sight – more than 2500 women racing around the park. The race was won by a 28-year-old girl called Jane Furness, who did the 4290 metres in 16 minutes 35 seconds, far ahead of her nearest rival.

The spring bank holiday weekend saw the first-ever joint Scout and Girl Guide camp to be held in Hertfordshire. It was known as 'Scougui'. The rain started as the 4000 children arrived on Friday and never stopped the entire weekend; it was the worst spring bank holiday weather for forty years apparently. Games and craft activities were planned, but not many took place, and signs outside some of the marquees read 'Water-skiing here'. The park was a sea of mud and took weeks to recover. It was a bad start to a disastrous summer.

We were planning to hold a concert in aid of Earth Life and the survival of the Cameroon rain forests; we had got a licence for 100,000 people and Rikki Stein was to be the promoter. It needed some big sponsors to get it off the ground and they are not easy to find. Sadly, it all fell through and we had no festival in 1984.

But the Classic Car rally was back. Peter Ellis arrived to put on another show and, although I was reluctant to work with him again, the event had been very profitable for us the last two summers and I did not feel I could turn it away. But Peter decided to run the event himself this year and offered us £5000 for the exclusive use of the park for the Saturday and Sunday. As we had made between £10,000 and £15,000 the previous two years, and only on the Sunday, I was not impressed and said that if he did all the gate-manning, car-parking and staking-out, I would consider taking £10,000. Peter came back saying that Burghley House had agreed to have them for £5000 and he would go there if I did not accept his offer. I said, 'Fine, don't let's waste any more time arguing – go to Burghley,' and got up and left the meeting. Peter came rushing after me and asked me to sit down again. I said I did not want to continue the discussion as he was so difficult to deal with. But I calmed down after a bit and went back in. Peter remarked that he did not think I had the necessary stamina for business discussions, and if I couldn't take it I shouldn't be in business. We continued arguing over the charges for a bit, but did not get anywhere as I refused to lower our fee and Peter refused to pay more than £5000.

We closed the meeting, but he rang up later and offered us £8000 plus a percentage of the takings over a certain figure, which we accepted. The event was a big success, as it always was, which made it even sadder that it had to be such a hassle each time. I rang up Peter Ellis's office to discuss how it had all gone a few days later and was told he had left the firm and that they were not planning to run any more events at Knebworth. That was the last I heard of him.

In June 1984, the Historic Houses Association held their first ever garden fair in our grounds. It was all thanks to Michael Calnan that our gardens were considered worthy of this honour but, sadly, he had made such a reputation for himself that he had been offered the job of assistant garden supervisor for all the National Trust's properties. It was a fantastic opportunity for him, and he accepted. We were very unhappy about him going: he had gone a long way towards putting the gardens back to their original Lutyens glory, and we would now have to find someone who could keep it going.

The garden fair was the same weekend as the Glastonbury Festival, which posed a problem for me. I longed to go to Glastonbury again, but I was supposed to be hosting the fair. I didn't know what to do. The thought of me wishing I was somewhere else all weekend was too much for David, however, so he promised to come home early on Friday and be on duty all weekend – and his parents would come up and help as well – so that I could go to the festival. Deciding it did not hurt to be selfish occasionally, I went. Glastonbury was certainly more my scene than a garden fair.

I carried on westwards after the festival and stayed with my mother in Devon; after my father's death I had tried to go down every three months or so to visit her. Henry was at Hartland working as an assistant art director on a film called *Water* with Michael Caine, part of which was being filmed on the Hartland cliffs. It was all supposed to take place on a Caribbean Island and most of it had been filmed on St Lucia. Henry was responsible for making the plastic palm trees stand up against the Atlantic gales and looking after the busloads of West Indians who had been brought in from Bristol. Luckily the weather stayed fine, and seeing the finished film it is difficult to tell which bits are St Lucia and which are Hartland cliffs. Our beach was known as 'Desolation Bay' in the film, which the family thought was a bit strong!

In August the English Village Sports Society held the semi-finals of their village olympics in the garden, and 6000 rural pubs throughout the country joined in. The events included turnip skittles, milkchurn-carrying and tossing the hay; it sounded rather a messy affair and I was anxious about the garden and hoped it would not rain. It did not and the event was a big success.

We staged an extravaganza in the autumn for the World Business Council, and 400 Americans came down for an 'Indian evening'. It was organised by Bob Hannah, a businessman from Chicago. He wanted a banquet with a vast marquee in the garden decorated in Indian style, and to welcome the guests in the courtyard we had the Scots Guards Military Band, snake-charmers, fire-eaters, knife-throwers, beggars, tiger cubs and even an elephant who gave rides. I had just been lent all the costumes from the television series of *The Far Pavilions* by Geoffrey Reeves, the producer, and was setting up an exhibition; they provided excellent costumes for our staff. J. Lyons, our caterers at the Barns, were confident that they could cook a good Indian curry for 400, and there was a cabaret consisting of dancing girls, musicians, a belly-dancer and a man who ate crushed glass, then lay on the broken glass and had a board of nails balanced on his tummy, with the American guests invited to stand on top of the board.

It all took a lot of organising and I was furious at having to go into hospital the day before the event for a major operation. But it apparently went off very well and was hailed by all as one of the best things we have ever done. I hope we will do it again one day.

The most exciting news of 1984 was the North Hertfordshire Council's decision in September to give us the go-ahead for the planning permission. A charitable trust was to be set up called 'The Knebworth House Education and Preservation Trust' to restore and preserve the house and gardens. The money from the sale of the land was expected to be over a million pounds. It had taken three years to get the Council to agree, and it was a great relief to us. It meant that the future of the house would be assured for the next seventy years, and at last we might have money to spend on restoring the inside of the house as well as repairing the structure. There were so many things that needed doing: new rugs for the main state rooms; safety doors which one could lock for the book-shelves in the Library, so we would not lose any more books; pictures to be restored and cleaned; and tapestries to be repaired. I would be able to start looking for antique curtains suitable for the large reception rooms; and old flags, banners and bed covers could be expertly washed and netted to prevent further deterioration. The gardens too would benefit. We needed more York paving to complete the herb garden, and perhaps we might even be able to replace the maze. A new yew maze big enough to cope with large numbers of visitors was going to cost £30,000.

It was an exciting prospect after the recent difficult years. With the Trust set up, it was worth investing in a qualified manager; Jane and I had done our best, but I had become exhausted with all the extra work and Jane did not have the experience or qualifications to run the business herself. The 1984 year had been a disaster financially: numbers had dropped to 79,850 and only 16,000 had visited the house. The agent that Humberts had been sending over once a week had been ill and we had hardly seen him for months, and BP was keeping David very busy in London. He left the house at seven in the morning and seldom came home before eight at night; he often had to bring work home as well. There was going to be a lot of extra work to be done at Knebworth, administering the Trust, selling the land, and planning for the hotel, and we needed someone well qualified to deal with all these new developments.

Jane left in December 1984, and soon afterwards John Hoy took over the running of the office. He was a Humbert and Flint employee, but was to work for us full-time, under contract. He was twenty-eight and had good qualifications, including five years' experience as assistant manager at Goodwood Estates in Sussex. Shirley Miller was doing very well in the accounts office with the help of Roy Eadie, who joined as part-time secretary of the Trust, and an assistant, Dawn Hickey; the accounts were up-to-date for the first time in fourteen years. John was going to need a secretary, so we hired Jacky Wilson, and Marion Hudson as part-time receptionist. The office was once more at full strength.

Freedom is having the time to do what one wants in life. Not many people have it, and many of those who do, do not know what to do with it. Now I had a manager again I decided to stick to promoting the house in various ways, such as travelling abroad, and chatting up people who could bring us business. I could also catch up on all the things I should have been doing in the house for the last two years. I loved my new-found freedom.

For my February trip in 1985, I decided on a two-week promotional visit to California, combined with some sun and fun. The pound was barely worth one dollar – very different from 1978 when we had gone with the children – but the strong dollar should mean that more Americans would be coming to Britain. Henry wanted to come too as he was between films and needed to do some research for a documentary on his favourite actress, Joan Fontaine. He had also started writing a film script of his own, and thought Hollywood as good a place as any to sit and write it.

We decided that I would work on the tourist promotion side and Henry would try and interest film location managers in coming over to England and using the house for filming. The present exchange rate would be an encouragement for them to do this. One day's filming would pay for our air tickets. Henry managed to find a friend who lent us his flat in Beverley Hills in exchange for Henry's maisonette in Marylebone, so we would not have to pay for hotels.

I had hoped for lots of help from the British Tourist Authority. They had been helpful on previous occasions, providing names and addresses of productive travel agencies and fixing up television, radio and newspaper interviews, but I felt they let me down this time. The New York BTA office sent me seventeen pages of travel agencies from all over California and a request for a sales report, but the list arrived on the day that I got to Los Angeles, not leaving me any time to fix anything up. Finding the list quite incomprehensible, I rang the BTA in Los Angeles, who produced ten agencies whom they knew to be interested in what I had to offer. This helped a bit, but I felt they could have done more. As a result, when a friend in New York suggested a public relations man in Los Angeles whom she knew, my first telephone call was to him. He came straight round to the apartment. She had warned me he might be expensive, but when I explained I could not really afford to pay him, he said he would not dream of charging me anything – perhaps a dinner together some time. I suppose I should have had more sense than to believe him.

He was very excited about all the material on the house. Henry had made six video films of the house and park, and I had brochures and photographs. In February, Knebworth had been featured for three consecutive weeks in *Country Life* and I had stocked up with copies of the articles. My new PR man took just about all the stuff I had. Every day I rang him to find out if he had any interviews for me, and every day he said wonderful things were just about to happen – he hoped to get me on to the Johnny Carson Show, or an interview with the *Los Angeles Times*, or the *Architectural Digest*. But it was always 'tomorrow'.

At last, on the day before I left for England, he rang up in great excitement. He had arranged an interview for me with a lady who was a freelance journalist, and she would be able to get me in to lots of newspapers. He had booked a table at L'Orangerie for the three of us; it was 'on me'.

I hope he and his lady friend enjoyed their dinner. It was the most expensive dinner I have ever eaten, let alone paid for, and the article that followed didn't bear much resemblance to what I had said. But it was my fault for falling for it.

To make up for that disaster, I had a big success with the first travel agency I visited. The manager was coming over to England the week that I got back, and he promised to bring twenty American tour operators with him to visit Knebworth. This he did, arriving at 9 a.m. the day after I got back to England. The first question every travel agent asked me was, did we have anywhere for Americans to stay? London was completely booked out for the entire summer. Unfortunately we do not. I have been tempted to have three or four couples to stay in the house but I know we are not really smart enough. We have no showers in the bathrooms, the ceilings are peeling off in all the rooms and there are stains on the carpets and curtains; we have no 'living-in' or professional staff, and although one can bring people in to help, one-off efforts can be risky – only I know where everything is and how I like things done, although by now Pattie is a close second. We have problems enough when we have our own friends staying for the weekends during the summer. The only guest rooms are in the public part of the house, and we have to make sure everyone is out of bed and their suitcases and clothes hidden in the bathrooms before eleven-thirty when we open to visitors. There have been some embarrassing moments when the guides have forgotten to check the bedrooms first and the tourists have seen more than they bargained for!

I also had a good interview with an Australian editor of *Vogue* magazine, who lived in Los Angeles, and *Town and Country* magazine in Los Angeles featured a photograph of our Banqueting Hall table by Baker Furniture while I was there. I was told that the table also appeared in the television series *Dynasty* in the dining room scenes. *The Shooting Party* had not come out yet in America, but it also had the Banqueting Hall table in it, and it was surprising how many people recognised it in the film as 'the Baker table'.

Back at Knebworth in April, I tried to keep a low profile. I made myself available for help if needed but did not encourage unnecessary interruptions from the office. One of the problems of starting again with a young and energetic new manager was that he was keen to try out lots of ideas, not realising that after fifteen years we had tried just about everything and it was difficult to drum up the enthusiasm and energy that we used to have for them. I found myself in danger of becoming negative and slightly cynical, but in fact it was just what we needed – someone new who was keen and capable.

We spent £30,000 in the spring of 1985 on 'Fort Knebworth' – a large wooden construction, 100-feet square and full of playground equipment – to give the adventure playground a boost. The old astroglide slide had completely worn through so we had to replace that as well.

In June we staged the wettest ever rock festival. Don Murfett, who runs the security firm Artist Services which had been responsible for security at all our previous festivals, put together a consortium to run the concert. Deep Purple, Meat Loaf and Scorpions headed the bill, and the licence for 120,000 people was granted on condition that we met the requirements of all the local authorities, police, Red Cross, etc. The police said it would cost the promoters £62,000 to cover the cost of their presence in the park, but we thought this was far too much, especially since the concert was being run by Don Murfett and he would have 350 of his own security men on duty that weekend. We did not see the need for or want 500-plus policemen in the park as well, and on top of the charge they expect their own marquee, lavatories, and food and drink for three days.

Everyone we spoke to agreed that a sum of £62,000 was exorbitant, especially considering we had never had any trouble at any of our festivals over the years. We felt the police were trying to prevent a concert from taking place, and there were a lot of stormy meetings when we tried to get the police to reduce either their charges or their manning levels, but with no success. Eventually we took the North Hertfordshire District Council to court, losing the case on a technical point, but winning a moral victory as the police agreed to reduce some of the charges. Ticket sales were not as good as expected and numbers looked more like 75,000, so in the end the police finally agreed to cut their bill to £32,000. The court case had left us without a licence, eight days before the festival, so a hurried meeting had to be called and luckily the Council reinstated the licence. I don't know what would have happened otherwise – it would have been very difficult to cancel the event at that late stage.

The festival was a great success in spite of the rain. We made a camp down in the arena, but whether it was these particular fans or whether rock concerts have changed since the last one in 1980, when we had the Beach Boys, the arena soon became uninhabitable from our point of view. The entire audience got to their feet when the first band came on stage at 11 a.m., and remained standing until 12 p.m. – I don't think it was just because the ground was wet. A shower of plastic bottles rained down on everyone's heads all day; they started off with the remnants of beer and cider in them, but as the day wore on and people could not be bothered to get out through the crowds they became full of pee instead, which was very unpleasant. So for the first time ever we retreated backstage to the guests' enclosure and watched the concert from there.

But I did stand on stage for Meat Loaf's performance. He had broken a leg in Australia a few weeks previously, after falling off a stage, and there had been some doubt as to whether he would be fit enough for the concert. He limped painfully up on to the stage but soon recovered and seemed to forget about the pain as the show took over. He is a large man, with an aggressive act, and every time he shouted 'F— you' at the audience, which was fairly often, a shower of cans, bottles and lumps of mud landed on the stage.

The floor was filthy and very slippery. At one point he fell over and I winced for his leg, but someone helped him up and he carried on, catching some of the missiles and throwing them back at the shouting audience.

I retreated to the guest enclosure after that. A lot of other people had had the same idea and there was quite a crowd, but some tables came in useful. About six of us stood on each table, the legs sinking into the mud, and it was quite a balancing act to keep it upright and can't have done the tables much good. Somehow one forgot it was pouring with rain. A lot of swabbing-down went on on the stage before Deep Purple appeared; they had not played together in England since the seventies and a lot of people had never heard them live, so they were a great attraction. The show finished with £15,000 worth of fireworks – the most spectacular display I have ever seen. Unfortunately, it woke the neighbours up for miles around, and one or two I met the next day said they thought a war had started.

It took all night to pull the coaches and cars out of the mud so that people could go home. The park was a quagmire, and the arena smelt like a pigsty for about three days and was covered with large black birds. Presumably there were some tasty pickings to be had, but it made the park look rather sinister. The litter was picked up in a week, but because of the mud a lot of it had got buried and as everything dried out and the grass began to grow it reappeared. We could have done with another clean-up a month later.

Six months later, in December 1985, David was served with three summonses from the Hertfordshire County Council. He was charged with breaking the licensing conditions as the music had been over the designated amount of decibels allowed by the public health authority, the lavatories had not been ready for inspection forty-eight hours before the festival began and they had been found to be in an unacceptable condition during the festival! I think the Council were getting their own back on us for taking them to court over the police manning levels in June.

The noise factor is very difficult to monitor as weather conditions, the cloud base and even a gust of wind can alter readings dramatically. I do not believe the lavatories have ever been ready for inspection forty-eight hours before, and they were only in a bad state because of the dreadful weather. A similar occurrence had taken place at the Green Belt Festival and we had not been taken to court then. We pleaded guilty, only because we needed to get the court case over quickly so that we could apply for a licence in time for 1986 – the Council knew they had us over a barrel. It annoyed David a lot, and he was fined £1000.

It all adds up to more hassle and makes it difficult to get another licence. I can never understand why, when an event gives so much pleasure to so many people and is on the whole well organised and peaceful, people in authority have to be against it and make it such a struggle to put on. We reckon we have worked hard for rock music over the years.

In the autumn of 1985, the National Gallery of Art in Washington staged a special exhibition called 'Treasure Houses of Britain', in which 250 houses were to be represented. Gervase Jackson-Stops from the National Trust had travelled the country looking round houses and making lists of objects he thought suitable to take over to America.

I rang him up in April and asked him if he wanted anything from Knebworth. He said he had been down and had a look around but had not seen anything suitable for the exhibition. Feeling rather slighted, I suggested a few items: the Ward picture of Sir Edward Bulwer-Lytton in his study, the Watts sketch of Lord Lytton, the silver throne of the Maharajah of Mysore, or the enamel Rajasthan animals. He sounded doubtful, but said he would try and get down again. He did come, but again without telling me and the house was shut up and many things put away. After that he said if I brought a few pieces of Indian silver to the Victoria and Albert Museum he would have a look at them. So I put part of the silver throne, a silver address casket in the form of a Ganges boat and the enamel animals into the back of the car, took a special insurance out to cover them in transit and drove them to the Victoria and Albert Museum. Gervase decided to take the silver ship. I was disappointed as I thought the throne was so much more spectacular and fifty years earlier, but I was pleased we were going to be in the exhibition after all. The ship had a couple of oars missing and some broken rigging, and had to be mended before being packed up and sent to America, but it is an unusual and handsome piece.

When I had been in California in the spring I was always being asked if we had anything going to the exhibition in Washington, and I felt it was quite important, with our house being open, that we should be represented.

We were invited out to the opening in November and David even took a week off from work to come too. British Airways did a special package deal, and 250 'stately home' owners all flew out on the same aeroplane. The plane was an hour and a half late taking off and I wondered if there had been an extra security check. It would have been quite a planeload to hijack. If it had crashed a lot of titles would have come tumbling down to eldest sons and the Inland Revenue would have had a field day! We sat *en bloc* on the aeroplane, and I felt the in-flight film should have been *Kind Hearts and Coronets*. One lady, Mrs Mockler, in her sixties, had never flown before and lots of strong drinks and encouragement were needed to get her on to the plane. I thought she was very brave about it.

The smart people stayed with friends, or at the British Embassy, and the rest of us were put up at the Washington Hilton. On the first evening we changed into crumpled dresses and dinner jackets straight out of the suitcase to go to a reception at the British embassy. We were a fairly mixed bunch, and a bit stand-offish to start with; the English do no like talking to each other unless they have been introduced, but when a few days later we were all given name tabs everybody suddenly started chatting to each other. At seven the first morning, we rang room service in the Hilton for breakfast. 'Sorry, lady, we are too busy this morning, you will have to eat in the restaurant,' came the reply. 'But I have never heard of a big hotel where one cannot have breakfast in one's room,' I complained. 'I am afraid there is no room service today,' said the voice and the telephone went dead. Much to David's embarrassment, I rang the manager and said we had been invited over to America to see the National Gallery exhibition and I thought it was unbelievable that a hotel such as the Hilton could not provide any room service, and anyway I was quite incapable of getting dressed without a cup of coffee first. Breakfast arrived about twenty minutes later, but only for one!

We were wined and dined for two days before setting off on a tour of Virginian historic houses, organised by the Kenmore Association, for the rest of the week. The exhibition was spectacular, sponsored by the Ford Motor Company and put together by Carter Brown, director of the gallery, and Gervase Jackson-Stops. It had taken seven years to organise, and each room was specially built in the style of the period to go with the objects. The silver ship from Knebworth was in a good position, I was glad to see.

A black-tie dinner was held one night in the gallery for 500 people, a senator hosted a lunch for us at the Capitol and Nancy Reagan invited us all to tea at the White House. We travelled everywhere in three ancient double-decker buses (to make us feel at home), and on the way to the White House we had a police escort on Harley Davidsons with sirens blaring. We were rushed past the red lights and through all the rush-hour traffic, feeling as if we were a party of excited schoolchildren on an outing. There was quite a bit of undignified giggling and rolling around in the aisles, and the citizens of Washington were left standing with their mouths open.

The Americans had suggested that we should bring tiaras for the Gala dinner, and there was a lot of whispering about who had and had not brought one. It was certainly thought not the thing to wear one, and I felt rather sorry for the unfortunate people who had got theirs out of the bank, taken out special insurance and then not felt able to wear it due to public opinion. One peer wore his coronation robes and was much frowned upon.

It rained for the entire week, and jumping in and out of the buses to look around the Virginia houses was a wet affair, especially as we had been told the temperature would be in the seventies and few of us had brought umbrellas and mackintoshes; luckily, gardens are not Virginia's strong point so we did not miss much in that respect. Everyone was very welcoming and we were well looked after. We would leave at 9 a.m. and drive through the wonderful fall colours of the countryside, visiting three or four houses during the day and spending the night in hotels or country clubs. The highlight was a night at Stratford Plantation in log cabins built for the directors of the Stratford Foundation – a private trust, entirely run by ladies, which looks after the property. The chalets had roaring log fires and were very comfortable, though the rain pattered down on the tin roofs all night. It rained at Williamsburg, which I was glad I had visited before with the children, and poured down in Charlottesville, where we toured the University of Virginia.

David flew home at the end of the week and I stayed on for a couple of days in Washington for a Baker, Knapp and Tubbs reception. Sir Humphrey Wakefield was supposed to be leaving me instructions at the Hilton Hotel, but when I arrived back there the hotel denied any knowledge of a letter or message for me. So, rather wondering if I was expected to be there at all, I booked myself into the Hilton and hoped that Baker would pay the bill.

The porter took my luggage up to my room and showed me how to double-lock and chain my door, and made me promise I would be sure and not let anyone in. Half an hour later there was a knock on the door. 'Wallpaper inspector here, come to inspect the wallpaper,' a man's voice said. 'Sorry, I'm busy,' I replied. 'It won't take a second,' he said. 'Go away,' I said, feeling rather like one of the three little pigs with the wolf. A couple of hours later came another knock on the door. 'Security here,' said a voice. I opened up, cautiously, leaving the door on the chain. A huge black man stood at the door in uniform, with a pistol strapped round his middle, and asked if everything was all right. 'I just wondered,' he said. 'Your television was so loud I thought you might be in trouble.' Next morning the housekeeper went along the corridor banging on everyone's door making them answer. 'Just checking everyone's all right,' she said. I began to wonder what normally went on in the Washington Hilton – it certainly wasn't very peaceful. Having nothing to do the next day, and still with no word from Humphrey, I spent a blissful day in the Space Museum, wishing I had the boys with me.

Humphrey rang up in an agitated state at five o'clock. 'Where are you? Why didn't you get my letter?' He had delivered a letter by hand to the Hilton a few days before, with instructions for me to stay in another hotel, and had organised a dinner party for me the night before. The Hilton had somehow managed to lose it.

But I made it to an enormous dinner at L'Enfant Hotel, which Baker hosted. Our Banqueting Hall table was one of their biggest-selling items, and everyone congratulated me and said how pleased we must be. Unfortunately, having sold the rights to Humphrey I was not as excited as I might have been, but I was glad for him, and he is always busy sending other business in our direction. Copying rugs, silver and china are the next projects, so maybe we will make some money for ourselves one day!

Chapter 17 Any other business

In October 1984 we held our first Trust meeting. It was a momentous occasion for David and me; after fifteen years of hard work and worry all our dreams and hopes for Knebworth had at last come true, and Knebworth House was now secure for future generations of Lyttons. The land in Knebworth village had been sold for over a million pounds, the money had been invested and a large amount of interest from the investments would be coming in every year. Without the major house and garden expenses, our own company debts would now have a chance to recover.

The Trust was made up of nine trustees: the Mayor of Stevenage, the Chairman of the North Hertfordshire District Council, the Chairman of the Knebworth Parish Council, our accountant Ralph Wagstaff, two City friends of David's, Lady Cobbold, Susan Blount (David's sister) and Henry. Because we lived in the house we were not allowed to be trustees.

The first meeting was held in the Banqueting Hall, around the now world-famous table. Allocations of the money from the expected Trust income were made for structural and interior repairs of the house, and the entire garden expenses would be taken over by the Trust. I was to be given an allowance to have pictures and furniture restored, and I could buy things for the house like rugs, carpets, curtains – and maybe even replace the hideous blue carpet-runners. It was all very exciting. It would take quite a few years, but with the major burden of house and gardens expenditure taken over by the Trust, we felt very optimistic again.

Looking back over the last twenty-five years, it has been lots of fun and a lot of hard work being married to David and living at Knebworth House. I have had to be far more practical than I would ever have been called on to be if we had lived in an ordinary house. I am a dab hand at painting, papering, caning, curtain-making and upholstery, amongst other things. I have gained in confidence over the years, and have learnt to travel and explore on my own and face television cameras and the press. I have learnt by trial and error how to feed large numbers of people, and I have carried furniture and lugged endless crates of food and drink back from the cash and carry. One advantage, or maybe disadvantage, of living in a large house twenty-eight miles from London is that it fills up with friends all the time. At weekends I am never sure who and how many will turn up.

It can be exhausting and I no longer feel as energetic or sometimes as enthusiastic as I used to, but life is for living, and we certainly do that to the full. If we had not put Knebworth on the map we would never have got the grants we needed to keep the house going, or the planning permission to set the Trust up and assure its future. The object of moving into Knebworth House was to keep the house in the family and to conserve it as part of the national heritage for future generations. After nearly 500 years we did not want to be the ones to give it all up – and we have achieved this. So far Knebworth has provided pleasure and interest to over three million people since 1970, and we hope it will continue to do so.

As a family it has brought us closer together. We have all played a part in preserving it, and the interest and excitements that go with the house have given the children a sense of history and an extra purpose to their lives. Luckily, Henry is the keenest of us all. But until it is time for him to take over, David and I will go on running Knebworth as directors of Lytton Enterprises, the company we started up in 1970. He will come home in the evenings and we will have our bath-time meetings, where I recount the happenings of the day. I like to think that the relaxing and soothing effect of the hot water at our board meetings has reduced disagreements over policy, prevented panic about finances and helped us to make the right decisions for the future – perhaps some other company directors should try it.